Born in Ayr, Scotland, in 1964, Gordon Muirhead joined the Parachute Regiment as a junior soldier in 1981 and gained his military parachute wings at the age of seventeen.

He covered all corners of the globe with the regimen – the Far East, Middle East, Europe, Mediterranean, and South, Central and North America on exercises or operations.

He was an officer cadet instructor at the Royal Military Academy Sandhurst, regimental sergeant major and commissioned as a captain in 2003.

Leaving the Army in the rank of major, he was made a Member of The Most Excellent Order of The British Empire (MBE).

Three Decades of Duty

The Comedy

GORDON MUIRHEAD

Three Decades of Duty

The Comedy

Vanguard Press

A CIP catalogue record for this title is
available from the British Library.

ISBN: 978-178465-033-9

*Although the author and publisher have made every effort to ensure that the information in
this book was correct at press time, the author and publisher do not assume and hereby
disclaim any liability to any party for any loss, damage, or disruption caused by errors or
omissions, whether such errors or omissions result from negligence, accident,
or any other cause.*

*Vanguard Press is an imprint of
Pegasus Elliot Mackenzie Publishers Ltd.*
www.pegasuspublishers.com

First Published in 2015

**Vanguard Press
Sheraton House Castle Park
Cambridge England**

Printed & Bound in Great Britain

To my darling wife, Janice, who stayed at home keeping the home fires burning brightly and bringing up our beautiful daughters whilst I travelled the world on behalf of our country.

The two years I spent as the regimental sergeant major of 2nd Battalion The Parachute Regiment should have earned you and the other wives at least a 'Mention in Dispatches' when the battalion completed four operational tours – Northern Ireland (twice), Macedonia and Afghanistan.

Acknowledgements

I would like to thank the British Army and particularly the Parachute Regiment for providing me with a fantastic career which took me all around the world to some very interesting places – and some not so interesting places where dangerous people lived. Without the travelling, the stories would not have been witnessed and recorded over the years.

This book is only made possible due to the diversity of people that serve in the British Army and the differing humours that are displayed on a daily basis.

CONTENTS

CHAPTER 4

ON OPERATIONS

CHAPTER 5   246
OFF DUTY

FOREWORD

Having served in the British Army as a regular soldier and officer for over twenty-eight years' service – firstly as a junior soldier at the age of sixteen years old until leaving many years later in the rank of major. I thought it might be fun to put pen to paper and describe some of the quips, antics, funny stories, and stories with serious implications that I have witnessed and heard of over those years during my military service. A lot of these stories are frequently retold at gatherings of soldiers past and present over a few beers, they will be familiar to very few outside of the unit involved.

There is a saying in the British Army that you always remember the good times and not the bad times. This is very true: you do remember the good times when you were sub-aqua diving in the Caribbean, on exercise in the safari lands of Kenya, or skiing in Norway – all paid for courtesy of the British taxpayer.

Very quickly you forget the wet, cold, hungry days spent in the middle of winter that were endured sitting in a blackthorn hedgerow in South Armagh, Northern Ireland, observing a suspect's house whilst eating cold rations with rain dripping off the end of your nose. A warm shower quickly washes away the aches and pains, bringing life back to numb limbs. Or the hot and sweaty patrols in Iraq and Afghanistan in 50-degree heat where time was spent searching for danger, which could come in the shape of an ambush or roadside bomb. Once safely back in the UK and sitting snugly in the local pubs of Aldershot or Colchester – a few beers later, the bad times don't really seem that bad.

The following short stories are written to give the people that have never served in the Armed Forces a glimpse through the keyhole into Army life and the humour that abounds there. It will also remind the serving and ex-serving soldiers of the times they had – good or bad, under different types and styles of leadership; we always managed to laugh about some of the daft things that we had to do.

All the stories have taken place over the last three decades – eighties, nineties, and the new millennium. At the time the majority of soldiers laughed, although perhaps not the individual who was at the centre of the gibe or the mischief.

The aim of the book is to narrate short stories so the non-military readers can gain some understanding of the type of people that fill the ranks of the British Army. To also give the reader an honest and open insight into what soldiers get up to around the world – on and off duty. Too often military books only concentrate on going somewhere and attacking something and receiving X amount of casualties. I have never read a military-based book that allows the reader to glimpse into the mind of soldiers and how they express themselves, regardless of the situation.

The average British soldier is by no means a saint and there are certainly some sinners within its ranks. However, I do believe they all know right from wrong and have a sense of honour, at least amongst themselves and for their regiment. More importantly, the book is to give the readers a chuckle or at least cheer them up in these current credit-crunching days and world strife.

In the sad world that we live in today, where political correctness seems to rule the waves and some people are reserved in what they say in fear of offending others, I have one thing to say – 'get a life and enjoy it'. Until you have experienced the training, education or operations that the youth of the British Armed Forces have endured over the last century, do not even try to suggest that any of these stories are sexist, bullying, or racist. Each story allows you to see some of the wit, humour and sarcasm by those that were in attendance and found it funny, regardless of the situation: whether it was in a benign or hostile environment.

Many books have been written about the British Army over the centuries; most of these books concentrate on specific battles or individuals. A lot of these books are written by highly accomplished intellects and academics who concentrate on the plans and theories of the commanders – all very good stuff, but at times far too serious and very drab on occasions.

INTRODUCTION

What Type Of People Make Up The British Army?

The British Army is a totally voluntary corporation that attracts civilians from all walks of life to its front door. Yes, there are the typical ex-private school pupils that make up parts of the officer corps – 'absolutely spiffing, one for the road, chaps' – sort of person. Thankfully, the majority of the officer corps today is not quite the image portrayed in the *Blackadder* series where Rowan Atkinson played an outstanding part. However, I dare say there are still a few chinless wonders around, hiding in some backwater of the Army. A large proportion of the officer corps now comes from state sponsored comprehensive schools and become excellent officers who are well respected by their soldiers.

The vast majority of officers do go through university and study to gain a degree. The quality and type of the degree achieved in their three- or four-year course might not hold up to scrutiny, but that is not their fault. Some of the degrees gained by these young officers to be are well earned – in the student bars up and down the country. If the country allows them to spend three or four years studying in a bar to allegedly better themselves, then who are we to quibble over standards? I think the education level of standards – or lack of them argument lies firmly at the door of No 10 Downing Street.

The soldiers and non-commissioned officers are born and raised from all corners of the United Kingdom. The majority are brought up and come from housing estates, small villages or towns from all corners of the country and have a normal upbringing – Scots, Irish, Welsh, Geordies, Cornish, Londoners, etc. A large proportion are well educated and only ever wanted to be soldiers from a very young age. Many families have had arguments with their sons and daughters who decide they want to join the Army due to the potential danger that might be faced by their loved ones.

What draws these young people to the Army's place of work is a whole debate on its own; for me it was pride in my country and an overwhelming desire from a young age to join the Parachute Regiment. Brought up on stories from *Commando* and *Warlord* comics and good old-fashioned war films, I was destined to join the Army. Others will express all sorts of reasons as to why they joined and served in the ranks of the British Army.

As of late there has been an increase in recruitment of soldiers from Commonwealth and other foreign countries: Nepal, Fiji, Jamaica, Australia, New Zealand, South Africa and Kenya. The better educated can become officers if they have the aptitude; the others join as soldiers.

In this book, all officers and soldiers in the stories are known as Lieutenant/Captain/ X, Y, Z or Private/Corporal/Sergeant X, Y, Z, etc. I thought it best not to bring embarrassment or identify those still serving – the personnel that were present at the time when the story was made will know exactly who the person is.

Tommy

I went into a public-'ouse to get a pint o' beer,
The publican 'e up an' sez, "We serve no red-coats here."
The girl's be'ind the bar they laughed an' giggled fit to die,
I outs into the street again an' to myself sez I:
O its Tommy this, an' Tommy that, an' "Tommy, go away";
But it's "Thank you, Mister Atkins", when the band begins to play,
The band begins to play, my boys, the band begins to play,
O it's "Thank you, Mister Atkins", when the band begins to play.
 I went into a theatre as sober as could be,
They gave a drunk civilian room, but 'adn't none for me;
They sent me to the gallery or round the music-'alls,
But when it comes to fightin', Lord! they'll shove me in the stalls!
For it's Tommy this, an' Tommy that, an' "Tommy, wait outside";
But it's "Special train for Atkins" when the trooper's on the tide,
The troopship's on the tide, my boys, the troopship's on the tide,
O its "Special train for Atkins" when the trooper's on the tide.

Yes, makin' mock o' uniforms that guard you while you sleep
Is cheaper than them uniforms, an' they're starvation cheap;
An' hustlin' drunken soldiers when they're goin' large a bit
Is five times better business than paradin' in full kit.
Then it's Tommy this, an' Tommy that, an' "Tommy, 'ow's yer soul?"
But it's "Thin red line of 'eroes" when the drums begin to roll,
The drums begin to roll, my boys, the drums begin to roll,
O it's "Thin red line of 'eroes" when the drums begin to roll.

We aren't no thin red 'eroes, nor we aren't no blackguards too,
But single men in barricks, most remarkable like you;
An' if sometimes our conduck isn't all your fancy paints,
Why, single men in barricks don't grow into plaster saints;
While it's Tommy this, an' Tommy that, an' "Tommy, fall be'ind",
But it's "Please to walk in front, sir", when there's trouble in the wind,
There's trouble in the wind, my boys, there's trouble in the wind,
O it's "Please to walk in front, sir", when there's trouble in the wind.
You talk o' better food for us, an' schools, an' fires, an' all:
We'll wait for extry rations if you treat us rational.
Don't mess about the cook-room slops, but prove it to our face
The Widow's Uniform is not the soldier-man's disgrace.
For it's Tommy this, an' Tommy that, an' "Chuck him out, the brute!"
But it's "Saviour of 'is country" when the guns begin to shoot;
An' it's Tommy this, an' Tommy that, an' anything you please;
An' Tommy ain't a bloomin' fool -- you bet that Tommy sees!

Rudyard Kipling

Has public opinion of the British soldier really changed that much in over one hundred years since Rudyard Kipling wrote the poem *Tommy* describing the soldier's opinion of how he was looked upon by the same people that sent him to war?

When the Argentinians invaded the Falkland Islands in 1982, the Great British Nation couldn't wait to send troops on the first tide, urged on by the British public. Entering Afghanistan was fully supported by the public in 2001 after the Twin Towers in New York were destroyed in a terrorist act of such magnitude it stunned the world.

How often do we see cheering crowds when the soldiers return and parade through their local towns to the beat of the drum after an Operational tour?

How often do we hear or read in the media that Soldier X, the brute, was refused entry to bars or clubs up and down the country?

How often do we read about soldiers in the local newspaper who have appeared before the magistrate for some misdemeanour?

How often do we hear stories that the government is not looking after the soldiers who were wounded on their behalf and the widowed wives that have been left to look after the children on their own?

The Military Covenant has recently been paraded by the current prime minister, David Cameron, and serving generals which promises better welfare, education and housing for the military community. I will leave the public to decide if we have been here before – only time will tell.

CHAPTER 1

TRAINING

The British Army takes training very seriously and spends a lot of its budget on training; soldiers can find themselves on many training courses every year. Over a full twenty-two year career, it would not be uncommon to spend three years or more on learning courses – the same length as some degree courses. Every person that joins the Army must do basic training which is relevant to their choice of career – infantry, drivers, storemen, medics, signallers, armoured corps, or artillery. The first twelve weeks of training is the same for every new recruit: it's where they learn to march, dress, shoot, live in the field, before branching off to their trade training – regardless of trade, everyone is a soldier first and trained to kill.

In Afghanistan a few years ago, a few Royal military policemen were flown into a forward operating base to investigate an accidental death in the Helmand Valley. When the Taliban attacked the base, they had to stand on the wall and return fire at the attackers along with the soldiers that were based there – everyone has to fight, particularly when there is a shortage of manpower.

Throughout a career there are certain courses that you must pass to gain promotion to the next rank; if you can't pass the courses you don't get promoted – simple, really. The courses are educational and prepare you for the next appointment that you might get – Section Commanders' Course, Platoon Sergeants' Course, Warrant Officers' Course, etc. These courses are essential and should ensure that soldiers get promoted at the right time, when they are ready for the new appointment (sadly not always the case) – when the wrong soldiers get promoted, the soldiers at the bottom of the ladder suffer due to incompetence of their new leaders.

There are many, many other courses that soldiers undergo throughout their careers: parachuting, skiing, jungle, driving, education, weapon teaching, map reading, drill, nuclear biological chemical warfare, medical, diving, signals, mortars, anti-tank, heavy machine gun; the list is endless.

The aim of all the training courses is so that the British Army can be as prepared for conflict at home and abroad to the best of its ability – whilst remaining within budgetary constraints. Budgetary constraints are a battle on their own, never mind Al Qaeda and its supporters.

1   COCONUTS THE SIZE OF A SPACE HOPPER

In the eighties a lot of soldiers from the Parachute Regiment went to RAF Brize Norton to be trained and qualified on 22ft steerable static line (SSL) parachutes. Normally, trained parachutists would jump from a Hercules C130 aircraft at 800 feet (nowadays it's 600ft), with an aim to be on the ground quickly but safely in about twenty seconds. Less time in the air means less of a target for the enemy to shoot at and disrupt the airborne soldiers disgorging from the aircraft above.

Some clever dick thought that if the guys were trained on steerable parachutes, then the lads could steer themselves, land closer together on the ground and be ready for action quicker.

The first flaw was easy to spot by any trained or untrained parachutist – jumping from 800 feet does not give you much time to sort yourself out and head in any direction with the other parachutists you have left the same aircraft with and have opened a canopy at the same time.

The solution was to jump higher from 1500 to 2000 feet. Although they would now spend longer in the air and the aircraft delivering the troops would be easily detected by radar.

The next problem was the landing – the 22ft SSL was designed for use with the Special Boat Service (SBS) so they could land in the sea, where a faster rate of descent didn't matter too much. However, a faster rate of fall on land meant harder landings for the paratroopers – not too popular with the troops.

The last part of this madness was telling all who jumped with this parachute that they were prone to slow openings and the extra jump height was needed for safety in peace time. Overall, not a fantastic offer for the soldiers and officers that were to jump with this new parachute attached to their backs.

Sergeant X was on his 22ft SSL course and had already completed three jumps with the new parachute and found no problems. Some of the landings had been slightly heavy but nothing to worry about.

On his fourth and final jump he got into the aircraft as before, he would be number 10 to jump. After thirty minutes of flying, the aircraft was heading into the jump run over Weston-on-the-Green near Oxford.

Inside the C130 all of the men were stood up with their equipment fitted and secured to their bodies. "Action Stations," was shouted out by the parachute jump instructor (PJI) and all of the men shuffled forward so that the number one of the stick (line of parachutists) was standing on the edge of the tail ramp ready to leap out into the void when ordered. "Red On!" yelled the PJI above the noise of the aircraft engines when the red light was displayed. The paratroopers knew that in the next few seconds they would be dispatched out of the aircraft. All eyes were glued to the para lights for the change of colour. "Green On, Go!" shouted the PJI when the red light next to the para doors changed to a fixed green light and the first man disappeared over the ramp edge into thin air. The rest of the parachutists followed in their stick order and were all dispatched within fifteen seconds.

Sergeant X followed the man in front down the aircraft until it was his turn to jump into what could be eternity. Arms across his reserve, legs together, chin in, jump forward into thin air, violently buffeted and thrown about by the slipstream behind the aircraft, one thousand, two thousand, three thousand, check canopy. On looking up, Sergeant X noticed that his parachute was taking its time to open fully. However, not to worry as he had been briefed on the parachute's history of slow opening. After about ten seconds of falling, the parachute finally opened, much to Sergeant X's relief. On looking around his airspace, he could see that he was extremely low and perhaps should have operated his reserve – just a few seconds before he hit the ground for another hard and heavy landing.

As Sergeant X was falling to earth at great speed without the benefit of a fully inflated canopy above his head, the PJI on the ground controlling the drop was going mad. He was screaming at the top of his voice through his loud hailer, shouting at the body falling to earth with what looked like a bag of washing trailing above his head to pull his reserve. Finally, the bag of washing opened and deployed into a fully functioning, billowing parachute and the body drifted to earth at the normal speed – thankfully.

He landed, rolled, stood up, before releasing himself from the parachute harness, gathered up his parachute into his arms and made his way to the rendezvous area. Looking up into the clear blue sky, he could see that the rest of the soldiers in his parachute stick were still at an altitude of over a thousand feet – which seemed strange to the sergeant. On walking closer to the rendezvous, he could see that a PJI was jumping up and down, clearly not pleased with someone. On reaching the rendezvous, the PJI was pointing and shouting at Sergeant X demanding to know why he never pulled his reserve parachute.

The realisation had finally sunk into Sergeant X: he had been too low and should have pulled his reserve parachute. Not wanting to lose face in front of other soldiers already at the rendezvous from previous aircraft drops, he replied, "If you jump it, you gotta ride it in," which left the parachute jump instructor with a look of utter disbelief written across his face.

Sergeant X was made a Member of the Most Excellent Order of the British Empire (MBE) many years later in the rank of captain for his outstanding work and compassion when dealing with families and the repatriation of sixteen members of the battalion that were killed in action during a tour of Afghanistan.

2   BEST BLUFFS ARE MEMORABLE

Officer Cadet Y was serving in his final year at the Royal Military Academy Sandhurst (RMAS); at this time in an officer's training they are scrutinised in all they say and do. Any un-officer-like behaviour could instantly stop them getting commissioned as officers of the Crown.

Cadet Y was in a relationship with one of the female cadets in the same Commissioning Course that he was on. One Friday night, the young couple must have had a steamy evening because he turned up on Saturday morning's parade with large, unsightly love bites all over his neck. Colour Sergeant X was in the process of inspecting the platoon when the academy adjutant turned up out of the blue and was asked if he would like to inspect the platoon.

The academy adjutant was a guards officer and not a particularly liked one because he was a little pompous and standoffish towards the cadets. More importantly, he had the power to get cadets back-termed or thrown out of the Academy for not behaving like officers and gentlemen on a whim.

Cadet Y was now starting to panic a little because he knew the academy adjutant would see the hideous love bites all over his neck and these were definitely not expected to be seen on a young potential officer. As the adjutant was coming along the ranks inspecting the cadets, they were all placed on that evening's show parade for various misdemeanours: trousers not pressed correctly, boots not shining enough, haircuts, etc. Eventually, he reached

Cadet Y and asked the question, "Why have you got large bruises all over your neck?"

By now Cadet Y had thought up an excuse that he hoped would satisfy the adjutant and was quick to reply, "Well, sir, when we were on exercise this week we were practising riot training. I was hit by potatoes that the crowd were using as missiles and I was unfortunate enough to be hit numerous times in the neck, sir." The adjutant asked him if he seriously expected him to believe this story, to which Cadet Y said, "Yes, sir." The adjutant peered down his nose at the young cadet, before turning away and carrying on with his inspection.

Months later the cadets were now in the final week of training waiting to pass out as second lieutenants on the Friday. During this week there is an official awards ceremony where the general in charge of the Academy presents awards to the best cadet, scholar, sportsman, writer of the course and a few others. Just before the general presents the official prizes, the academy adjutant presents a few spoof prizes that the cadets are not aware of. The best action hero presentation goes to Officer Cadet Z for his gung-ho part in an attack on the final exercise, etc. The adjutant stood on the stage in front of the two hundred seated cadets and asked Cadet Y and his girlfriend (Cadet F) to both stand up and identify themselves to the audience. He and his girlfriend both slowly stood up, wearing bright red faces of embarrassment, not knowing what was coming next.

The adjutant announced that the next presentation was for the best bluff excuse he had heard throughout this commissioning course. He then regaled the story of the morning inspection and the excuse that Cadet Y had told him about having large black bruises all over his neck. The adjutant remarked at how shocked he had been to see the bruises and how similar they looked to teeth marks and not potatoes. Strangely enough, the bruises looked similar in size and shape to that of Cadet F's mouth.

Both were applauded by all of the cadets at the ceremony and were asked to step forward onto the stage by the adjutant to accept a presentation which turned out to be a potato peeler.

3   DIRTY FACES

One of the oldest and first field craft lessons that any new recruit in the British Army gets taught is the application of camouflage cream to the hands and face. The cream is used to darken the skin so that the soldier can blend in with the environment and not present a glaring target to enemy soldiers on operations.

Corporal X had recently been posted as a training instructor to Pirbright, teaching the next generation of junior soldiers destined to fill the ranks of the Parachute Regiment. Corporal X was one of life's naturally funny characters, who got bored easily and made light of most things. A few years earlier he had fought in the Falklands campaign, serving in Sergeant McKay's platoon, who was awarded a posthumous Victoria Cross for his part in the night attack on Mount Longdon.

When applying camouflage cream, you can't have too much or too little: you need just enough to break up the shape of the face and hands so that you are more akin to your surroundings. Too little and a shiny face can easily be seen; too much and a totally blackened face sticks out in nature. He briefed the section of ten new recruits sat at his feet who were hanging onto every word that this war veteran told them.

After a few minutes, Corporal X told his section, "Stay there, lads, I am going for a quick pee behind that bush over there." He walked away from his section and stood beside the bush knowing that the young soldiers could still see him when he unzipped his trousers. He pulled his trousers down to his knees so that he could urinate standing up, with his buttocks on show to the recruits.

All the recruits could see Corporal X facing away; they all noticed that both of his buttocks had been tiger-striped with camouflage cream. On seeing this, the new recruits started pointing, giggling; and the laughter got louder.

Corporal X asked, "All right, lads, what's so funny?"

The young recruits replied in between giggles, "It's your bum, Corporal, it's covered in camouflage cream."

Corporal X told them, "In a sniper threat area you can't be too careful, lads; you never know who is watching and you will always need the toilet at some stage."

He managed to keep a straight face and finished the lesson. Later that night, before the young recruits went out on their first field exercise, ten new recruits were in the toilet asking each other, "Do you think I have too much or too little on my bum?"

In the meantime, Corporal X was in the staff room telling the rest of the training team about the prank he had just played on his section of new recruits.

4   ANGELS IN THE WOODS

Whoever said that there should be no difference made between men and women in the deployable areas of the British Army need to have their heads examined. Whilst stationed at the Royal Military Academy Sandhurst, Colour Sergeant X was lucky enough to be selected to be the male platoon instructor for a female platoon in their second and third terms.

It was a position of trust for male instructors to be given the appointment to lead these young, impressionable females through their training. Not an enviable appointment for the overly eager colour sergeant who wanted his team to win the inter-platoon competitions in the final term against the other male platoons. A fact of life is that the male platoons will do better than the female platoons at Sandhurst due to the physical nature of the competitions. Shock horror, I can hear from the politically correct brigade already.

Likewise, on exercises the majority of lady cadets were not too keen to stay in the field, living in trenches for extended periods of time if they could help it. For a start, women are more hygienic than their male counterparts who do not mind living in a field and stinking to high heaven for days on end – the majority of women do mind.

At the very end of the cadets' year at the Academy, they go abroad for a two-week final exercise on their final leadership phase. The platoon was fortunate enough to be sent to Southern Germany for their final exercise. At this stage of training, a cadet would need to commit a major atrocity to be failed and not be commissioned. When the exercise finished, they only have a further two weeks in the Academy before they pass out as commissioned officers.

The formal orders to the cadets on the exercise is minimal, because they should be trusted to get on with the mission, due to the fact that some of them will be in their regiments in a month's time as fully fledged second lieutenants and bona fide platoon commanders. Colour Sergeant X had given the cadets their final set of orders, which was to set up an observation post (op) overlooking a crossroads, and report back all enemy movement through the crossroads by radio to their HQ. They were given twenty-four hours to practise any rehearsals, issue their own orders, pack their kit, march the fifteen kilometres to the area where the op position would be located and have it set up by noon the following day. Officer Cadet Y was in charge of this mission; she went about her business getting the platoon prepared and ready to deploy. The real platoon commander and colour sergeant left them to it and planned to check on their progress in the op position just prior to noon the next day.

The next morning Colour Sergeant X marched to where he expected to find the cadets in their op position; sure enough he found a good position well camouflaged and dug in. The only problem was there were no female cadets to be seen. There should have been twelve camouflaged future female platoon commanders peering out of the op but there were none. All their webbing and bergans (rucksacks) were in the position but there were no cadets or weapons in sight.

He sat down on the ground, pulled his map from his trouser pocket to have a look and work out where the female cadets could possibly be. There was nothing obvious on the map that would attract the females away from their op position.

The colour sergeant decided to walk down to the nearest river, which was about 800 metres away, and see if he could find them replenishing their water bottles as it was a hot day. When he got closer to the river he could hear a lot of giggling, female, English voices, and he knew he had found them. As he emerged from the tree line at the edge of the river, he couldn't believe his eyes. There were twelve naked female cadets frolicking around in the river, splashing around having a great time. He let out his deepest scream of "What the hell is going on here?" which silenced the giggling and had the girls scrambling back into their uniforms and putting their equipment on in an instant.

Once the girls were fully clothed and kitted up, he took the officer cadet in charge to one side to ask her what the hell she was playing at. She explained that, as the commander, she decided that the girls were filthy and needed to wash themselves and their hair, so she made a command decision to let them have a swim and get cleaned up before occupying the op position. At this point the colour sergeant exploded and went into a major rant regarding her lack of leadership, mission security, responsibilities as a commander, etc.

To make matters worse, the girls hadn't noticed that while they were in the river having a great time splashing around, a small crowd of German lads had noticed them and were queued up fifty metres away, spying on them through the bushes. The colour sergeant was quoted telling Officer Cadet Y, "The only thing of value that you have produced under your leadership and command today, is the biggest and best peep show in Southern Germany. God only knows what the enemy has seen."

Thankfully, no photographs were ever taken, otherwise the national newspapers could have had a field day and twelve female officer cadets would most likely not have passed out as commissioned officers two weeks later.

As the years progressed and experience was gained, some of these officer cadets went on to have fantastic careers in the British Army – reaching the rank of Lt Col and others have been made Members of the Most Excellent Order of the British Empire (MBE).

5 PRIOR PLANNING AND PREPARATION PREVENTS PISS-POOR PERFORMANCE

Every infantry regiment in the British Army has two colours – the Queen's Colour and a Regimental Colour – they are basically flags on poles that you will see on big parades like Trooping the Colour or Changing of the Guard at Buckingham Palace. Whenever the colours are on parade it is quite a special time militarily. If soldiers are dressed in civilian clothing and the colours are marched past, they should stand to attention; if they are dressed in uniform they salute. In the olden days units would stand around the colours and defend them to the last bullet – which happened a few times in British military history.

Any parade that is going to include the colours being marched on incorporates a lot of drill and parade rehearsals before the big day to ensure it will go without a hitch.

On this particular parade, His Royal Highness The Prince of Wales was going to be the inspecting officer, so a lot of extra preparation and rehearsals had taken place. The regimental sergeant major had specially selected the colour party for this Royal parade, which consisted of two officers, a warrant officer class two, and two colour sergeants – all very reliable men.

After weeks of rehearsals the day arrived. The regimental sergeant major went ahead of the main parading soldiers to ensure everything was in place before his colour party arrived at the parade ground. The parade was taking place at RAF Wattisham – about an hour's drive from Colchester.

The regimental sergeant major was standing at the edge of the parade ground when a colour sergeant from his sister battalion came sprinting towards him in his best uniform. When he reached the regimental sergeant major, he could hardly talk for laughing – eventually he explained that his warrant officer in charge of his colour party had left his uniform trousers in Colchester. The regimental sergeant major's first thought was, "I hope this is a joke; we are on parade in fifteen minutes and there is absolutely no chance of getting back to Colchester in a round trip of two hours to collect his trousers."

The warrant officer had indeed forgotten his trousers, but fortunately had the wit to go round the Army camp he was now in and find someone of a similar size and height so he could borrow his trousers for the parade – which turned out to be loaned from a private soldier from the Army Air Corps.

The parade went extremely well and there were no hitches, His Royal Highness never knew how close he was to seeing a warrant officer parading in front of him dressed in his Y-fronts.

6   WHAT'S APPROPRIATE – HORSES FOR COURSES

Eight years previously, Colour Sergeant Y had been a corporal instructor at the depot of the Parachute Regiment before he became an instructor at the Royal Military Academy Sandhurst. The Parachute Regiment Depot is where the training of future paratroopers takes place, a factory that changes civilians into men that will perform controlled acts of violence when called on to do so, on behalf of Her Majesty's government around the globe.

Sandhurst, on the other hand, was full of gentlefolk who would eventually lead soldiers – but very few of the officers would lead parachute soldiers. To that end, the course and surroundings were tempered to a more sedate and civilised manner within the Academy grounds.

Colour Sergeant Y naively thought that a few tricks he had learned in his depot Para days could be implemented into how he ran his platoon at Sandhurst. As a corporal, if he needed to speak to his recruits quickly he would shout "Corridor"; the recruits would promptly stop what they were doing in their rooms and appear in the corridor, standing to attention. All within ten seconds, otherwise press-ups came into play as a punishment until all the trainee soldiers were present.

At Sandhurst he explained what "corridor" meant to his platoon of twenty-six female officer cadets and how he expected them to be in the corridor within ten seconds when they heard him calling "Corridor" – all looked at him quizzically. "Any questions on the command – Corridor?" asked the colour sergeant. None of the cadets said a word to him before they were dismissed.

A few days, later he needed to speak to his platoon quickly on an important issue that needed to be passed down from the company commanders' meeting.

"Corridor!" bellowed the colour sergeant as he walked into the platoon's accommodation. Within ten seconds all the girls were standing in the corridor awaiting the important information from their instructor.

He nearly fainted; the girls were stood in the corridor in various states of undress, skimpy underwear, stockings and suspenders, some just out of the shower with towels that barely kept them covered, etc. With eyes popping out of his head, he had to ask all of the girls to go back to their rooms, get covered up with more clothing and come back in five minutes. The girls went off to their rooms, giggling like children, while the colour sergeant went into his office and put the kettle on for a much-needed cup of tea.

Five minutes later he re-briefed them that if he ever shouted "Corridor" again, they were to come out into the corridor wearing clothes appropriate to having a male in their presence who was not their boyfriend.

Throughout the remaining nine months of their training, the colour sergeant never once called "Corridor" again. If the college sergeant major had appeared on the platoon floor and found the girls being briefed dressed so scantily, the colour sergeant would have been sacked on the spot.

7   MOTHERS AND THEIR ADORING SONS

The company sergeant major was sitting in his nice new office in a training establishment that had just been opened to cater for the need to recruit junior soldiers to fill the ranks of the British Army. All young soldiers were called students and were stationed in the establishment for twelve months before moving on to adult service and phase two of their training. They were all earmarked for the Teeth Arms of the Army – tankies, gunners, infantry and paratroopers.

The telephone rang and he picked it up; on the other end of the line was the irate mother of Student X who was wondering why her son had not been home for over two months. The young students were classed as minors due to the fact they were under the age of eighteen. They had to write a letter to their parents asking them if they could go home at weekends; most of their parents would reply saying that they could or could not. Sadly, some of the young students were from broken homes and had no place to go. However, the vast majority came from normal loving families and the parents wanted to see their children as often as possible.

The company sergeant major had a file where he kept all the parent letter replies stating that the sons or daughters could go home at the dated weekend. Looking through his file, he found a whole batch of letters regarding this student and his mother – according to these letters he had been home every weekend for the last two months. Without a letter, the young students were not allowed to stay out overnight from the college. There was a bed check at midnight to ensure all students staying the weekend were in bed and accounted for to ensure none were missing.

Smelling a rat, he reassured the parent on the other end of the telephone line that he would get to the bottom of it and told her he would call her back once he had found out why her son hadn't been home.

Student X was called for and brought before the company sergeant major for an interview without coffee. He was a typical Londoner that thought he was a bit of a wide boy, one of the very few students that had just turned eighteen years of age prior to passing out of the junior establishment and moving on to his next phase of training.

The company sergeant major asked Student X, "When was the last time you were home?"

The young lad quickly replied, "Last weekend, sir."

The company sergeant major asked, "And when before that were you home?" The student replied that he had been home every weekend for the last two months.

The company sergeant major looked at the young student and asked him, "If that is the case, why has your mother just called me to find out why you haven't been home for two months?" He leapt from his chair and demanded to know where he had been spending his weekends, because it clearly wasn't at home or in the college. The company sergeant major ranted that one thing the British Army did not need was any more liars within its ranks. He told the young soldier that if he didn't tell him exactly where he had been staying at the weekends over the last two months, he would get him thrown out of the Army within a week due to lack of integrity on his part.

Student X nearly collapsed at this revelation and the reaction by the company sergeant major. Flapping and not wanting to get thrown out of the Army, the young student told him that he had been spending his weekends at a house in Leeds with some girls. When the company sergeant major got to the bottom of the story, it became apparent that it wasn't girlfriends that he was staying with, but hookers in a dodgy housing estate. He had been spending all of his cash and time in a house of ill repute every weekend for the last two months instead of going home.

Having been around the world a few times, the company sergeant major was surprised but not shocked at the young student's behaviour; he was also wise enough to know that the young lad had not gone to Leeds on his own. He wanted to get the names of his accomplices and catch all of them for the sake of their parents.

The company sergeant major asked him, "Who else was with you at these love parties?"

Student X realising that he was in a world of hurt but not wanting to admit it or grass on his mates who were with him, told the company sergeant major, "No one, sir, just me on my own."

The company sergeant major started yelling at the lad, "If you think I believe that then you must think I button up the back of my neck," getting the desired result. The young student's bottom lip began to quiver and there was a tear in the corner of his eye.

Picking up the telephone, the company sergeant major looked at Student X and told him, "You have got exactly five seconds to tell me who your accomplices are. If you don't tell me, I will call your mother right now and tell her you have been spending your time and cash at the weekends with whores in a brothel in Leeds."

Student X quickly blurted out: "Students A, B, C and D."

All the students were brought before the company sergeant major for a talk about morals and standards expected in the British Army. They all spent their last few weeks at the college doing extra duties at nights prior to their passing-out parade.

The company sergeant major telephoned the young lad's mother and guaranteed her that her son would be home this weekend and he was very much looking forward to seeing his family.

8   TATTOO ARTIST AT WORK

Colour Sergeant X came out of New College accommodation at the Royal Military Academy Sandhurst one sunny summer's morning to inspect his platoon of potential officers. They were all formed up in three ranks facing towards the lower lakes in the Academy grounds, dressed in shirt-sleeve order – denims, stable belt, beret, with shirt sleeves rolled up. As he approached the platoon, the duty cadet called the platoon smartly to attention and asked the colour sergeant if he would like to inspect the platoon. As usual, the instructor started the inspection and picked people up for boots not shiny enough, trousers not pressed correctly, creases in shirts, hair too long, fluff on berets, loose threads on shirts and he placed them on show parade that night. Every cadet hated show parades, because it meant getting back into uniform at 2200 hours at night and parading at the college guardroom to be inspected again by the duty colour sergeant.

As he progressed along the front rank, he noticed all of the cadets now had small tattoos on their right forearm which none of them had yesterday or any of the days since they had been in his platoon. The colour sergeant exploded into a rage, yelling at the cadets and telling them that officers should not have tattoos, as it was un-gentlemanly, unsightly and a lower-rank vocation. He also noticed that they all had the same tattoo and it was an Everton badge – his favourite team.

"What's the meaning of these tattoos," he bellowed at the duty cadet, noticing for the first time that he had one on his forearm as well. The cadet quickly explained that the whole platoon thought so highly of him that, in his honour, they all went together to the tattoo parlour to get the same tattoo that he himself had on his forearm. At this remark he nearly fainted, thinking this was the last straw for his Army career; he would get removed from post for poor leadership by setting a bad example on his part and allowing this to happen.

On closer inspection of the tattoos, it was with the greatest of relief for the colour sergeant when he noticed that the tattoos were in fact not real – they were only hand drawn on with a felt tip marker pen and were washable. As the duty cadet shouted out, "April fool," the colour sergeant was so relieved that he had to smile and laugh along with the giggling platoon.

Later that night, vengeance was sweet as the platoon colour sergeant spent a few happy hours running the platoon ragged up and down the hills of Barossa, and around the lower lakes within the Academy grounds, carrying logs as payback for their little joke – which had nearly given him a heart attack.

9   RSPCA

Sergeant X was a training instructor in charge of the training team that taught new recruits in the Territorial Army in the Regiments Depot. His immediate boss was called Captain Y, who was an ex-regimental sergeant major now commissioned into the Parachute Regiment.

The sergeant was very experienced and was very well thought of for his exploits at Goose Green with Second Battalion the Parachute Regiment. The captain was a generation above and very well respected for his service in Aden and early tours of Northern Ireland in the 1970s with First Battalion the Parachute Regiment.

Captain Y had a little white Jack Russell terrier that went everywhere with him – running, to the office, training with the recruits. Unfortunately, the dog would nip at the heels of unsuspecting recruits or staff instructors, which was becoming a bit of a nuisance.

Sergeant X decided that he would play a joke on Captain Y by writing a letter as a wind-up. He copied a letterhead from the RSPCA and addressed the letter to Captain Y, before posting it in Farnborough. The content of the letter was a complaint against his dog, which had been nipping members of the public and soldiers in training. The letter warned him that if the dog didn't improve and stop biting people, then there was no option but to have it put down in the interest of public safety. Sergeant X had told the other members of the training team what he had done and awaited a response from the captain to his letter.

A few days later, the captain came into the office without his dog, which was very unusual. So Sergeant X went in and asked the captain where his dog was. The captain replied, "Yesterday I received a letter of complaint from the RSPCA against my dog saying it had been biting people, so I had no option but to have it put down."

At this revelation the sergeant nearly collapsed onto the floor. He stammered, "You have done what? You must be joking."

The captain kept a straight face and replied, "Well what else could I do? If it bit a recruit it might bite a child. So last night the wife and I took it to the vet and explained what it had been doing and they agreed. So they put it to sleep by injection."

The sergeant was now as white as a sheet and sweating not knowing what to say. He eventually mustered up the moral courage to confess that it had all been a joke, he had written the letter himself and not the RSPCA.

The captain quickly pounced and shouted, "Gotcha." He had known all along as he had overheard the sergeant telling the other members of the team what he was doing – his dog was alive and well at home.

The sergeant was so relieved that he hadn't put his dog down he was physically shaking and unable to speak for a few minutes. Until eventually he replied, "Don't attempt to play a trick on a fox when you are actually a chicken." The whole training team laughed long into the afternoon at the sergeant's expense.

Captain Y was made a member of the Most Excellent Order of the British Empire (MBE) a few years later for his hard work during forty years' service to the regiment.

10   GETTING LOST IN THE CROWD

Part of officer training takes place at a place called Longmoor Camp in Southern England; here the officer cadets are taught how to operate in an urban environment. The training area is a small village with real fully functional houses, shop, pub and a security base outside the village. The camp is well maintained and could be mistaken for normal streets that you would find in the surrounding villages.

The cadets spend a week there; the first part of the week half of the cadets are nominated as exercising troops and the other half are nominated as the civilian population that live in the houses. Later in the week they then reverse roles for the remainder of the training.

The cadets being exercised live and operate from the security base and are split into normal platoon formations and are taught, trained and tested in how to deal with shootings, bombings, searching vehicles, searching the public and how to operate in a riot situation.

The cadets acting as the civilian population are given make-believe names; they are briefed to play the part stated on their new identity cards and to dress accordingly. Some are nominated to be the bar owner, barmaid, gardeners, milkman, taxi drivers, electricians, shopkeeper, petrol pump attendant: generally people in everyday life scenarios.

Throughout the week the cadets acting as civilians are told to set up incidents and wait for the security forces to react. They would set up bombings, sniping shoots and smuggle the weapons away in prams being pushed by mothers, hassle the troops for a reaction, hide and transport weapons. The cadets being tested as security forces would be given orders to be in certain areas at set times, so that they would be sniped at or weapons would be moved at that time so they might find them. It is fantastic training for the officer cadets on both sides of the training and very good experience for the future platoon commanders of the British Army.

On the final day of the exercise there is a full-blown riot which wouldn't have looked out of place in Belfast in the early 1970s. The security forces are all kitted out in full riot gear: shields, baton guns, body armour, wooden batons and helmets with riot visors fitted. By this stage they have been taught how to organise crowd snatch squads, form baselines, shield drills, baton rules, operate vehicles in riot situations and how to deal with petrol bombers.

The cadet civilian population are briefed to be rioters and to do their best to keep the security forces out of a certain street. On riot day, soldiers from outside units come in to boost the rioters' numbers and help to make the riot as realistic as possible, so the exercising cadets get maximum benefit from the experience and exercise. For this task they make a barrier out of old cars, boxes, tyres, bricks, stones, wood and anything they can get their hands on. To increase pressure on the exercising cadets, they burn tyres, throw missiles, petrol bombs and attack their riot shields.

The soldiers from the outside units that turn up on the day of the riot relish the chance to attack and abuse the officer cadets being tested; they are more than happy to attack the riot shields and beat the security forces. The ammunition used as missiles against the security forces is potatoes. On the street corners a farmer delivers and piles up tons of potatoes for ready use by the rioters. Getting hit by a potato that has been thrown by a soldier, who is trying his hardest to injure an officer cadet, is quite painful and leaves a black bruise on arms and legs that are not protected by body armour.

Throughout the week the cadets company instructing staff has also been acting as the civilian population or security forces with them during the incidents. On riot day the company commander briefed the cadets and staff that they were to clear the road from street X to street Y in order for the engineers to come in and search a house at the end of the road. Once all the orders were issued, the company commander finished off by saying that all instructing staff were to wear white tape on their arms so that they could be identified by everybody as instructors.

Colour Sergeant X listened to the orders and was surprised when the company commander said that all instructors should be identifiable by having white tape on their arms. He thought to himself there was no chance he was putting white tape on his arms so that the rioting cadets on the other side could single him out for extra potato target practice.

At the end of the riot, Colour Sergeant X laughed his head off as every member of the instructing staff that had worn white tape around their arms had been targeted by the rioting cadets and soldiers. Every one of them had been heavily pelted with potatoes; their arms and legs, which had no body armour protection, were covered in painful-looking deep black bruises – similar in pattern to a leopard.

He never had a single bruise – being indistinguishable is sometimes best.

11   MASTER CHEF ON MANOEUVRES

Corporal X was a very experienced soldier who had been around the world on various exercises and been on many operations, including the Falkland Islands Campaign of 1982. He had recently been posted to the training depot to train new recruits and was put in charge of a section of twelve young men who were straight from civilian life. Under his guidance, leadership, and instruction the majority should pass out of training twenty-eight weeks later all being well.

In the early days of training the budding recruits spent a few days living out in the woods to acclimatise and get used to living outdoors. It is surprising the amount of youngsters who have never spent a single night living out in a tent, etc. A lot of us took living out for granted as we grew up in the country and had spent many weekends camping in a tent.

As fledgling paratroopers, they were also taught basic survival techniques in case they needed to use them in some far-off land in the future on behalf of Her Majesty's government. The survival techniques taught were basic methods in how to snare rabbits, catch fish, what plants and shrubs could be eaten safely and were nutritious.

A lot of the recruits were city dwellers who never knew where meat and vegetables actually came from – some had never seen a real cow in a field. Once they had been shown how to kill and cook a rabbit, they were all introduced to their live rabbit and issued vegetables. They were told that was their dinner for the night – there were a few 'you must be joking' faces in the audience.

Corporal X took his squad away to a section area where they would dispatch the rabbits and make their dinner for the night. The first issue encountered was the unwillingness of some recruits to kill their dinner. As the night grew late, they all decided killing a rabbit was better than starvation for the night. Their next issue was the rabbit was too big for their mess tin. One group of three recruits that were quite squeamish were not willing to chop their rabbit into smaller pieces so they looked around for a larger vessel to cook the rabbit stew in. They found what can only be described as an old metal bucket lying half-buried and rusting in the ground, which they dug up and washed out. Once it was washed out and scrubbed to get the rust off, it didn't look too bad – or so they thought anyway.

Whilst carrying out his rounds checking on the new recruits, Corporal X came across these three individuals who were looking pleased with themselves at their efforts at making dinner. They had the rabbit in the pot, with all the vegetables, and supplemented it with nettles and it was bubbling away producing a lovely aroma. Corporal X asked them where they got the container from and, when they explained, he pointed out, "I hope you washed that out and boiled it before the chicken was put in to kill all the germs."

The recruits all replied, "Yes, Corporal, as per the instructions on how to kill bugs and sterilise by boiling." They hadn't; once the chicken was cleaned it had been put straight into the makeshift pot with all the veggies. Once the stew was ready, the three recruits scoffed the lot between them before getting into their sleeping bags for the night.

Around midnight, Corporal X was patrolling around the section area making sure everything was all right and the young recruits were all OK. Before he got to the area where the three 'Cordon Bleu' chefs were, he could hear moans and retching noises from twenty metres away. As he reached them, all three were either writhing around the ground or bent over on hands and knees being sick – or trying to be sick, as they had already retched everything up that was possible.

Corporal X knew straight away what the cause was and the lads were taken straight to the hospital in Aldershot, where they were all treated for food poisoning; they were in a bad way for about a week.

The moral of the story is only eat properly cooked chicken when outside and listen to what you have been told – Kentucky Fried Chicken is probably best, unless in a survival situation.

Many years later, Corporal X was awarded a Mention in Dispatches (MID) for bravery against the enemy during a tour of Afghanistan in the rank of captain.

12   IGNORE SAFETY RULES AT YOUR PERIL

One of the most important lessons all soldiers learn is never to point a weapon of any description at a person unless you mean to use the weapon against them. Nice and simple rule, where could you go wrong? Another important lesson is not to use live ammunition systems when teaching a weapons lesson. Both very simple lessons and all soldiers know them, so there should be no accidents. WRONG.

Colour Sergeant X, who was from an old traditional regiment, was teaching the 66mm anti-tank rocket system to a platoon of officer cadets behind a range hut on the Brecon firing ranges in Wales. This particular weapon system fired a high-explosive projectile capable of destroying an armoured vehicle. To save money, the Army had converted some of the used 66mm rocket launchers to fire a 21mm metal bolt from the weapon. The weapon functioned just like the real weapon: when fired, it had a back blast that exploded out the rear and fired a metal projectile out the front which had a tracer element so that you could see where the metal bolt went – target hit or miss. The bolt never had an explosive content and was a cheap training aid to save firing expensive real 66mm rockets – nonetheless it could be lethal in the wrong hands.

On this particular day, Colour Sergeant X had been rushing around all over the place and thought he was too clever to adhere to the above two weapon-handling rules. He decided to teach his lesson using a live 66mm rocket system which still had a live 21mm bolt inside the weapon. All the cadets gathered at his feet, poised with notebook and pencil ready to write down the information on the weapon system.

The lesson was going extremely well, the cadets were asking questions and the instructor was answering them back with the correct information. Moving on with the lesson, he then taught them the firing procedures for the weapon system.

At the point Colour Sergeant X was demonstrating the firing drills, there was a bright flash, a blast of air, smoke and a loud bang as the 21mm bolt fired from the weapon system hit a young cadet sitting at the back of the lesson. The bolt went straight through the front of his chest and was sticking out of his back in the shoulder area, fully embedded in his body.

The cadet was rolling around on the ground, clearly in great pain and shock, and blood was soaking through his uniform. The colour sergeant was heard to say, "Shit I didn't mean that to happen." The moral of the story is to always adhere to simple rules that are there for a reason and should be followed to the letter at all times. Thankfully the cadet made a full recovery and went on to have a very successful career in the Army – the colour sergeant did not.

13   MIDDLE EASTERN PROMISE

The Royal Military Academy Sandhurst is renowned for training officer cadets from different countries around the world – Africans, Arabs, Far East Caribbean and Muslims. Some of these cadets are not as enthusiastic as you would expect to find in such a prestigious establishment. A few are only there because they have been ordered to attend by their fathers to gain a little grounding in life. However, to be fair, there are some who do pass the course on their own merit – Cadet Z was certainly not one of these future officers.

Colour Sergeant X was unfortunate enough to have Cadet Z in his platoon. He was a member of the royal family from a Middle Eastern country and had absolutely no intention of spending any more time in uniform than he could help. He had been ordered by his father to complete the twelve-month course at Sandhurst – if he was to get any inheritance.

For the past six months Colour Sergeant X had been having his patience tested to the limit with this cadet. The colour sergeant was a very professional instructor and wanted his platoon to win or do very well in the inter-platoon competitions.

The weak link in his platoon was Cadet Z, who was only interested in getting up to London at weekends. There he could sample the best delights that the West had to offer a very wealthy Arab who enjoyed the excesses only money can buy.

The final straw for Colour Sergeant X was at the end of a morning's fitness session where Cadet Z was last again. Not only was he last, but he started to walk the last few hundred metres to the finishing line. The cadet had made the biggest error he could have made by showing no effort at all on his part or commitment to the platoon in the eyes of Colour Sergeant X.

The colour sergeant went straight across to the cadet so he could vent his anger and annoyance; he gave him the biggest bollocking of his young life. The cadet was not used to being spoken to like this and was somewhat shocked and taken aback. The colour sergeant held nothing back and called him every name under the sun – a fat, short, useless piece of offal not fit to walk on the hallowed grounds of Sandhurst.

After a few minutes of verbal abuse, the cadet regained his composure and replied to the very angry colour sergeant, "I may be short and fat but I have lots of money." This induced a full-blown rage by the instructor which the young prince would likely never forget for the rest of his life.

14   BATTLE OF THE SHITS

Private X had only been in the Army six weeks and did not fully understand the intricacies of regimental rivalry. During his first few weeks of training all he seemed to do was drill, learn to salute, halt, turn and march up and down the parade square, getting shouted at by his sergeant. Drill is considered an important part of military life in some circles within the Army, but not by all soldiers – some despise it with a passion.

Early in all recruits' training they are tested on the drill square to ensure all can march in a straight line and salute as an individual and as part of a platoon. Private X's platoon sergeant was a member of the Parachute Regiment and was surprisingly good at drill; he was determined that all the recruits in the platoon would pass the drill test first time.

Sergeant Z was a member of a famous Guards Regiment and was also determined that all of his recruits would pass the drill test first time as well. In the sergeants' mess there was a sweepstake for the platoon that achieved the highest number of recruits that passed the drill test on their first attempt. All the platoon sergeants wanted to win the sweepstake and impress the regimental sergeant major – more importantly, the sergeants had all put twenty pounds into the sweepstake and three hundred pounds was there for the winning.

Private X and his platoon were stood at the edge of the drill square formed up in three ranks, waiting and ready to be marched on for their drill test. Besides his platoon, there was also a Guards platoon formed up waiting their turn for the test as well.

Just as Private X and his platoon were called forward and began marching onto the drill square for their test, the sergeant from the Guards Platoon called out, "Only two things fall from the sky – bird shit and paratroopers." He was hoping to put the marching recruits off their step and fail the test.

The guards recruits thought this was hilarious and started to laugh out loudly until the Para sergeant replied, "Never mind those, lads, we all know two things stay on the ground – dog shit and crap hats." The Para Platoon marched on with pride and the Guards Platoon fell silent. The Para sergeant won the sweepstake in the sergeants' mess and couldn't wait to rub his victory into the sergeant that had tried to put his recruits off their step.

15   HOW NOT TO DEAL WITH THE MEDIA

Corporal X was a very keen and enthusiastic non-commissioned officer serving in his regiment's training depot instructing new recruits. The media were very interested in all Army training at this time because of a recent spate of bullying and racist cases that had hit the national headlines.

The training establishments were keen for journalists to visit and interview recruits when given the chance; they could see for themselves and report that nothing was amiss with recruit training. Corporal X was selected along with another two corporals to be interviewed by the journalists at a press conference held that night in the depot.

The corporals attending the meeting were dressed in their best uniforms to look the part and impress the media with their appearance. A total of twenty journalists turned up with an array of cameras and tape recorders. The interview was going as well as planned. The colonel and officers stood behind the chosen corporals, beaming every time they answered a question politely and in line with the new Armed Services Equal Opportunity and Diversity Policy.

The meeting was going splendidly until one of the journalists commented that all questions were being answered parrot-fashion and he did not believe that everything in the training establishment could be perfect. There must be something that the recruits were not good at and would need to be pushed harder to achieve success.

Corporal X volunteered an answer and agreed that the recruits were not good at everything; the commanding officer leaned forward wondering what he was going to say. A journalist asked the corporal to elaborate. "Go on, Corporal X, I am sure the officers and everyone else in the room is very keen to hear of any imperfections that the recruits have that might require extra training." The media at the time were trying very hard to link any extra training that wasn't in the curriculum to bullying.

Encouraged, Corporal X volunteered that some recruits could not pass the Army swimming test and had to be given extra swimming lessons, which was not in the programme. The journalist asked if there were any trends that could explain why they couldn't swim. The corporal replied, "Yes, they are all of African descent." The journalists couldn't write quickly enough into their notebooks and the commanding officer spilt his tea.

In the newspaper the next morning the quote was in print for all to see – *Ethnic minority soldiers can't pass Army swimming test*. In the training establishment a study had to be done to find out why some ethnic minorities weren't as good at swimming as others. Corporal X had an interview with the commanding officer without coffee the next morning, where his naivety when dealing with the press was pointed out.

The young corporal had stated a fact and the training establishment was actually doing its best to get the recruits through the swimming test, without adding in extra lessons for all of the recruits who didn't need them.

16 MUFFLED MUTTERINGS

The officer cadets had been deployed on an urban training exercise at Longmoor village for a few days and had already been taught all the necessary skills and practised what they had been taught to operate in a built-up area. The exercise had entered its final phase and the platoons were now being given orders which they carried out under the command, control and planning of the cadet platoon commander.

The colour sergeant instructor listened to the orders being issued to the platoon from the cadet platoon commander. He had been given the mission to raid a house in one of the nearby streets inside the village where received intelligence indicated that a known terrorist was likely to be in hiding.

The cadet commander gave a good set of orders; he had thought through the scenario quite well and issued his orders accordingly to achieve the mission. He nominated soldiers to stop the traffic driving past the house during the raid; soldiers were positioned front and rear of the building in case the terrorist tried to escape from a door or open window. He split the platoon into groups and allocated soldiers to search specific rooms and areas; he nominated arresting soldiers and issued handcuffs. He ordered a section to be ready to deploy as anti-riot troops armed with shields, batons and helmets, just in case the neighbours in nearby houses took exception to a local guy being arrested.

The civilian population was being played by other cadets who had been briefed that they were to occupy the house, hide the terrorist inside, but make it spicy, something different; use their imagination and don't let the security forces find the terrorist straight away.

The rehearsals were complete once the troops had practised and practised until they all knew what they were doing, where they would go in the house – left, right, or upstairs. The plan was simple – a team entering would rush the front door and smash it down with a sledgehammer. The troops behind them would then all file into the house in the order that they could search the house and every room within seconds to catch the terrorist wherever he was hiding.

As the platoon approached the house, the first thing they noticed was the loud music blaring out and the flashing disco lights from within. Once the cadet commander was happy the cut-off groups were at the rear of the house and the traffic had been stopped on the road, he gave the order for the sledgehammer soldiers to rush forward and smash the front door in.

As the sledgehammer soldiers reached the front door of the house and had just raised the sledgehammers ready to smash their way in, it was opened by a female cadet playing the part of a madam. She stood in the open doorway dressed in a mini skirt, stockings on display and a basque showing her ample cleavage. The madam asked in a very slow and sexy voice, "Can I help you?" The two soldiers holding the sledgehammers stood there rooted to the spot, with dribble running down their chins.

Watching from behind a hedge, the cadet platoon commander glared in amazement and annoyance at the soldiers who had been foiled by a woman and an open door. He quickly rallied the rest of the platoon with a "follow me" order, as he raced to the door pushing the sexy cadet out of the way so that his soldiers could all get to their allocated rooms, search for and capture the suspected terrorist. Rushing upstairs, he ran into his own nominated bedroom and found to his amazement a male dressed in the tiniest black G-string, wearing a gimp mask over his head and handcuffed at the hands and feet to an upright bed frame. In the middle of the room there was another naked male kneeling on his hands and knees. He was dressed in a similar G-string, a leather mask and a dog collar around his neck. The leash from the dog collar was being held by a gorgeous female who was standing astride the male. She was wearing high heels, stockings and suspenders, tiny knickers and a basque. In her other hand she held a horse-riding crop and was smacking the man on his knees kneeling before her – who was crying out with each smack.

It took the cadet in charge a few seconds to take in what he was seeing and to focus his mind on the mission and find the terrorist. He ripped the gimp mask from the male handcuffed to the bed and discovered that he wasn't the terrorist – he told all the soldiers to search under the beds and in the cupboards. It took him a while to realise that the terrorist was in full view and kneeling in the centre of the room wearing a leather mask beneath the thighs of a gorgeous female cadet.

Only in the UK could officer training at the prestigious Royal Military Academy Sandhurst be enhanced by cadets using their imagination and adding a brothel into a terrorist scenario.

CHAPTER 2

IN BARRACKS

Soldiers cannot remain on operations or exercise indefinitely and do spend quite a large amount of their time in barracks. The single or married soldiers living unaccompanied live in the camp where they have a locker, bed space and eat in the cookhouse. Married soldiers generally live in local Army married quarters near to the base, which are provided at a lower rental rate than normal civilian council rates. Some soldiers have purchased and own their houses where they can live once they have been given permission by the commanding officer to live away from the umbrella of the military.

Whilst the units are in barracks the soldiers carry out administration of themselves and the unit's equipment – weapons, vehicle maintenance, etc. They also do in barracks training, fitness, classroom work, lectures, ranges, driving and local area training.

Normally they have the nights and weekends off, unless they have been nominated for a guard duty or work-party detail.

17   EARLY BIRD CATCHES THE WORM

In the early eighties homosexuals were not allowed to serve in the Armed Forces; if discovered, they would be disciplined, charged and thrown out of the Army.

Sergeant X was serving as the provost sergeant for his unit when he heard rumours that there were practising lesbians serving in his unit. He was responsible to the commanding officer and the regimental sergeant major for the maintenance, discipline and upholding of standards in place at that time in the unit. Sergeant X was upset that there might be lesbians in the vicinity, as he saw this as a personal challenge against his authority as the local unit law enforcer. He decided it would be his personal mission to find them, get proof and get them kicked out of the Army.

Late one Friday night, Private Y was lying on his bed in the guardroom; he had just finished two hours standing at the gate checking soldiers' ID and car passes to allow them entry to the camp. He was woken by the guard commander, who told him that the provost sergeant had a job for him. Wiping sleep from his eyes and combing his hair he went through to the guardroom office where he met the provost sergeant.

The provost sergeant greeted the young private and told him he had a very important job for him and he would brief him in the Land Rover. They both got into the Land Rover and drove away from the guardroom. As he got into the Land Rover, Private Y had noticed that there was a ladder tied to the roof of the vehicle.

Once they were driving, Sergeant X told the young soldier that they were going to the female accommodation just around the corner; when they get there ultimate stealth would be required. At the female accommodation block the sergeant pulled the Land Rover in to the roadside and turned off the engine and headlights. He turned to face Private Y and explained all about lesbians and how they were not allowed to serve in the British Army. Sergeant X pointed to a first-floor window and told him that it was his belief that there were two lesbians in that room right now committing a homosexual act and he wanted to catch them at it.

The sergeant briefed Private Y that he was to quietly get the ladder off the roof of the Land Rover and place it against the wall under their window without making any noise. Once the ladder was against the wall, he was to silently creep up the ladder and peer in through the window. When he saw the lesbians and they were in the process of committing a homosexual act, he was to give the sergeant the thumbs up, who would be standing at the bottom of the ladder. Sergeant X would then quickly race into the building, up the stairs and arrest them in their room.

The soldier put the ladder against the wall and tentatively started to climb up. On reaching the top of the ladder, he cupped his hands around his face and looked in through the small gap in the curtains. What he saw had the young lad's eyes popping out of his head: there were two young female clerks lying on a bed, clearly in the middle of making love to each other.

The sergeant was stood at the bottom of the ladder looking up at the young private, who had now been peering in through the window for about fifteen minutes. The sergeant quietly whispered up the ladder, "Have they started yet?"

Private Y quietly replied under a hushed breath, "No, no, not yet," as he continued to peer through the window, not believing his luck and what he was seeing in front of his very eyes.

After about thirty minutes, the soldier eventually came back down the ladder and told the sergeant all he could see was a girl asleep in her bed. The two girls were never caught by the overzealous provost sergeant.

18   KNOW YOUR AUDIENCE

Sometimes officers and soldiers can say the most stupid things at the wrong time, in the wrong company and place. Captain X was the adjutant of his battalion, responsible for discipline and manning of the battalion. He reported directly to the commanding officer and worked with him on a daily basis.

This particular officer was known as a posh jock by the soldiers, which meant he was from Scotland and came from a family with money and allegedly had all of the right connections. He did believe he was from a higher DNA level than the normal soldier.

At Christmas, the British Army has a tradition that the warrant officers and sergeants' mess get invited to the officers' mess for drinks and the following year the other mess returns the invite. Whichever mess is hosting pays for all of the drinks on the night, so each mess tries hard to drink the other dry when invited in. On this particular Christmas night's drink party, the officers were in the sergeants' mess, where the beer and wine was flowing very easily and quickly.

By late evening the majority of the soldiers in attendance were heading towards being drunk, having started drinking at two o'clock in the afternoon. Captain X was clearly the worst for wear. Because of his posh accent the sergeants loved taking the mickey out of him continually, which he never realised. He held a very high opinion of himself, which was completely different to how the soldiers actually thought of him. Captain X thought he was the bee's knees and a very experienced officer; he had served in the battalion for three years, which was laughable because not a man in the sergeants' mess had served for less than twelve years.

These parties are always packed shoulder to shoulder, smoky, boisterous, noisy, loud music, laughter and general banter. Sometimes there can be the odd break in conversation when things go quiet and everyone in the room can hear your conversation. In one of these lapses of quietness, Captain X was chatting to some of the younger sergeants and made the mistake of stating that he was probably the hardest man in the battalion.

Once the room got over the shock of such a bold statement in the company of seasoned veterans, Captain X found out that he wasn't actually the hardest man in the battalion after all. He was quickly picked up by three sergeants and thrown out of a window in the bar, his belt and beret following him through the window and he was given the advice, "Don't come back to the sergeants' mess until you have grown up a little bit more, sonny." The commanding officer who was present at the drinks party found this hilarious and stated, "What a ludicrous thing to say in the sergeants' mess, silly young man."

Captain X was made an Officer of the Most Excellent Order of the British Empire (OBE) many years later for his hard work and planning in Afghanistan in the rank of colonel.

19 GOOSE-STEPPING INTO TROUBLE

As we all know from the tourist brochures and television, a lot of royal households are guarded by soldiers and guardsmen of the British Forces throughout the year. The troops that guard these palaces are not always members of the Household Division or Guards who take a particular pride in this station in life.

At times of the year other regiments and even the RAF have taken their turn at standing outside guarding Buckingham Palace, Windsor Castle, and Edinburgh Castle on this royal duty. I think it takes a special kind of person to stand still outside for hours on end; some soldiers do not like it because they have a low boredom threshold. Perhaps the Guards Division is trained to empty their minds for hours on end because they are extremely proud of their chosen duty and seem to enjoy it.

Admittedly when you see Trooping the Colour or Changing of the Guard at Buckingham Palace it is done very well and does represent Britishness to visiting tourists – red tunics, bearskins, marching bands, all very stirring stuff. What the tourists don't see is the hours of painful rehearsals, shining of boots, pressing of uniforms that the individual soldiers and officers undergo to maintain the highest of standards expected by the visiting tourists and royalty.

Private X was a member of a very famous County Regiment that had a long and distinguished history. His battalion had recently taken up post as the six-month battalion that would assist the Guards with public duties throughout the winter.

On a lovely white crisp winter's morning, he found himself on parade at the rear of Windsor Castle doing sentry duty in his best dress uniform, guarding the Queen who was in residence. Private X had only been in the Army for about a year; half of that had been his training and therefore he was a very junior and inexperienced soldier. Born in the PlayStation age, he didn't do boredom; he found sentry duty extremely boring standing still on this guarding malarkey. When on post you are allowed to march about ten paces, do an about turn and back again so you keep the blood circulating around your feet – in the snow and frost he was chilled to the bone. Well, ten paces, an about turn, a further ten paces was not enough for this young, cold, and very bored soldier. He decided he would do his own marching about when he felt like it and it wouldn't just be in a straight line there and back.

He took it upon himself to march away from the sentry box for ten paces, do a right turn followed by a left turn, then another ten paces about turn, repeating the process again over the next thirty minutes. Once he was content with the pattern he had made, he went to the centre line and marched forward five paces, a left turn for five paces, followed by a further ten paces and an about turn. Once content, he then did a similar pattern on the bottom of the centre line. Just as he had completed the pattern in the snow to his satisfaction, he returned to the sentry position to continue his duty unnoticed.

He had stood at his post for about ten minutes when he saw out of the corner of his eye a sergeant and a corporal running through the snow and heading in his direction. When they got there, he was grabbed by the two of them and taken away to the guardroom, under protest. All the sergeant could say was, "You stupid idiot, what have you been playing at?"

Private X replied, "I haven't done anything, I have been stood on sentry duty for the last hour."

The sergeant asked, "Have you left your post and marched around the area to the front of your sentry box?"

"Yes, Sergeant," replied Private X, " I was a little bored, so I went a little further out than I was briefed to march by the duty corporal."

The sergeant started to lose his temper at this point. "Have you any idea of the seriousness of what you have done?" he bellowed into the young soldier's face – who just looked bewildered.

Allegedly, a member of the Royal household had looked down from an upstairs window and wondered why one of the sentries was firstly marching through the snow in the courtyard, and secondly, was there any reason why he was making a Swastika shape in the snow as he marched up and down around the place?

What happened to the young soldier is now lost in folklore. However, I am pretty confident he never had a weekend off for a very long time.

20   FUNERAL PRACTICE

You would think that funeral practice for soldiers killed in action would be a very serious affair – which it is; but pranks are still played on soldiers during drill rehearsals.

After the Falklands War, the families of the soldiers that were killed in that far-off land were given the option to bring their dead relatives back to the UK for burial. This was the first-ever British campaign that families were offered this service. Normally, dead soldiers were just buried in a foreign field in whatever part of the world they found themselves fighting for Queen and Country. The War Graves Commission would then look after them in subsequent years.

Private X joined the battalion three months after his unit returned from fighting in the Falklands War. The battalion and his new company had fought in the best traditions expected of its forefathers who had fought in North Africa, Normandy, Sicily, Arnhem, crossing the Rhine, Palestine, Suez Canal, Aden and Borneo. One morning on parade, the company sergeant major informed the soldiers on parade that members of the regiment that had been killed in action on the Falklands Islands would be returned to the UK for reburial in Aldershot Military Cemetery. At the time a lot of the soldiers that had fought with the battalion were still recovering from injuries in hospital, were on sick leave or light duties. They were not fit to participate in the funerals, which caused a shortage of manpower for funeral bearers' duties. The company sergeant major informed them that all available manpower fit for duty would be needed to form firing parties and coffin-bearing duties – including all the new recruits who had recently joined the company.

When soldiers join a unit that has just returned from a campaign, it is difficult for the new soldiers to fit in, as they feel left out. The older members who were in the campaign continually talk about their exploits, which makes it difficult for new lads to interject – "What do you know, crow, you weren't down south," [meaning Falklands] was often the cry towards the new guys from the older sweats for the next few years.

Private X was allocated to coffin-bearing duties – which meant he would be carrying a young 23-year-old lance corporal to his final resting place in Aldershot Military Cemetery.

In the best traditions of the British Army, the drill rehearsal for the military funeral would be carried out to the finest standards expected – which meant ten days of practising dressing/carrying/lowering coffin drills until it went like clockwork.

For the drill rehearsals an empty wooden coffin is used, so that all bearers get the drills right, are able to march correctly and in step with a coffin on their shoulders. For the lowering of the coffin into the grave, the sergeant decided that they would use the vehicle inspection pit in the unit garage where they could practise lowering the coffin into the grave.

Practising with an empty wooden drill coffin isn't that difficult. However, for realism, sandbags were added once the lads had gotten to grips with the drill movements required. This is done so that the coffin weighs approximately the same as the soldier about to be buried. Drill becomes quite difficult when picking up and lowering a coffin that now weighs between ninety to one hundred and twenty kilograms – not easy.

All week the drill had been going very well, so the sergeant in charge of the coffin that Private X was allocated to decided to play a joke on the young eager soldier. The sergeant said to him, "I notice you aren't wearing your South Atlantic Medal ribbon on your uniform; you couldn't have served in the campaign?"

Private X was now slightly embarrassed in front of the other coffin-bearers who had all fought in the campaign. He replied, "That's right, Sergeant, I was still in training and only joined the battalion a few months ago." This caused much laughter from the older soldiers, who called him a crow and a war-dodger – which annoyed him immensely, but there was nothing he could do.

The sergeant said, "OK, that's fine, don't worry about it. I will make you feel part of the battalion." The sergeant explained to the burial party that instead of carrying the coffin with sandbags, he would like all coffin-bearers to feel what it would be like to have a real body in the coffin. Private X was volunteered to be the first to try it: he was pushed and squashed into the coffin before the lid was closed and lifted into the air. In the garage the coffin was lowered into the inspection pit and Private X was lowered into his 'resting place'. The sergeant put his finger to his lips and whispered to the lads to go quietly and get spare tyres, which they placed on top of the coffin so that he couldn't get out.

Once there were enough tyres in place so that Private X couldn't escape, the sergeant sent the others for a smoke break. Ten minutes later they all returned and Private X was brought up from the inspection pit and released – he was very much relieved to be out in the fresh air again and out of the confined space.

The sergeant passed Private X a glass of port and said to all of the soldiers present that he may have missed this campaign, but he will have lots more campaigns to attend if he makes a career in the British Army.

They then raised a toast to those that had fallen and for those that would fall in the future.

21 STAR TREK FAN

Private X was being charged through the military system for fighting in the barracks: he had gotten himself into a bit of trouble with another soldier, but felt that he shouldn't be getting charged. His side of the story was that he never started the fight (I never heard of any soldier admitting to starting a fight in my twenty-eight years' service) and was only retaliating against an older soldier that had picked on him. The fact was, his opponent had ended up in the medical centre requiring medical attention – regardless of who started it, he had gone way over the top and inflicted serious injuries to a fellow soldier. Private X was still unrepentant and believed he was innocent.

The process to charge an individual in the army is a lengthy experience; normally the company commander – a major – can deal with all cases within his company as long as it is not too serious. In this case, the major decided he couldn't deal with it, which meant the decision was passed up to the next level – to the commanding officer, who is a lieutenant colonel.

When soldiers are sent on to a commanding officer it is a big deal, as he has the powers to lock a soldier up in a military prison for twenty-eight days with no pay – considering the officer has never had any legal training, it is quite a unique position of power.

Soldiers on commanding officer's orders are normally paraded thirty minutes before the allocated time and inspected by the regimental sergeant major before being 'marched in' in front of the commanding officer. Service dress, medals, bulled boots, no beret or belt is the normal attire. Regardless of how smart the soldier is, he normally gets a 2200 hours show clean parade that night if the commanding officer doesn't award a custodial sentence.

Once the commanding officer is ready to see the soldier he gets 'marched in' in quick time by the regimental sergeant major screaming in his ear, "Left, right, left, right, mark time, get those knees up, halt, left turn – Private X placed on report, sir." Nowadays the soldier is asked to enter the commanding officer's room and is offered a chair for the proceedings – innocent until proven guilty. The commanding officer then has a myriad of paperwork to go through on his desk appertaining to the case. There are lots of questions and answers and ticking off boxes so that both sides of the evidence can be heard and a fair trial is reached. Eventually, the case reaches the most important question, which normally ends in the commanding officer saying, "I have heard the case and can deal with it myself; will you accept my award or do you elect for trial by court martial?" This is where the soldiers must decide if they are happy for the commanding officer to potentially award them a maximum of twenty-eight days' jail sentence or decide to go for a court martial, which has the potential to award them a much longer custodial sentence and could lead to discharge from the Army.

All soldiers in this position have thought it through before the question is even asked. Private X was still seething inside, but knew the consequences of sticking to his guns if he pleaded his innocence – going for trial by court martial could end in disaster, so he decided to accept the commanding officer's award.

The commanding officer then looked at Private X, gave him a good bollocking for inflicting damage on one of his soldiers and warned him about appearing in front of him again – "I award you fourteen days' jail with loss of pay. Have you anything to say?" asked the commanding officer flatly.

"Beam me up, Scotty," Private X replied.

At this remark the commanding officer went ballistic and asked the regimental sergeant major to take him away to the battalion jail and requested that the provost sergeant teach him a lesson for being flippant. An hour later, Private X was soaked to the skin in sweat through his service dress having run around with a 60lb shell on his shoulder for the last hour – but he was still feeling better because of his little retort in the commanding officer's office.

22   WHO CHEATS WINS

Every Christmas when the British Army is in barracks, the majority of units have an officers' mess versus the warrant officers' and sergeants' mess game of rugby or football. The game is all about goodwill and having fun in the festive season prior to standing down for a good stint of Christmas leave. However, neither mess wants to lose and everyone who plays in the game gives it their all to make sure their team wins.

This particular year the officers' mess had an exchange officer from Australia who was about six feet six inches tall, musclebound and must have weighed about 125kgs. More importantly, it was rumoured that he had played rugby to a very good standard back in his home country.

The regimental sergeant major decided that he wasn't having this big lump of muscle rampaging around the rugby field trampling his sergeants into the Aldershot mud – Christmas spirit or not.

A quick and simple plan was hatched in the sergeants' mess that would stop this captain from playing in the game.

On the morning of the rugby match, the captain was walking past the battalion guardroom dressed in his rugby strip and boots ready for the game. Shouts rang out from the duty corporal that a prisoner in one of the cells was going berserk and wrecking the place – could he come in and help. The captain quickly dashed into the guardroom to assist where he could and ran into the prison cell where, in an effort to calm him, he grabbed the rampaging prisoner who was in the process of smashing his locker against a wall. As soon as the captain grabbed the prisoner, he stopped struggling. The cell door was slammed shut and locked behind the gallant captain – he remained there for the duration of the rugby game. Before the eyehole on the cell door was closed, the captain had both of his hands wrapped around the prisoner's neck and had him pinned to the wall. He threatened to strangle the prisoner if he wasn't let out. On the orders of the regimental sergeant major, this fell on deaf ears and the sergeants' mess went on to a glorious victory on the rugby pitch. Later that night, when the sergeants' mess were invited into the officers' mess for Christmas drinks, the captain had been released and found the funny side of it – luckily.

23   FIXING WINDOWS ALDERSHOT STYLE

Corporal X was a typical quartermasters corporal that had served in the same battalion for over twenty years' Army service: short, slightly overweight, scruffy, misshapen beret, unpolished boots; he wore coveralls all day, not uniform, as a symbol of his seniority and to wind up the regimental sergeant major. He did not care one fig for promotion or what his next annual confidential report would say. He was at his promotional ceiling and happy in his world, just hanging on for a few more years to get his pension before sliding off into civilian life and obscurity.

In his younger days, whilst serving in the battalion fifteen years before, he had been awarded a Mention in Dispatches for his actions and bravery fighting against the Argentinians in the Falklands War of 1982. Everyone in the battalion knew and respected this older, quick-witted and wiser corporal – all knew he was to be avoided and not messed around.

Corporal X was employed in the quartermasters' department as the battalion's carpenter, a person that came in very handy if you needed anything mending or fixing. In the early eighties the pubs in Aldershot closed at 1400 hours on a Saturday and never reopened until later that evening. Therefore there were lots of thirsty soldiers with nowhere to go, so parties in the single living accommodation were organised for Saturday afternoons. These parties or speak-easies almost always ended up in a punch-up between soldiers and furniture getting damaged and broken.

On a Monday morning Corporal X was very popular; if he could fix the damage to the furniture or accommodation, it would save the soldiers getting huge official bills from the quartermaster. In the eighties, soldiers were poorly paid and a few hundred pounds for barrack damages was a large amount of money.

On this particular Saturday a chair had been thrown through a window and Corporal X had been put to task by Support Company to find and fit a new window before the quartermaster found out. A four-foot square window and frame would have cost a few hundred pounds; the individual who caused the damage was very pleased to employ Corporal X on a window-stealing mission at a fraction of the real cost which he would need to fork out if it was discovered.

Montgomery Lines in Aldershot was a brigade-sized barracks consisting of six individual units accommodated in four identical barracks and accommodation blocks. The lines were built in the sixties and the men shared four to a room. The accommodation layout was identical in every camp, which meant that the windows were the same. Getting caught stealing from another brigade unit was not clever, but Corporal X had stolen windows and frames on numerous occasions before.

Corporal X, dressed in coveralls with no beret on his head, picked up his ladder and walked to the unit across the road disguised as a workman. A lot of the neighbours from the camp next door were away on exercise and the camp was more or less empty. He walked up to the first accommodation block and went inside for a quick look to see if anyone was around. All seemed quiet, so he went back outside and put his ladder against the wall and climbed up. He worked away unscrewing and lifting the complete window from its frame before taking out the remaining frame. Once he had finished, still undetected, he picked up his ladder, new window and frame before he started to stagger back to his own accommodation across the road under the strain of his ill-gotten gains.

As Corporal X was crossing the path to get back to the safety of his own camp, he heard a high-pitched wail of "YOU THERE". By now he was sweating under the weight of the heavy window and ladder; with his head down he was only concentrating on putting one foot in front of the other. From just behind him he could hear someone shouting at him. Thinking he was rumbled, he turned slowly to face the voice with dread. He was ready to explain that he was a civilian workman on a job.

On looking up from the ground, a spotty second lieutenant from the Intelligence Corps appeared in Corporal X's vision. The young officer was obviously straight out of officer training at Sandhurst: daft looking and badly shaped beret, trousers too far up his leg, brand new single pip on his shoulder epaulettes. Before Corporal X could speak, the young officer was ranting on about the correct compliments being paid to all officers in the form of a salute. Pointing at Corporal X, the second lieutenant called out, "You, Corporal, you just passed me on the path and did not pay me the correct compliments. What sort of unit are you from?" he accused.

Corporal X looked the young officer up and down with distain and snorted back, "You look very smart, sir, and I am sure your mother is very proud." He then turned and staggered away, leaving behind a second lieutenant with a gaping mouth, not having received the compliments (salute) he had expected.

24   HELPING THE POLICE WITH THEIR ENQUIRIES

When you entered Aldershot there was a large green sign about six feet wide and four feet in height at the roadside that simply stated: *Aldershot Home of the British Army* – it's probably gone now due to some idiot council decision or ridiculous human rights act. For many years it had a Divisional HQ; was home to the Parachute Regiment, 16 Parachute Brigade, which changed its name a few times and diminished its capability as each new formation took its role and place in history; plus various other training regiments. There were literally thousands of troops stationed in and around the town; there still is a large amount of troops posted there today, but nowhere near the amount that used to be stationed there. The Parachute Regiment was posted to another garrison town in the UK, which has allowed other units the pleasure of serving in such an old military town.

Defence cuts do not have any sentimental value – only cruelty for the soldiers that served in the regiments and formations destined for the scrap heap.

When large numbers of troops from different regiments are stationed in the same garrison town, there will always be frictions between each unit, as every soldier believes his unit is the best. This is good and bad. Good in the fact that pride in a unit is essential – only a second-rate soldier would admit to not being in the best unit. Bad in the fact that when regimental rivalry enters public houses, the outcome is inevitable – fisticuffs, black eyes all round, and police intervention.

During the 1980s, whenever there was a serious fight in the town the Royal Military Police would quite often be approached by the local civilian police to organise an identity parade, to see if the culprits were in one of the units so they could be identified and brought to justice.

On this occasion the police had been informed that, the serious fight that took place in one of the local bars the previous Saturday night, had been caused by soldiers from the battalion. An identity parade for the whole battalion had been organised for the Monday morning – nowadays this could not take place due to the legality of the identity parade.

The regimental sergeant major marched onto the parade ground in front of his battalion of six hundred and fifty men and halted, before calling the soldiers to the position of attention. He then briefed the soldiers that a very serious assault had taken place last Saturday in one of the local bars in town. Information had been received that soldiers from this battalion were responsible and he requested the culprits to step forward as it would save everyone a lot of wasted time. No one stepped forward. He then continued with his brief, explaining that very shortly the person who was assaulted would come on parade and walk up and down every rank until he had seen every face in the unit. If he placed his hand on your shoulder, you would be escorted off the parade ground to be interviewed by the police. He also explained that the victim had been seriously assaulted and wished his identity to be kept a secret, so he was also in disguise.

The battalion of six hundred and fifty soldiers could only look over in total disbelief as the police escorted a male onto the parade ground. He was hobbling on crutches, he wore a thick dark coat that reached down to his knees, and he had a brown paper bag on his head with holes cut out for the eyes so he could see where he was going.

The brown paper bag on his head with the holes cut out for his eyes made him look ridiculous and it only took the first young paratrooper to get a fit of the giggles before the whole parade began to laugh out loud at this idiotic attempt at witness protection. The regimental sergeant major tried his best to keep the soldiers in check but even he saw the funny side of this ridiculous disguise.

In the end the victim turned round and stormed off the parade ground to get away from the guffaws of laughter as quickly as he could get his crutches moving, with the police trailing beside him.

Later, it was discovered that there were no soldiers involved in the assault in the town; some clever civilians had mentioned to the police that soldiers from the battalion were definitely involved. The easy option was to get a military identity parade formed up so the police could be seen to be following leads.

25   ALTERNATIVE CAREER CHANGE

When soldiers leave the Army once they have completed the amount of service years they signed on for, it is customary for them to have a leaving interview with the commanding officer. He gets marched in to see the commanding officer for a quick chat on his last day – thank you for your loyal service, all the best for your new endeavours in civilian life sort of chat.

Some soldiers really enjoy their years in the services and experience great adventures around the world on operations or on exercise. Some soldiers leave a little disgruntled because their career wasn't going the way they thought it should, or they became disillusioned for one reason or another. They all believe they will do much better in civilian life where they will make millions of pounds – great, only time will tell.

Corporal X was the latter: he had served for twelve years in the battalion, had enjoyed his career but was now disappointed that he had not been promoted to sergeant on the last annual promotion board, so he decided to sign off and leave the Army.

The commanding officer had known Corporal X for quite a few years and knew the reasons why he was leaving – but truth be told, he just wasn't ready to be a sergeant at this time. There were more capable non-commissioned officers ready for promotion ahead of him – although he probably would have been ready in another three or four years' time with the benefit of more experience behind him. Corporal X was known for being outspoken and for not being the brightest in the class – so the commanding officer wasn't sure how the leaving interview was going to work out.

Corporal X was sent in to the commanding officer's office by the regimental sergeant major for his leaving interview, whereupon he was welcomed in and offered a chair. Throughout the interview Corporal X was a little more withdrawn than normal, which wasn't what the commanding officer expected. They chatted about all the good times they had during the period they had worked together over the years in various parts of the world and if he was sure he was making the right choice by leaving the Army.

When the commanding officer reached the final question, "What are you going to do when you leave and join the civilian workforce?" Corporal X replied, "I am going to be a lion tamer, sir." The commanding officer was a little surprised by this reply and asked him how he had thought about his new choice of career. Corporal X replied, "Well, sir, I am fed up being a clown in this bloody circus so I thought I would try a different avenue."

The commanding officer wished him the best and threw him out of his office before he burst into laughter. In between fits of giggles, it took the commanding officer five minutes to tell the story to the adjutant and the regimental sergeant major in the next office.

26   IS THERE EVER ANY JUSTICE?

Private X was marched in front of his company commander to be charged for an offence under Queen's Regulations in that he failed to obey an order given to him by his platoon sergeant. He was being charged because he was caught in an out of bounds area having been told by the platoon sergeant not to go there as it was out of bounds at the time.

In this case the out of bounds area was a pub in the local town which was being watched by the police – it was suspected that drugs were being sold on the premises. Drugs and the Army do not mix and if any soldier takes drugs he is automatically discharged from service.

The sergeant was looking after his men, but Private X thought he knew better as the pub was his local and he felt that he should be able to drink wherever he liked. In the Army an order is an order and must be complied with or face the consequences.

Therefore, Private X found himself on disciplinary orders with his company commander. The soldier defended himself and stated that he felt in his own down time he should be able to go wherever he pleased. The sergeant gave evidence stating that Private X was informed with the rest of the platoon on his nightly brief – the pub was out of bounds.

When all the evidence had been heard, the company commander quickly concluded that Private X had in fact disobeyed an order and should be punished. "Private X, do you accept my award or wish to go for trial by court martial?" asked the company commander. Private X knew he was in the wrong; the only reason he was in the pub was because he was trying to get a date with the barmaid and he knew he had no option but to accept the commander's award, otherwise he might end up in a world of hurt.

"Yes, sir, I accept your award," said Private X.

The commander then tore a strip off the young lad for disobeying orders and awarded him a hundred pound fine. He noticed that the young soldier kept bending forward slightly and was looking under his desk. The commander shouted, "Stand still and look at me while I address you, Private X. Why are you looking under my desk?" to which the young private replied, "Sir, I am looking under your desk for justice because I can't see any coming over the top of the desk." At this remark he was marched off to the jail for an hour's extra fitness with the provost sergeant.

27   FITNESS POTATOES

Major X was an outstanding company commander who was in charge of the hundred officers and soldiers within his fighting company. He was an old-fashioned officer with the right moral values: honesty, integrity, and a passion for looking after his soldiers – because of this, he was greatly respected by his soldiers. He believed in the Officer Corp's motto 'Serve to Lead', which is drummed into all the officer cadets at the Royal Military Academy Sandhurst when they go through on their commissioning course. Sadly, some officers believe that the men are there to serve them, which is totally wrong.

His only failing was his forgetfulness, and lack of ability in organising himself – he was always too busy sorting out other issues that he would quite often forget all about where he was supposed to be and doing what.

Every Friday morning his company always completed a ten-mile speed march with bergans weighing 35lb around the Aldershot training area. The ballast for bergans was normally sealed sand in bags or lead weights that soldiers had made purely for fitness. All the soldiers enjoyed this, as it was a great way to finish the week before serious partying downtown over the weekend.

Major X had been asked by his wife that morning to collect some shopping and she handed him a shopping list to get the items from the shops before he came home: later that night they were hosting a dinner party. He thought he would get the shopping in the morning so it was done and he wouldn't forget later on in the day.

Having completed his shopping, he drove into camp, where he noticed that his company were all formed up outside with bergans on their backs clearly ready to head out on a march. Seeing the company sergeant major he thought, "Shit today is Friday and it's the company march that I should be on." He headed straight past the company, trying to walk casually whilst carrying his recently purchased shopping until he was out of sight, then sprinted to his office to get his PT kit, bergan and get back on parade to meet the timeline. When he finally found his bergan it was empty – he had forgotten to repack it for the march after the recent exercise. Looking around the office, he searched for any items that he could put into the bergan to achieve the minimum 35lb weigh-in. He knew the company sergeant major would make every man weigh his kit on the scales, including him. He started filling his bergan with books, spare clothing, anything that he could find to try and make the weight. He was still short of weight, so he decided that the 20lb bag of potatoes that he had just bought would do just the job. He stuffed the potatoes into every crevice and pouch so that they were hidden and he would make the weigh-in.

Now confident that he had enough weight in his bergan, off he went to meet the company sergeant major and the company for the march. As he approached the company, they came to the position of attention for the normal formalities. "Good morning, sir, would you like to weigh your bergan in front of the men?"

"Certainly!" boomed Major X, as he confidently took his bergan off his shoulder and placed it on the scales.

The company sergeant major lifted the bergan onto the scales and peered at the dial. "Your bergan is 45lb this morning, sir; it's a little on the heavy side. Do you want to take some weigh out?"

Major X realizing that he couldn't open his bergan in front of these steely-eyed paratroopers otherwise they would see the potatoes, so replied, "No thank you, Company Sergeant Major, I will go as I am, thank you." Deep down he was thinking, "Shit this is going to be a hard march, as all the others have 35lb and are all very fit soldiers."

The company sergeant major always sets the pace and leads from the front on these marches and lets the officers cut about encouraging the men if required. Once out of the urban jungle of Aldershot and onto the sandy tracks of the training area, the pace was always increased so that all soldiers and officers got physically stretched. As the company was marching along, some of the soldiers kept finding the odd potato lying on the track, which is something you wouldn't normally see. Eventually, one of the private soldiers noticed where the source of the potatoes was coming from and discreetly pointed out to all soldiers in his vicinity – Major X's pouches had come undone and his cargo of potatoes was now bouncing out onto the track.

Two hours later, on return to barracks and sitting in his office, Major X was chatting to the company sergeant major and he remarked, "I thought, considering the extra weight I carried around today, the march wasn't that difficult, Company Sergeant Major. You are getting easier on the men." The company sergeant major, who now knew what happened, had brought scales with him to the office and asked the company commander to recheck his bergan weight. Major X picked up the scales and reweighed his bergan to discover it was 20lb lighter than it should have been.

Before he could work it out, the company sergeant major let him know that everyone in the company knew and his potatoes were now spread over ten miles of the Aldershot training area.

That night, when Major X got home, he walked into the house and his wife asked him for the shopping – he had left the shopping in his office and forgot to buy any more potatoes. How the dinner party went is anyone's guess.

28   SMARTLY TO ATTENTION

Private X was an old-school soldier who had served in the battalion for approximately fifteen years and still held the lowly rank of private soldier. This was a rank that he was happy to be at; he had no career ambition whatsoever. In fairness, he kept himself fit and remained a very professional soldier in all duties that he had to undertake – he was still serving in a fighting company, which he enjoyed very much. He was a hard-drinking soldier born and bred in Glasgow, known for his whisky drinking when off duty. All the new soldiers looked up to him because he had been around the block quite a few times and was a very experienced soldier who had been on numerous operational tours around the world.

On returning from leave, Private X had missed the 1400 hours parade and was now being charged for lateness – which was very unlike this old crusty soldier. As a senior soldier he took this as an extreme insult and felt he had let others down by setting a bad example and the company sergeant major had no option but to charge him.

When he was stood in front of the company commander and asked to explain why he was late back from leave, Private X explained the following: "Well, sir, it was like this. As I was leaving the bar in Glasgow Central Station to get on my train to London I heard a band strike up 'God Save the Queen'. As you would expect any professional soldier to do, I felt it best to do the right thing and show respect for our sovereign. So I stood rigidly to attention on the platform until they had finished the music, by which time my train had left the station and I had to wait four hours for the next train. So you can see, sir, it wasn't my fault and I am sure you would have done exactly the same thing yourself."

The company commander looked across at the company sergeant major, who always remains in the room when soldiers are charged – he just raised his eyebrows. The commander expunged the charge and Private X escaped without punishment. Once he had gone, the commander asked the company sergeant major what he thought of the story, to which he replied, "A load of old bollocks, but ten out of ten for originality," which they both found hilarious.

29   PERSONAL SECURITY

Sergeants X and Y were two of the biggest pranksters that lived in the sergeants' mess; they were always winding each other up and playing tricks on fellow mess members. If anyone left their room open, they would come back and find their belongings in disarray. There could be talcum powder all over the room, trouser legs on their uniforms tied into tight knots – very childish.

All who lived in the mess knew it was them that were doing it, but no one ever managed to catch them in the act. Sergeants X and Y were very security conscious and never left their own rooms open, so no one could get back at them to return the favour.

Sergeant Z had just come back from having a few beers downtown and had neglected to lock his door. On opening his bunk door, he found that his whole room had been rearranged – bed in a different position; his bedside locker and fridge on top of his bed, alongside his laundry basket; every shirt in his locker had knots tied tightly into the sleeves. He was not in the least impressed.

The next morning at breakfast he told everyone who were sat around the table, explaining what someone had done to his room and asking if anyone knew anything about it. All present shook their heads in denial and giggled – particularly Sergeants X and Y.

That weekend, Sergeant Z was the battalion orderly officer, which meant that he had to stay the weekend on duty in case of any call-outs or issues within the battalion. All others were stood down and went home for the weekend to wherever their wives and families were living in the UK.

Seeing as though all mess members would be away for the weekend and the mess would be empty, it was time to give the two sergeants a bit of their own medicine and see how long they laughed or liked it.

On Friday night, once all had gone, Sergeant Z nipped upstairs and found that both of them had locked their room doors. He went outside and noticed that they had both left their small room window open – they both lived on the first floor. However, this would not be an issue.

So the plan was laid: he needed to get a ladder, climb up and get in through the small open windows to their rooms. He thought long and hard about what would be a nice surprise for the two young sergeants returning to their rooms after the weekend.

It was now in the height of summer and getting hot, which was probably why the two jokers had left their windows open for the weekend.

Sergeant Z collected a ladder from the quartermaster's yard; he placed it against the wall and climbed up to the first window. He squeezed himself through the window, reaching down to unlatch the opening to the large window so he could get into the room. Once in the room, he turned on the water tap and placed the waste paper bucket in the sink and filled it to the brim. Once full, he proceeded to throw the water all over the carpet soaking it thoroughly. He continued throwing buckets of water onto the carpet until he was satisfied that the carpet was thoroughly soaked for his purpose.

He opened his jacket pocket and pulled out a packet of cress seeds, which he liberally threw all over the soaked carpet. Once satisfied, he wrote on the wall: *reap what you sow*, and climbed back out the window, securing the big window and leaving the small window as it was.

Sergeant Z moved the ladder along the wall and placed it under the window of the next culprit, before climbing up to gain entry as before. Once inside the room, he pulled out a plastic bag from his jacket that contained a mackerel fish that had been gutted. He opened the fish and reached down behind the sink where he draped it over the hot pipe that provided hot water to the hand basin. He wrote on the wall: *something fishy going on here.* Satisfied that this was a good hiding spot for the fish, he left the room, securing the windows and leaving all as he had found it.

After the weekend the pranksters returned. Sergeant X opened his room door and found that he had what looked like a lawn all over his carpet. When Sergeant Y opened his room he nearly puked at the stench that met him as he entered.

Both went ballistic at their discoveries. Next morning at breakfast they both demanded to know who had done such a thing when they were away for the weekend. Everyone sat at the table shaking their heads in denial and giggled. Sergeant Z commented that there had been a lot of pranks played in the mess recently and suggested whoever was doing it should stop before it got out of hand. Normality finally returned to a happy sergeants' mess.

30   CAREER PROSPECTS

Lance Corporal X was entering his nineteenth year of service and was employed as a provost lance corporal in the battalion guardroom, looking after prisoners who were locked up. He had done this job for quite a few years and was very experienced at it. Although having served for nineteen years and only reaching the rank of lance corporal, he hadn't been very successful in his military career – particularly as most guys at the nineteen-year point would be warrant officer rank, which was four ranks above him.

For whatever reason, Lance Corporal X just never moved up the promotion ladder – truth be told, he just wasn't very efficient, confident, or conscientious in whatever he did.

There were three prisoners being kept in the guardroom jail for the next few weeks; they had been sentenced and jailed by the commanding officer for twenty-eight days each. One of the prisoners felt that he had been harshly treated and should not be in jail, so he decided that he would make a run for it the first chance he got.

Three times a day the prisoners would get marched over to the cookhouse for breakfast, lunch, and dinner. When they left the guardroom, they would wear a steel polished helmet, backpack filled with 30lb of sand and carry a WOMBAT shell weighing 60lb on their shoulder. The WOMBAT shell was a drill anti-tank practice round made of brass and wood.

Prisoner Z had decided that he would make his escape after lunch when they came out of the cookhouse. He had noticed that Lance Corporal X would always have a large lunch as it was free and he always took his time coming out of the dining room as the last man. Prisoner Z's escape plan was simple: he would eat nothing at lunch so he still had an empty stomach and could run faster to get away from Lance Corporal X, who had just stuffed himself. They always put the packs and helmets back on when they came out of the dining room, so instead of putting anything on he would casually walk to the exit door as normal and sprint away as soon as he was outside.

Prisoner Z picked a Sunday for the day to escape, as there would be a lot less soldiers around in the camp who might interfere with his escape plan. On the given Sunday, they were marched over to the kitchen for their lunch as normal. Once inside the dining room, the WOMBAT shells were placed on the floor, helmets removed and packs taken off and placed beside the door. The prisoners were fallen out and told to go and get their food from the hot plate and sit at the nominated table.

Prisoner Z took some food from the hotplate and sat down at the table, but he just pushed it around his plate to make it look as though he had eaten something. Lance Corporal X never noticed anything. After twenty minutes, lunch was over and the prisoners were told to stand up, get outside and put their packs and helmets on.

The moment had arrived for Prisoner Z: he walked casually to the door and picked up his pack and helmet and took it outside. As soon as the fresh air hit him, he threw the kit onto the ground and sprinted across the road and leapt over the wall to freedom. By the time Lance Corporal X came out from the dining room he was nowhere to be seen. The remaining prisoners formed up and it took Lance Corporal X a few minutes to realise that the kit on the floor and one less prisoner meant one had escaped. He stammered at the remaining prisoners, "Where is Prisoner Z?"

They looked at him playing dumb and answered in unison, "Don't know, Lance Corporal X."

The remaining prisoners were marched back to the guardroom and locked in the jail whilst Lance Corporal X reported the escaped prisoner to his sergeant. Allowing a prisoner to escape whilst in your custody was a big black mark against a provost corporal.

Later in the day, Lance Corporal X was sat on the steps in front of the guardroom with his head in his hands. The sergeant asked him if he was all right to which Lance Corporal X replied, "It's my career, Sergeant. It's now in tatters." Perhaps he should have worried about his career fifteen years previously.

31   DELIVERIES WITH A PERSONAL TOUCH

Warrant Officer Class 2 X had been working his company of 120 men very hard lately, ruling them with an iron rod since taking up his appointment as the new company sergeant major. This particular company had always been known for having an unruly streak which seemed ingrained in its history and never seemed to change over the years – regardless of who was in charge. He had decided that he would break this tradition and get them all fully back into line with the rest of the battalion during his time in post.

This raising of the standards in discipline had not gone unnoticed by the senior private soldiers who had spent a few years in the company. What's more, they didn't like the extra bullshit, as they saw it – it was interrupting their normal steady way of life.

So they decided it was time to play a game on the company sergeant major to wind him up to see if they could break him.

The first inkling that anything was amiss towards the company sergeant major started when he received a telephone call from the battalion guardroom requesting that he came to the front gate to collect his packages.

The company sergeant major told the guardroom that he had not requested any deliveries or packages; the guardroom confirmed all his personal details, confirmed that the items were addressed to him and he should come and see for himself. He put his maroon beret on his head and marched across to the guardroom, where he met the corporal who had just telephoned him.

There was also a guy stood there from DHL asking him to sign for the packages. The company sergeant major explained that he had not ordered anything to be delivered to the camp. The DHL guy confirmed his details and said he must have ordered them, which the company sergeant major denied. In the end the DHL guy and the company sergeant major had a heated stand-up argument about signing for and accepting the packages, which turned out to be a garden shed. The company sergeant major stated that he lived in the sergeants' mess, so why would he want to buy a garden shed? The DHL guy said that he didn't care.

In the end, the company sergeant major refused to sign for the garden shed and eventually a very annoyed DHL guy took the goods back to his warehouse.

Over the next month the company sergeant major was inundated with deliveries consisting of more garden furniture, women's clothes, bondage equipment, gym equipment and applications to join all sorts of clubs from squash clubs to the local swingers' club.

Being quite a clever individual, he quickly suspected that someone in the company was trying to wind him up, but he was also clever enough not to rise to the bait, as he knew it would only get worse if he reacted.

The private soldier that was doing all the ordering on behalf of the company sergeant major was having a right old giggle to himself – scouring the classified sections in magazines and ordering anything that could be delivered to the barracks.

The company sergeant major decided on a simple plan of action to stop this. He stood out in front of the company on a morning muster parade and briefed the company: "Thank you very much for the nice presents that someone in the company is ordering and getting delivered to the barracks on my behalf. I have decided that for every present that arrives in camp addressed to me, the weekly Friday ten-mile march will increase in direct proportion until the deliveries stop arriving." He emphasised, "For the slower members in the company that means that if I get three presents this week the march will be extended by three miles to make thirteen miles on Friday's march." The soldiers stood in silence at this plan of action.

In fairness to the private soldier and the company sergeant major, they both now saw this as a challenge of stamina and stubbornness – both were extremely fit. The final Friday march before normality returned was for nineteen miles. At this stage, one of the older soldiers gripped the young private and told him to stop ordering kit for the company sergeant major. It had gone on long enough, plus the marches were getting out of hand and taking too long on a Friday, which was cutting into their weekend leave.

Thereafter no more kit was delivered to the barracks and the company sergeant major was firmly established as a strict disciplinarian within the company.

Colour Sergeant X was sitting in his office when he received a telephone call from the regimental sergeant major informing him that the Royal Military Police were in the camp and wanted to interview him. Apparently, twenty mattresses had been found floating in the Basingstoke canal in Aldershot and some sport fishermen had complained. The Royal Military Police wanted him to help them with their inquiries.

Colour Sergeant X was the company quartermaster sergeant responsible for all kit, equipment, and accommodation stores placed in his charge for X Company.

He was interviewed by the policemen and denied all knowledge of how any mattresses would end up floating in the canal, as there are strict disposal instructions for environmental waste like foam-filled mattresses. He admitted that the week before he had told his new store man to get rid of twenty soiled mattresses. He asked the policeman why he was being interviewed and was told the mattresses that were found in the river had X Company written on them in indelible ink. Seeing as this is X Company, it didn't take much working out where the mattresses had originated.

The store man was called into the office for interview and asked by the policeman, "Did you throw twenty mattresses into the Basingstoke canal?"

Private Z replied, "Yes I did, two days ago, why?" The policeman looked at the young soldier and asked him why he had done it. He replied, "I had just started a new job with the colour sergeant who I wanted to impress, so I loaded them up and got rid of them." The policeman then pointed out the environmental rules and regulations to the young soldier and sent him on his way.

The Royal Military Police were satisfied by their questioning that the young soldier had done it but without any kind of malice. The colour sergeant was told to get his guys down to the canal, retrieve the floating mattresses and dispose of them properly – case closed.

Once the police had left, the livid colour sergeant dragged the young store man into his office to find out what he was playing at. The lad informed him, "Well, you told me to load up the mattresses into the truck and get rid of them – so I did."

The colour sergeant replied, "Yes, I know I did but as a store man I thought you would know to take them to the Ordnance camp for proper disposal." The young soldier apologised for dumping the mattresses in the water and said he would confirm everything that he wasn't sure of in the future.

Before he left the office, the colour sergeant asked him if there was anything else he was unsure of at the minute, to which he replied, "I am not sure what licence you need to drive the truck but I don't have any current driving licences."

At this revelation, the colour sergeant just rolled his eyes and thanked his lucky stars that the policemen had not delved too deeply into the whole story, otherwise they would both have been in a world of pain and probably under arrest.

33   CHRISTMAS SURPRISE

Before soldiers are stood down for Christmas leave or on Christmas morning if they are abroad on an exercise or operations, they are woken by 'gunfire'. Gunfire is tea laced with dark rum and is served to the soldiers when they are still lying in their beds by the officers and sergeants from their unit.

This is a tradition that has taken place every Christmas for many years in all of the British services. The officers and sergeants come into camp early in the morning and meet in the cookhouse, where the chefs issue each company tea urns and bottles of rum. The rum used to be issued through the military supply system until the 'bean counters' decided to stop it; nowadays the commanding officers buy the rum out of their allocated fund so the tradition can continue.

Once all the officers and sergeants are gathered, the commanding officer normally wishes them a happy Christmas and toasts them and the battalion with a glass of port, before they leave the cookhouse and make their way to their respective platoons and company accommodation. The regimental band is split across the companies so that there is some music and loud drum banging to help wake the sleeping soldiers. At 0600 hours in the morning, waking sleeping soldiers is not a pretty sight, particularly if they have been in the town drinking the night before they go on leave. Finding women from the town in the accommodation at this time of the morning is not uncommon;

they are woken, made to leave the camp and undertake the 'walk of shame' as they leave the barracks.

The Mortar Platoon decided that, instead of them being woken and surprised by the loud drum banging in the early morning, they planned their own surprise. This platoon has had a long-standing reputation for housing a number of gay soldiers, which has made it infamous throughout the British Army over the years. Whether it ever did or not is open for debate, as there was certainly none serving in it during the late eighties; it was also a reputation that a lot of the soldiers played along with.

The soldiers' surprise was simple enough; they would empty a room of all its furniture and beds and cover the floor with wall-to-wall mattresses and duvets.

In the early morning the trumpets, drums, loud music, yelling could be heard throughout the accommodation block, as the officers and sergeants made their way through Support Company bedrooms, waking the sleeping soldiers with hot mugs of 'gunfire' and wishing them all a happy Christmas. When the company commander and the company sergeant major burst into the Mortar Platoon accommodation, they didn't know what to do. There were a dozen naked soldiers lying spread-eagled across a carpet of mattresses snoring away, smelling of beer from the previous night's drinking. The company sergeant major bellowed out loudly, waking the sleeping soldiers, who all giggled at the look of surprise and shock on their bosses' faces. They covered themselves and sat up to accept their mugs of gunfire, still giggling, which turned into loud laughter by all, including the company commander and sergeant major who realised it had been a joke.

The reputation of the Mortar Platoon had been preserved for another generation.

34   STITCH IN TIME

When a soldier passes out of training he is classed as a trained soldier; getting posted to his first unit can be quite daunting, to say the least. He has left the organised training regime where a daily programme dictates his life and routine – and entered into the life of the unknown, where he and his battalion could be posted anywhere around the world in peacetime or on operations.

Fitting into a close-knit unit for the first time, where new recruits are looked upon as unknowing, inexperienced and uneducated in the ways of war, can be challenging. They are seen as an unknown quantity until they have been tested by the older members of the platoon they have joined. It can be ten times harder to fit in when the new soldier joins a unit that has just returned from an operational tour or war where some of the soldiers in that platoon were killed or injured. When young soldiers are posted to their first battalion, it becomes their battalion and is ingrained in their souls for the rest of their lives.

Private X was posted to his battalion only weeks after they returned from the Falklands War. The battalion fought with distinction and had sadly lost twenty-three men killed in action and over fifty wounded. On return they were given an extended leave period before returning to their Tidworth Barracks to pack up and move to Aldershot, where Private X and five of his mates joined them.

On arrival in the battalion lines, the new recruits were met by a corporal, allocated to their new company and marched over with all of their baggage to meet the company sergeant major. When they met the company sergeant major he was exactly what you would expect – short, stocky, well dressed and grumpy. He welcomed the young soldiers to the company and told them to remember this was their company and to work hard in everything they did. He then threw each of them a green square of cloth material about three inches square across his table. He told them that it was a DZ flash, "Which denotes this battalion from all others in the British Army and I want it sewn on your para smocks by tomorrow morning's 0815 hours muster parade – every member of the battalion wears this on their right upper sleeve."

As the new soldiers were being marched across to the company accommodation by the corporal, Private X asked his mates if any of them had a sewing kit so they could sew this green patch on their smock – none of them had.

The corporal allocated Private X to the middle floor (5 Platoon), taking him in and showing him his locker and bed space within his new platoon so he could unpack and settle in. The accommodation was quite nice – not luxurious but enough for the young soldier's meagre possessions. The room was in two halves with four beds on both sides and one bunk for the section non-commissioned officer. The rest of the platoon was over on the rugby pitch playing or watching a rugby match against another unit.

Later that evening, when the other soldiers returned to the platoon accommodation, they all came into the room to ogle the new recruit – some were friendly and others not quite as friendly, which Private X couldn't understand, as he had worked hard for six months to pass all the training to serve in the regiment and battalion.

In his room there were two other soldiers who chatted to him; he asked them individually if they had a sewing kit that he could borrow so that he could sew on his DZ flash – they both replied that they didn't. The lance corporal in the bunk told him he never had one either – he was limping, as he had been shot in the knee during the fighting in the Falkland Islands.

This left Private X in a bit of a dilemma because on the other side of the partitioned room there were three soldiers and none of them had been particularly friendly towards him so far. To make matters worse, out of the three soldiers, one of them was limping due to a gunshot wound in the buttocks and another had lost an arm at the shoulder. In the back of his mind he heard the company sergeant major telling him to make sure the badge was sewn on by the first parade in the morning.

So the young soldier gathered his confidence and walked around the partition to ask his neighbours. The first soldier, who had been shot in the buttocks, was asked if he had a needle and thread he could borrow to sew on his DZ flash – "F**k off" was the reply. Undaunted, he asked the next soldier who appeared not to be injured – again "F**k off" was the curt reply. Private X had planned ahead and had decided not to ask the guy with one arm in case it offended him, so he turned round and went to walk back to his bed space.

As he walked away the soldier with one arm asked, "Why haven't you asked me for a sewing kit?" Private X turned around and asked him if he had one and was met with a torrent of abuse. "Why the f**k would I have a sewing kit with only one arm?"

Private X could only apologise and walk back to his own bed space with his tail between his legs.

As he was walking away he could hear the three of them talking. "We better watch that loud-mouthed crow," (derogatory term for new recruit).

Eventually, Private X found a sewing kit on one of the other floors and sorted himself out for his first company muster parade the next morning.

Many, many years later, Private X rose through the ranks of the Army to become a battalion regimental sergeant major, before commissioning and reaching the rank of major. He was also made a Member of the Most Excellent Order of the British Empire (MBE) for his service during an operational tour in Afghanistan and for his hard work during peacetime.

35   ONE IN THE EYE

Now and again the officers invite the sergeants' mess into their mess for a games night or vice versa. It is really just a social gathering to get them all together and have a little fun; it is surprising that you sometimes don't see soldiers in your unit from one week to the next. When a unit is busy, they can be spread across the globe or the UK; some companies can be on an operation, some on an exercise, and others may be on leave. So whenever there is a chance to get them all together, a prudent commander takes the opportunity and grabs it with both hands.

The games nights are good fun and include all sorts of different games, ranging from bar diving, where you stand on the bar and leap out as far as you can where your mates catch you; alcohol draughts where the glasses of red and white wine are the draughts and your opponent drinks them when you jump over his; mess rugby and tug of war; the list is endless. There is always an inter-mess boat race with beer and a yard of ale drinking competition. Both messes like to win, but it is really irrelevant, as the aim is to get the entire command element of the battalion together to have some fun, in an environment away from the prying eyes of the civilian population, where they can let their hair down and relax.

One night in the officers' mess during the small hours after a games night, a few of the younger officers were still standing at the bar drinking and all of them were quite drunk. One of them told a story of how he had been drinking tequila with his girlfriend on his last weekend at home in London. He explained that he placed a small glass of tequila between her breasts, put some salt on her neck and placed a piece of lime between her lips. When all the items were in place, he would lean forward and pick up the glass from between her breasts using only his teeth, drink the tequila, lick the salt from her neck and finally suck the lime from her lips. She loved it and would giggle while he was doing it.

The next morning the same officers were spotted walking around the battalion lines with vivid red blood-shot eyes. The adjutant who is responsible for officer discipline asked them to explain what had happened to their eyes. They sheepishly looked at the adjutant and explained the story of how one of them had been drinking tequila with his girlfriend and they had thought up an alternative way to drink it in an all-male environment. They explained that they had been drinking the tequila, sniffing the salt from a teaspoon and squeezing the lime into the corner of their eyes. They told the adjutant they had christened the game 'Hardman'; the adjutant told them they were idiots and gave them each five extra duties for looking idiotic in front of the soldiers. The game was banned from ever being played in the officers' mess again.

36   THE FOLLY OF IDENTITY CARDS

In the British Army every individual is issued with an identity card which has his Army number, date of birth, a photograph, and blood group printed on it. It is unique to the individual soldier.

Company Sergeant Major X was a fine figure of a man, just what you would expect from a warrant officer class two serving in one of the traditional regiments. He was very proud of his regiment and in particular the traditional part they played on ceremonial duties. He was fortunate enough to be stationed in Edinburgh Castle at the time of the Tattoo and his company had been selected to be part of the ceremony. For weeks he drilled his men until they were immaculate in the execution of their drill movements and precise in their arms drill. They were eager and ready to perform in front of the huge audience that is attracted to the Edinburgh Tattoo every year.

On the first big night of the Tattoo, he marched his company out of Edinburgh Castle gate onto the display area, chest bursting, drum beating, crowd applauding, cameras flashing, and his company performed their part to perfection. Ten minutes later, once their display was finished, they marched off the parade square to the area where their bus waited to take them back to the barracks for the night and a well-earned beer.

As they were getting onto the bus, an old American lady accompanied by her husband approached the company sergeant major to let him know that she thought they were fantastic and looked really smart in their red tunics and bearskins on their heads. He was bristling with pride until she said one of his men had dropped something in the street as they marched down the hill and that was why she had followed them to the bus area.

The company sergeant major told the old lady that he doubted that any of his soldiers would drop anything in the street, but accepted the item from the lady. Once the last of the lads were sitting in the bus, he climbed aboard and sat down ready for the journey home. He realised that he had been handed an Army ID card by the old American lady. The company sergeant major jumped up from his seat and wound himself into a rage: firstly he had been pulled up by an American lady tourist and her husband in the street; secondly, someone in his company had lost their ID card on his parade.

The bus load of soldiers could only look on and listen in bewilderment as he frothed at the mouth, swearing, and finger-pointing. Unthinkingly, he warned the seated soldiers, if he ever found out who the ID card belonged to they would be charged and placed on report.

Sometimes the obvious is too obvious. He earned the nickname 'empty locker head' for this incident – the name and photograph on the ID card would surely have identified the perpetrator!

37   WASTAGE OF TIME

At times the British Army can produce the best non-commissioned officers in the world, but some 'numpties' still manage to get promoted way above their capabilities – they simply cannot see the wood for the trees.

Sergeant X was very keen but not quite the sharpest soldier in the battalion; if he had been blessed with more common sense and applied more thought, he might have gone further up the ranks. He was a member of the Mortar Platoon, which was a very keen and professional platoon that was highly thought of Army-wide for their professionalism. Sergeant X decided that he wanted a better and quicker way to camouflage the vehicles when on exercise than the current system the platoon already used. So he decided he wanted large hessian sheets painted black and green stripes that could be pulled over the complete vehicle for speedy camouflage. On the whole a good idea, apart from the fact that hessian gets very heavy when wet and it doesn't hold paint very well. The amount of material required to cover each vehicle was about twenty metres square.

The Mortar Platoon started painting the hessian on the Monday and only finished it five days later on the Friday. Every time they applied paint to the material it ran through, leaving very little paint on the hessian and pools on the grass underneath. They used over fifty gallons of green and black paint to get the desired effect.

The young soldiers kept mentioning this to the sergeant who was having none of it. "Get back to work and stop trying to skive," he would bellow at the men. So the soldiers carried on pouring the paint and attempted to rub it into the material before it ran through and out the other side of the hessian.

It then took another week for the hessian to dry. When they tried to fold it, it was like folding cardboard – it had become solid. Eventually, when they succeeded in getting it folded, the smallest size they could force it into was a cube about two metres square, which nearly filled the trailer the vehicle would have to tow. Where the hessian sheet had been painted and laid out to dry, there was a square of solid paint underneath about an inch thick where the grass should have been.

The platoon had painted a total of eight of these sheets at the same time. When the quartermaster saw the damage and the large black and green squares of solid paint left behind on his lawn he went ballistic. He called for Sergeant X to find out whose idea it was to paint the hessian in the first place and find out what its purpose was. Once Sergeant X explained that it was to camouflage the vehicles quickly, he understood but he did not understand why he never asked for a more waterproof-type material.

In the end a lot of time and effort had been wasted, the sheets were too big and heavy to be used and were eventually binned. The Mortar Platoon under the supervision of Sergeant X spent another week chipping the paint off the grass area, and it took weeks to get the lawn back to normal.

38   MESS FUN

One Friday night in Colchester, a warrant officers' and sergeants' mess were having a stag formal dinner – stag means mess members only, no wives or partners. However, in the twenty-first century there are now female sergeants in the mess and stag really now just means without partners of any gender. It was a full regimental dinner, all mess members were wearing their bright red mess dress with their miniature campaign medals on their chests, candelabra, mess silver, a very grand affair. These dinners can have any number of fine food courses with five being the minimum: sitting at the table can last up to four hours. Copious amounts of wine and port are always drunk at the table during the meal; these nights are fantastic and can be splendid fun.

The regimental sergeant major, who is the head of the warrant officers' and sergeants' mess, had decided that because it was only mess members in attendance at the dinner, a bit of self-generated mess fun should be extradited from within the diners. Earlier in the evening when no one was around, he had sneaked into the dining room and placed a playing card under every mess member's place mat – ace of spades, seven of diamonds, etc.

On these occasions there is always a speech from the regimental sergeant major at the end of the dinner to thank the chefs for a splendid meal, and to celebrate or pass on some information to the seated mess members. On this occasion when he stood up to speak, he first explained that everyone should look under their place mats and there they would find a playing card.

He then explained that a sergeants' mess should be able to entertain itself and tonight that was what they would do – the rules of the game were the following:

Whoever had the playing cards that were nominated was to stand up and entertain the mess with a joke, funny story, or a song. The remaining seated mess members would become the senate, and the senate would be asked to vote with thumbs up or down as to how good the individuals joke or story was. If the senate voted with thumbs up then that was good entertainment; if the senate voted with thumbs down, then the individual was fined a bottle of port for boring the mess. The regimental sergeant major had cunningly recorded all the playing card numbers of the mess characters that he knew would provide good entertainment – after all, the aim was to have a good laugh and nothing else. When the speech was over, he gave the mess members five minutes to think up some form of entertainment before the first individuals would be asked to entertain the mess.

The first few nominees had stood up and told very funny stories, which the senate had all voted well on. The next playing card on the regimental sergeant major's list belonged to a female sergeant who was an administration clerk and a good laugh. A very nice girl but a wild card when she had too much to drink; at this stage of the evening she had drunk a few glasses of wine.

The regimental sergeant major called out the five of clubs; Sergeant X jumped up out of her chair and shouted that it was her. She then told the seated mess members that she wanted to tell a story about her and her girlfriend from last Friday night. She called across to the regimental sergeant major asking if that would be all right – which he agreed. Everyone in the mess knew that she was a lesbian and lived with her partner; however, it just wasn't talked about.

She started her story by saying that she and her girlfriend had been downtown clubbing last Friday night. They had a great night out, drinking and dancing, which had resulted in them both worked up, so they cut the night short so that they could get home to bed early and make love. Army rules had changed by this stage and homosexual relationships were allowed under the Equal Opportunity and Diversity rules that had been implemented.

At this point there was complete silence as the Mess members listened to every word that Sergeant X was saying.

She carried on with her story, explaining that she had been woken up early on Saturday morning by her girlfriend screaming beside her in bed. She explained that she asked her girlfriend what the matter was, to which she replied, "I have got a lump."

Sergeant X asked her, "What do you mean you have a lump?" to which her girlfriend replied, "I have a lump down below," as she pointed downwards with her finger. Sergeant X then told her girlfriend to lie back and open her legs so she could have a look.

You could have heard a pin drop at this point in the sergeants' mess.

Sergeant X was using her arms, going through the actions of getting her girlfriend to lie back on the bed and opening her legs, just in case anyone in the senate wasn't clear on what she had just said. She then went through the motions of opening her girlfriend's legs with her hands and she pushed her head forward as if she was having a look and said, "That's not a lump, that's my chewing gum from last night."

The whole mess was speechless for about five seconds before it erupted into applause and she received a standing ovation. The senate voted with thumbs up on that story.

Army tailors can be relied upon to ensure all soldiers look different on Royal parades.

CHAPTER 3

EXERCISES

The British Army is very fortunate to have some of the best training areas in the world. There is a saying: 'it isn't training, if it isn't raining'. In the UK bad weather is almost guaranteed and is ideal for adding a little more pressure to soldiers that are undergoing difficult training exercises. The training areas in Scotland, the north of England and Wales were made by Mother Nature and are ideal for finding faults in a soldier's personal administration in the field and for finding faults in commanders' plans. If you can train and succeed in these areas, you will be successful anywhere else in the world.

The British Army trains in the Arctic, desert, jungle, and Western European theatres, so that it always has some troops who are trained to operate in the differing climates. The Arctic has been described by many as aggressive camping because the soldiers live in tents for the majority of the time spent in the snow. A very harsh environment to operate in and lots of training is required so that the soldiers can learn to live and fight in the extreme weather. The jungle is an environment that you either love or hate. It is a place where you should never starve if you know where to look. You are always soaking wet through, rain or sweat; the jungle is never quiet and visibility is generally a few feet ahead due to the thick foliage which causes major issues when navigating. The desert can be a killer due to the heat and lack of water. Travelling long distance is generally by vehicles that continually have mechanical problems due to the extreme heat. Western Europe is probably the friendliest of the environments because it is where the British Army calls home.

The best part of being on an overseas exercise to France, Belgium, Holland, Italy, Canada, USA, Brunei, Hong Kong, Cyprus, Kenya, Belize, Australia, New Zealand, Botswana, Egypt, Poland is the R and R (rest and recuperation). The British Army has always given soldiers a few days off at the end of an exercise so they can go and explore a bit of the country. Join the Army to see the world.

39   NATIONAL EROTIC DANCING CHAMPIONSHIPS

Throughout the British Army there is a tradition/culture that wherever they are in the world they always have a party (piss up) at the end of the training exercise. This is particularly true when taking part in an exchange exercise with soldiers from different nations. These parties always end up being very drunken affairs and both nations try to out-drink each other in a sort of macho contest – normally games of some description form part of the evening's entertainment organised by the attending soldiers.

In the early eighties the company found itself training in an area of Southern France with a French Parachute Regiment that had recently returned from Beirut. The unit had received quite a few soldiers killed in action during its tour, but were in high spirits and thought very highly of themselves for their actions. The British Company had only returned from the Falklands conflict nine months earlier and thought very highly of themselves as well. So the scene was set for two outstanding units competing against each other to be the best militarily and socially.

The exercise had proved to be very physically demanding, involving lots of parachute drops and marching very long distances through the Pyrenees area of Southern France in small groups for days on end. Throughout the exercise a growing admiration on both sides had taken place: the French were no longer seen as 'cheese-eating surrender monkeys' and the British were no longer just 'Le Beef'.

At the end of the last part of the exercise, the company sergeant major from the British Company and the 'adjutant' from the French Company agreed that they should hold a piss up out on the training area. That way the soldiers could let off steam in a neutral location that would not attract any unwanted attention from the local gendarme in case it got out of hand – both veteran warrant officers knew it would. Over the training period it was easy to spot that all levels of rank had been trying to get the upper hand and prove they were better than their counterparts.

Once all the teams had made it to the final rendezvous after parachuting into an area below Toulouse, those who had survived the drop uninjured and evaded capture had covered a distance of over one hundred miles. The British had the greatest respect for the French parachuting skills because the Drop Zones (DZs) that they had been using throughout the exercise all seemed to be just random areas, covered in trees, buildings, streams, roads, cows – called hazards. The British Drop Zones in the UK on the other hand are a little less 'sporty' as they are all located on dedicated training areas and are pretty much hazard free in comparison. So quite a few of the Brits had found themselves hung up in trees, bouncing off buildings, landing in rivers – something they were unaccustomed to. Some of the soldiers from both nations, who had been injured during the parachute drop, had completed the infiltration march. They saw it as failure if they couldn't complete the mission and get to the rendezvous with their team mates.

So, after four days of evading capture, all the parachutists had made it to the final checkpoint and logged in – all soldiers looked the worse for wear. Soldiers limped through injury, twisted knees, bad feet due to the distance with clothes in tatters – a group of men that had been physically challenged but had gone the distance. They all needed a good feed and rest.

This was now the last night before the UK troops were flying back home and the warrant officers had organised a large piss up for all to relax and cement strong relations with each other. Organised for the two hundred and fifty soldiers present was enough beer and wine to float a battleship. BBQ stands were piled high with meat that the soldiers could throw on the charcoal whenever they were ready for it. The night started out quite slowly, as the troops were a lot more tired than any of them would care to admit.

However, as the night progressed and a few more beers were drunk, which helped to ease the aches, pains and blistered feet, laughter returned quickly. The more they drank, the more boisterous and louder the soldiers became. All soldiers were briefed by the warrant officers to go and collect some firewood from their surroundings and a large fire was built in the middle, which became the central area for all to gather round. The French started off singing their haunting regimental songs, which sound fantastic when sung around a camp fire by over a hundred Frenchmen. The Brits never came near with their efforts at 'Swing Low Sweet Chariot'. Next were the tests of strength, press-ups, heaves, dips, and arm wrestling competition. The arm wrestling ended in a fight as the French bloke accused the Brit of holding the table; a few joined in from either side, but it was soon stopped after a little blood was spilt. By this stage of the night the soldiers were totally drunk and ended up eating raw meat and passing it round for a bite – instead of cooking it on the BBQ.

One of the lads decided that it was time to challenge the French to a 'dance-off', which sounded a bit weird at 0200 hours in the morning in the middle of a French forest, surrounded by two hundred-odd drunken paratroopers. Not wanting to back out of a challenge, the French equivalent of John Travolta was pushed forward as their dancing representative.

A British Corporal stepped forward and explained the rules of the dance, which was called the 'Dance of the Flaming Arseholes'. This was translated to the French, who listened intently, not believing what they were hearing. It was not really a dance, more like a test of fighting through the pain barrier if you got it wrong. The dance consisted of a member from each nation facing each other – dropping their trousers and being issued with a sheet of toilet paper that measured fifteen sheets long. The toilet paper was tucked into the bum so the competitor had a trail of toilet paper hanging from his rear like a long tail. Once both soldiers were ready, the paper was lit at the exact same time. As the flame raced towards the buttocks, the first person who pulled the toilet paper out was the loser – hence the dance's name. Both soldiers were ready and the paper was lit; as the flame started to race up the paper behind their legs, both soldiers started to dance and sway so the paper didn't touch their legs. As it neared the buttocks they were both swirling around trying to keep the flame away from their butts. Eventually, a cry of "sacre blu, monsieur" from the French soldier rang out as he frantically pulled out the paper away from his buttocks to stop himself from getting burned.

This caused great hilarity as the French had never seen this game before, but they seemed to like it and more guys were pushed forward to represent their unit and country.

So the British Army and the French Army competed for their honour in a wood in Southern France and the outcome of the competition was finally settled by the 'Dance of the Flaming Arseholes'. Who won is actually irrelevant, as fantastic team building had been cemented throughout the whole of the exercise. For the sake of peace in Europe, the winning side shall remain a closely guarded secret only known to those that were there on the night.

40   SEARCH AND RESCUE

The company had only recently completed another Northern Ireland tour and had just returned to barracks after the normal four weeks' post-tour leave. The soldiers were briefed by the company sergeant major that they were all going to Newquay in Cornwall to conduct a week's adventure training. Adventure training in the British Army is quite rare and is looked forward to by all whenever they get allocated any, as it can be great fun.

The training normally consists of rock climbing, canoeing, wind-surfing, hill walking, caving, diving, etc. It is a good week away from military training to give the soldiers a chance to breathe and not just think Army scenarios/training. It is always a relaxed week where the nights off are plentiful and so is the chance to get out for a few beers and fun. For young soldiers full of energy, Newquay could not have been a better place to go for adventure training, particularly as it was the middle of summer and it is well known for being one of the UK's premier party towns.

The company arrived and set up a tented camp and field kitchen in an area of land about four hundred metres from the sea, where they would stay for the week. Quite an idyllic spot and morning fitness was enjoyed by all – less those that sported a hangover from the previous night's partying.

The sea around Newquay is well known for attracting surfers because of its waves – some say it is the best area for surfing in the UK. However, it also has a terrible riptide which can be quite difficult to get out of if it catches you and drags you out to sea.

One of the platoons was programmed to go sea canoeing for the day, so they collected their canoes, paddles, splay decks, life jackets, helmets, packed lunches and drove off in the minibuses to the site chosen by their platoon sergeant.

Once they got to the area, they unloaded the minibuses and carried all the canoes and kit down to the beach, where they would go through a period of instruction before they got into the canoes and out to sea. The platoon sergeant was a very keen canoeist and wanted to show his young soldiers what they could do out on the water if they learned the basic canoe skills.

After a few hours of instruction, it was time to get out on the water and see what they had learned. The first soldiers dragged their canoes down to the sea's edge, pulled up their splay decks around their waists, and donned their life jackets and canoe helmets. Dragging the canoes behind them to slightly deeper water, they all climbed into the canoes and followed the instructor out into the sea like ducklings behind their mother. As they went further out, the water was becoming quite choppy, but everyone seemed all right at first and they coped with the lapping waves. The morning got windier and the waves got taller and within twenty minutes all of the budding canoeists, including the instructor, were upturned and in the water.

Now that all the lads were in the water they had very little chance or experience to get themselves back into the canoes; there was only one choice – swim for shore. The instructor was starting to panic, as it was clear they were caught in the riptide and none of the lads could swim against the tide to get to the beach. The instructor was responsible for the safety of the men plus all of the canoes and equipment. After fifteen minutes trying to battle through the waves to shore and getting nowhere, some the lads let go of their canoes, took off their splay decks and ditched the paddles which were hindering them as they tried to swim ashore. There was now a situation that was obviously getting quite serious: the soldiers had now been in the water for more than thirty minutes. The weaker swimmers were starting to panic and the instructor was going mad at them for ditching the kit, plus trying to keep them all together.

Fortunately a corporal had been left on the beach and was looking out to sea and watching the potential disaster taking place. After ten minutes watching the guys in the water, he realised they weren't waving at him for fun and he raised the alarm by firstly calling the coastguard and then the company commander.

Once the coastguard had been alerted, the corporal spotted some surfers nearby that turned out to be Australians on holiday. He ran across and explained to the surfers that all his mates seemed to be capsized and weren't able to swim back in due to the riptide. Immediately, they all picked up their surfboards and headed out into the crashing waves. Over the next twenty minutes or so the surfers paddled back and forth to the beleaguered soldiers. They brought them in one by one by getting the soldiers to hold on to the back of the surfboards as they paddled.

When all the soldiers were safely ashore, it was a great relief to the instructor. However, he was still in panic mode as all the canoes and associated equipment were still out in the sea. As he stood there, a great big yellow Search and Rescue helicopter landed and the crewman ran over to see what the problem was. It was explained to him that the soldiers had been in trouble but were all now safe. The crewman gave the instructor a good telling off for not understanding the sea state, taking out too many inexperienced canoeists and for wasting the aircrew's time. He then turned around and stormed off, yelling behind him that a bill for the helicopter callout might be on its way to him and his unit.

The instructor was by now feeling quite sheepish, having narrowly avoided a disaster by the skin of his teeth; he now looked very foolish in front of the young soldiers he had almost drowned. To make matters worse he could see the company commander and the company sergeant major marching towards him with purpose. When they reached him, the company sergeant major asked what had happened and then ripped into him for almost drowning the soldiers and threatened him with a court martial.

Meanwhile, back at the company tented area, the remaining soldiers had their adventure training cancelled for the day and were brought together and informed of what had happened to the budding canoeists. Every section commander was briefed and allocated an area of beach line to patrol and wait for the missing canoes and equipment that should be washed in when the sea calmed.

Corporal X and his section walked along the beach road and over the sand dunes to get to the area that they had been allocated. When they got there, Corporal X briefed his section that they would all take turns walking along the allocated beach area for thirty minutes at a time. If any of the kit was washed onto the beach, they were to collect it before any of the nearby civilians tried to claim it for themselves.

As the corporal stood in front of the men briefing them, he became aware that they weren't listening to him and their attention was concentrated on something else behind him on the beach. He quickly told them to pay attention. One of them said, "But look over there, Corporal, everyone is naked behind you." He looked around and noticed for the first time that he had been allocated an area which was a nudist beach.

Not wanting to upset beach protocol, the section very quickly stripped off without a word from Corporal X who had stripped as well. The rest of the day was paradise as they sunbathed naked, chatting to a few beautiful girls enjoying the gorgeous weather.

Later, as the section dozed in the lovely Cornish sunshine, they were rudely woken by a very loud bellow from the company sergeant major who had just appeared on the sand. "Corporal X, what the hell do you think you are doing?"

The corporal replied, "Well, sir, when in Rome do what the Romans do."

The company sergeant major very curtly replied, "I will give you bloody Romans, now get your clothes on while I speak to you."

At the end of an epic day, a dozen soldiers had nearly drowned; a Search and Rescue helicopter had been called and cancelled. Australian surfers had come to the rescue and most of the company had spent a warm summer's day on a nudist beach in Cornwall.

For the soldiers that were on the adventure training exercise, they would always look back very fondly on the trip to Newquay. The only person who would not was the canoe instructor, who ended up paying for the lost equipment – none of it ever washed up on the beach. Perhaps if the company had paid more attention to the surf and not the nudists some of it may have been recovered – who knows?

41   YUM YUM

The soldiers found themselves on a Norwegian car ferry zig-zagging up the Irish Sea en route to an exercise in the west of Scotland. The whole battalion group plus stores were spread aboard half a dozen ships, along with the rest of the brigade. The reason the ships were zig-zagging was to do with anti-submarine drills that were being practised by the Royal Navy, who were escorting the ferries and affording them safe passage for their part of the exercise.

The ships had left Portsmouth harbour about a week earlier and still had another week to go before the troops would be disembarked in Scotland. On a North Sea car ferry there is only so much you can do in a car hold full of trucks/vehicles/pallets of stores before it gets quite boring, as space is very limited. So the routine became platoon fitness in the morning followed by weapon/map reading lessons, etc. The afternoon was more training until about 1600 hours when the ship laid on tea/coffee and cakes and that ended the day prior to showers and dinner at around 1900 hours in the evening.

The ferry was 100% civilian-owned and manned by civilian staff, chefs, waiters and engineers, who tried their best to look after all on board as well as they could. In the evening the bar used to open at around 2000 hours after dinner and closed around midnight each night. The soldiers who were not used to this quite enjoyed their time on ship, as it wasn't very onerous. As time went on and boredom took hold, the majority of soldiers were in the bar each night having a good time.

The only problem with these landlubbers was that after a few beers at night they would normally have a kebab or a bag of chips as they headed back to their barrack block. On board ship there were no such takeaways, so they would feel hungry when they went to bed each evening.

Privates X and Y decided that they would need to find food this particular night, so when the bar closed they staggered off to find the galley (kitchen). When they got there, they couldn't believe their luck – the door was unlocked. They stumbled in but were disappointed to find that all the cupboards were padlocked and couldn't be opened. Private X was busy trying all the locks for a second time when Private Y said, "Turn around." As Private X turned around, he couldn't believe his eyes – there was a trolley with tray after tray of little white coconut cakes with a cherry on top. Both soldiers looked at each other and started to giggle like children. They asked each other what should they do and quickly decided that they would take a bite out of each cake so they would look like half-moons and no one should notice. After chomping over two hundred bites from the cakes, the two soldiers had more than their fill and wandered off to bed thinking no one would notice in the morning.

At 1600 hours the next day, all on board ship were sitting in the dining area waiting on the normal tea/coffee and cakes – only beverages turned up that afternoon. One of the lads asked a waitress where the cakes were. She leaned over and said, "Someone had broken into the galley last night and eaten them all." Private X was quick to remark what selfish twat would do such a thing. Private Y could only look away and sip his coffee in silent disgrace.

42   HUCKLEBERRY CREEK WILDLIFE

The platoon was deployed on an exercise in the mountains of Washington State, USA, in an area called Huckleberry Creek. Here they were to be taught methods and techniques that might help them in a survival situation by instructors from the US Special Forces. The first part of the course was held in a temporary camp which was made out of timber, and canvas cabins which had a small stove in the middle to keep them warm in the night. Here they would learn all the theory before going out into the field and putting the theory lessons into practice.

On arrival at the camp they were shown around and briefed on the administration rules within the camp. It was the start of winter and there was already two feet of snow in the camp. The instructor briefed everyone, that whilst living in the camp the most important rule that should never be broken was the securing of the bin lids to the large wheelie rubbish bins, which had security straps provided. He explained that, because it was the start of winter, some of the bears hadn't started their hibernation and they would be on the hunt for any food that they could find. The smell from unsecured waste bins full of discarded food could attract the bears into the camp: when hungry bears and humans meet there can be big problems. The camp was in the middle of the forest and wildlife wandered wherever it wanted.

The soldiers were allocated their cabins and unpacked their kit. Corporal X told Private Y to go to the wood pile that had been pointed out to them on the tour of the camp and collect enough logs for the fire to last them through the night.

Private Y was always playing practical jokes and pranks on everyone. He put his warm jacket on and zipped up his boots and as he was leaving he commented to no one in particular, "I hope no hungry bears get me." Ten minutes later, Private Y raced back into the cabin room and slammed the door shut behind him. He locked the door and spread-eagled his body against the door and frame as if to keep a demon from breaking the door down. He was panting, out of breath and hardly able to speak. "Bear, bear, there's a huge friggin' bear out there!" he shouted to all in the room.

All the soldiers just laughed at his statement. Corporal X told him, "You are just so predictable."

Private X replied, "No, No, I swear there is a huge bear out there, you have to believe me," as he clung and pressed his body to the door, shaking with fear.

After a few minutes of him swearing that there was a bear outside, Corporal X told him to move to the side so he could have a look. Corporal X opened the door and stepped outside, only to be faced by a huge brown grizzly bear that stood up on his hind legs and let out a blood-curdling roar in his direction. He quickly turned about and slammed the door shut, locking it behind him and telling the others to pull their beds and lockers across to block the door. Private Y just said, "See I told you."

Outside, a few rifle shots rang out – the camp guard had been alerted and fired warning shots at the bear, which made its escape back into the wood unharmed.

Private Y couldn't wait to tell the story of how he had to wrestle with the bear and get back to the cabin to warn his mates – not quite the same story his mates told.

43   VERY QUICK-WITTED

The military band was formed up on the edge of the parade ground ready to march on for their full and final rehearsal. They were dressed in their finest red tunics with shiny buttons, medals, shiny boots, glistening instruments and bearskins placed on their heads that hid their eyes. Carrying their musical instruments, they looked every inch part of the London tourist posters that were plastered over the walls of the underground rail network. The band was under the eyes and gaze of the regimental sergeant major, who was employed to scrutinise the parade, to make sure that everyone knew the parade drill movements so that no mistakes would be made on the big day in front of the public. A parade should go like clockwork, leaving all of the civilian spectators marvelling at the military precision of the occasion. Performing a major parade in central London in front of thousands of civilians and tourists from all corners of the planet is very serious business for the Household Division.

The regimental sergeant major had been involved in large-scale parades for over twenty years, from when he himself was a young guardsman learning the trade that he enjoyed. He was now in the position to oversee parades and he would not let the best traditions of the British Army go downhill during his tenure of office. Over the years he had developed a very experienced and keen eye that could spot the smallest of details, which were not quite right or looked out of place on any parade.

The parade was formed up with the military band offset to one side playing stirring tunes by Wagner and Bach from yesteryear. Allegedly, he noticed that one of the musicians in the band was a coloured chap of African descent and he was beating the big bass drum. He was dressed in military service uniform with a large leopard skin draped over the top of his uniform and the big bass drum attached at the front. This is normal issue uniform for a bass drummer serving in a military band. In the early eighties it was very unusual to have coloured chaps in the Household Division's band.

Looking across the parade ground at the band and the individual with the base drum, he thought something looked out of place: the solitary dark face dressed in an Army issue leopard skin uniform just stood out. Once the band had stopped playing and all was deathly quiet, the regimental sergeant major marched over towards the young musician. He pointed his pace stick in the drummer's direction and bellowed across the parade ground in his best drill voice, "Who told that bass drummer to come on my parade dressed in his civilian clothes?"

The troops on parade and the individual all laughed at the regimental sergeant major's quick wit, which relieved the tension, easing their aching limbs and toes during another long and tiring parade rehearsal for the benefit of the public.

44   SHAKING LIKE A LEAF

There is a Parachute School called Kingsfield Airfield near Limassol in Cyprus which used to run a two-week freefall parachuting course for soldiers based on the island. The course aim was to get the soldiers to parachute fifteen times and encourage the more capable soldiers to experience freefall. It was a very popular course which was run and organised by soldiers seconded from their units – a two-year posting and all they needed to do was fall gracefully through the clear blue skies of Cyprus for a living. They were actually very highly accomplished free-fallers in their own right and excellent instructors.

Back in the 1980s the way you progressed to freefall parachuting was through a much more stringent testing method than the accelerated freefall course that you can do today. Nowadays you can be taken straight up to 12,000 feet, where you leap out of an aircraft with two instructors that teach you on the way down – perhaps not for the faint-hearted. In the 1980s to get to freefall you needed to complete three stable spreads, which meant you still exited the aircraft with a static line attached from the parachute to the aircraft, back arched with your arms and legs spread so you were stable in the air. The reason this was taught was so that the parachute would deploy cleanly from your back in a safe manner whilst falling in freefall through the air. Once the instructors were content that you were stable in the air, you moved on to 'dummy pulls'. This was the same as a stable spread with the addition that you had to bring both your arms in whilst maintaining a stable spread position, keeping your legs wide and your back arched. Your left arm went above your head and your right hand went to the dummy pull handle on your chest harness. Both arms had to move in together so that you stayed stable and your body remained horizontal with the ground. Once your hands were in position and you were gripping the yellow dummy handle, you pulled and both your arms went back to the stable spread position, gripping the handle in your right hand – simulating pulling the parachute handle that would operate a freefall parachute. Once you had completed three good dummy pulls, you were deemed ready for your first five-second delay freefall parachute jump.

Progressing from static line parachuting to freefall parachuting is a major step and some soldiers don't like it and have no desire to progress to that level. When you have a static line attached to the aircraft the parachute will always open regardless of what you do outside the aircraft. When freefall parachuting, the only person that can open the parachute is the person falling because there is no static line and you are not attached to the aircraft. The freefall part of the course for those that wanted to progress further meant they would start on five-second delays, which meant they exited the aircraft and fell for five seconds before they pulled the handle to operate the parachute. Once they had completed three good five-second delays, they progressed to ten-second delays and finally fifteen-second delays – gaining more height at each level. By the end of the course the soldiers that had done well and liked freefall were jumping from heights of around 6,500 feet and falling for fifteen seconds before pulling the handle to open the parachute and safely float to the ground.

The parachutes that were being used on the course were called air conical parachutes, which got the name from the shape of the canopy when inflated – a very safe and efficient freefall parachute. The yellow parachute handle was held in place on the chest harness by elasticated material that needed a good positive pull to get it out for the parachute to open. When operating the handle, it pulled a steel cable out of its tube, which led to a pin that held the packed parachute in place. Once this pin was pulled out, a coiled spring attached to the packed parachute would reassert and push the parachute out, allowing wind speed and air to fill the silk material and jerk the parachute open.

The soldiers were coming to the end of the course, which they had thoroughly enjoyed and had a fantastic time; if they weren't parachuting or packing parachutes, they were sunbathing in the glorious Cypriot weather.

Private X was now onto fifteen-second delays and loved it. He exited the aircraft at 6,500 feet and plummeted towards the ground at speeds of 120mph. At this speed you need to wear goggles so you can see your altimeter on your wrist, see what you are doing and enjoy the view. As he neared the 'pull' height of

2,500 feet, he brought his arms in and pulled the handle before moving his arms back out into the stable spread position.

The guys on the ground were looking up watching Private X falling and getting larger by the second as he neared the ground. They were all looking up and thinking to themselves that he was getting a little low and should have pulled by then. A few more seconds and the guys were all on their feet looking up and shouting, "Pull your handle, pull your handle," as they started to panic. When Private X was at around 500 feet above the ground his parachute cracked open and he floated safely to the ground.

When he came into the parachute packing area where all the soldiers were standing, his face was as white as a sheet; he was shaking and threw his parachute on the ground. "That's it, I am never parachuting again!" he yelled out for all to hear.

One of the other solders asked, "What the hell happened and why did you pull so low?"

Private X explained, "I brought both my arms in to pull the handle as normal; I thought I had pulled the handle cleanly and moved my arms back into the stable spread position, waiting for the jerk as the parachute opens. Realising that the handle wasn't in my right hand, I looked down and saw the yellow handle flapping around in the wind and when I tried to pull properly I couldn't get my hand on the handle because it kept moving and fluttering in the wind. By the time I managed to grab the handle and pull, I was very low and nearly shat my pants."

During the seconds when he thought his parachute was about to deploy, the time it took him to realise it wasn't and to react, he had continued to plummet in freefall an extra few thousand feet in height before his parachute opened.

That night Private X had a few beers in The Drop Inn before parachuting the next day.

Private X was awarded a Military Cross (MC) for bravery and leadership during operations in Iraq many years later in the rank of colour sergeant.

45   BUDDY/BUDDY SYSTEM

One of the most dangerous places to go inside when there are lots of bored soldiers about with plenty of spare time on their hands – is a portaloo. A portaloo is exactly what it says – a portable toilet that you see at any rock concert or gathering of people in the UK.

A few years ago they were all put in place on training areas across the UK and the days of soldiers digging holes to bury their toilet waste was at an end due to the environmental green people.

The platoon of soldiers were on their final deployment training exercise on Salisbury Plain, preparing for their next tour of duty in Iraq. They had just broken up for lunch and were sitting around, awaiting the next part of their training to take place.

After being in the same location for one week of continual use by over thirty soldiers two or three times a day, you can imagine it isn't the most hygienic place to visit. At this stage it was always wise to go to the toilet in pairs – just like girls on a night out but for different reasons. You went inside the toilet whilst your mate stood outside to make sure no one tampered with the portaloo – buddy/buddy system at its best.

After lunch they had about an hour before the next phase of training was due to start, so the guys sat around lounging, some dozing, some chatting, whilst they digested their superb lunch of delicious range stew.

One of the lads noticed that a vehicle had just pulled up and three soldiers from another regiment wearing black hats had just stepped out of their vehicle. One came over holding a map and asking for directions on how to get to wherever – clearly lost. One stayed with the vehicle and the other walked towards the portaloo. On seeing the lad heading over to the portaloo, the soldiers that had been idly chatting woke up their dozing mates and nodded towards the direction of the toilet.

As the guys all became fully awake and aware that a soldier from another unit was going to their portaloo on his own – it was like watching a sleeping python that has just woken and become instantly aware that a nice juicy chicken was walking towards it, unaware of the danger it was in.

Once the lad got inside the portaloo and closed the door, confirming it was locked by the click of the bolt, that was the signal for about ten of the guys to sprint the twenty metres to the target. As they neared the target, they all came together and formed into one moving mass as they collectively leapt into the air, impacting on the side of the door. This projected enough force for the portaloo to fly backwards and land on its side. From inside the portaloo all that could be heard was a scream of terror.

The running soldiers all returned to where they had been seated a few seconds earlier and continued chatting away again. At the same time the two soldiers from the other unit ran to help their friend and get him out of the upturned toilet. As they wrenched open the door, the soldier within stood up, still with his trousers around his ankles, covered in blue dye and the weekly waste of thirty soldiers. All he could say was "you bastards", which caused great hilarity around the soldiers that had carried out the attack.

The soldier was taken straight to a nearby stream, where he was pushed in to get cleaned up. His mates helped him as best they could until even they started to laugh with great hilarity. The unfortunate soldier took a long time to see the funny side of the practical joke – if he ever did.

46   SQUEAK SQUEAK

The platoon sergeant's Battle Course is arguably the most important career course for an infantry non-commissioned officer. The tactical part of the course lasts seven weeks and takes place near the town of Brecon in Wales. This training area is one of the best testing grounds that Mother Nature could have devised and has helped to shape the British Army infantry and parachute soldiers for a few generations. The course is very physically demanding and teaches non-commissioned officers to think tactically under pressure when they are tired, wet, cold, and physically exhausted.

The course is a pass or fail course – if you fail you are not eligible for promotion and if you pass well with a distinction it can help to get you promoted quicker. So the course is taken very seriously and can make or break a young soldier's career.

The course was started by the Parachute Regiment many moons ago as a testing ground to ensure natural leaders were being trained and developed to meet the challenges of the modern battlefield and lead the soldiers within the regiment. The rest of the infantry never used to have a Battle School and over the years muscled in, and by the end of the 1970s the Parachute Regiment Battle School ceased to exist and the Infantry Battle School in Brecon was born.

All non-commissioned officers that attended the course were substantive corporals and allowed to wear the local rank of sergeant chevrons on their uniform for the duration of the course.

As the course progresses, there is always a number of soldiers that get returned to unit (RTU'd) for various reasons – injury, failing progress tests, not making the grade. One of the physical tests is a march over the Brecon Beacon Mountains carrying rucksacks and weapons. The march is over a distance of approximately twenty-five miles and ascends/descends over some of the highest peaks before it reaches the famous Penny Fan, which is the highest peak in the Beacons. This march always proves to be a challenge to a lot of soldiers who come from regiments that don't really do much of that sort of thing.

The march is treated as a Command Appointment, which means that one of the students is put in charge of the mission to get the platoon from A to B in the quickest time. So in effect it is an inter-platoon race, but also a pass or fail for all of the individual soldiers that don't meet the course time.

Sergeant X was from a fine County Regiment who was currently posted to Germany working in the Armoured Infantry role, which meant that they drove everywhere in their Warrior armoured personnel carriers and didn't do many long marches on foot. He was nominated to be the platoon commander for this task, an appointment he was dreading because he wasn't the fittest bloke and he would be expected to lead by example and assist the weaker members of the platoon around the route.

Sergeant X issued a good set of orders to his platoon on the route to be taken, water stops and timings he expected to meet, etc. So in the early morning darkness the platoon found itself sitting in the back of an old Army four-ton truck trundling out to the start point of the march. On arrival at the drop-off point, Sergeant X got the soldiers off the trucks and organised into formation; rucksacks on, they headed off at a good pace under his command.

After an hour, Sergeant X was starting to feel the pressure of his rucksack straps cutting into his shoulders and his feet were getting sore already. At this point they hadn't even climbed the first peak and they all knew they had four major peaks to climb before the end of the march, which would take them at least another eight hours. All the time the instructor who was accompanying the platoon was badgering Sergeant X with requests for information to put him under pressure. Sergeant X decided to have a quick water stop so he could gather his thoughts and rearrange his rucksack, which he was sure was heavier on one side. The instructor pointed out that this stop was not part of his plan and it would change his time appreciation. After ten minutes they set off again and reached the bottom of the first hill an hour later. Sergeant X was dreading this climb as he was expected to lead the men up. Shoulders forward, leaning into the hill, off he went at the front of his platoon. After a few hundred metres he started to tire due to his poor personal fitness and slowed the pace of the march. Every member of the platoon was now on his shoulder and walking along behind him as he staggered forward under the weight of his pack. He called another water stop half way up the hill so he could have a rest. The instructor was starting to lose his rag with him as he was wasting time with too many stops. Some of the brighter students in the platoon realised that they were wasting a lot of time and would not meet the course time, which would mean they would all fail the test.

Eventually, they got to the top of the first hill after a fellow student took Sergeant X's rucksack and carried it up for him; other students were physically pushing him up the hill. Once at the top, another stop was called and his kit was redistributed so he carried less weight. Off they went again; in about two hours and after numerous water stops they reached the base of the second peak. This time they managed to get to the top of the peak after many water stops and Sergeant X being stripped of all his equipment and being pushed and pulled to the top. By this time he could hardly speak, never mind be in charge; the instructor was giving him a hard time and putting him under real pressure.

Kit redistributed, off they went again and as soon as they started to climb the next peak Sergeant X was flagging again. His kit was taken off him again and he was now walking up the hill with no kit on whatsoever, as it was now being carried by the others, who were now not in the slightest bit impressed with his performance. Sergeant X was getting lots of verbal abuse from the instructor and fellow students regarding his lack of leadership and moral courage. He called a halt and got the platoon together and sat them down. Sergeant X stated, "I have had enough of this shit. Sergeant Y take over the platoon." He then sat down on his rucksack.

The platoon looked on dumbfounded as the instructor ripped into him for giving up, deserting his position and lack of leadership. The instructor shouted at him, "Let's get on with the march. Sergeant X are you a man or a mouse?" to which he replied, "A mouse."

Instant Fail.

The battalion left the UK in early January when there was still snow on the ground and arrived in Cyprus several hours later after a long flight in a C130 Hercules aircraft. They were only on the ground for about four hours before they continued their journey to Kenya. In Cyprus the soldiers were issued water, rations, blank ammunition, mapping and parachutes. They were conducting a strategic insertion exercise to deploy troops quickly from the UK into a foreign country at short notice.

The exercise scenario was to insert troops into the African bush as quickly as possible to rescue expat farmers that were being systematically killed off by local freedom fighters – that scenario didn't need much imagination. Once the farmers were located, they were to be brought out to a central location and evacuated out of the country. For the exercise, the regimental band was playing the part of the farmers and the freedom fighters. The insertion had to be by parachute to deploy the amount of troops to the area that were required for the mission within the time frame – the troops had to be on the ground within twenty-four hours to save maximum lives.

The area they were parachuting into was two thousand feet above sea level, which meant the air was thinner and parachutists descend quicker, which equates to harder landings. When the aircraft descended into Kenyan airspace the soldiers were all hooked up and ready to jump. The aircraft doors were opened and the heated air blasted in from the outside, so different from the cold winter of UK they had left several hours previously. As they flew along the Rift Valley the scenery from the air was breathtaking.

When they approached the drop zone the 'green light' came on and the troops started to shuffle forward and leap from the aircraft into the blazing heat of Africa. The troops that jumped from the aircraft at the end of the stick all landed in and around a tribal village which marked the end of the drop zone. Once the soldiers hit the ground and rolled over they noticed the tall Masai warriors standing nearby on one leg, watching the proceedings. They were dressed in bright red clothing with lots of beads around their necks; they seemed to like standing on one leg like a stork and they all carried long spears. The soldiers called out "Jambo" to the Masai, who just stared back blankly, probably wondering who these people were that had just descended from the sky.

Now safely in the country the soldiers had to get on with their mission and locate the farmers that they had been ordered to find.

Corporal X had been tasked to move as fast as possible and locate a family that were located in the Samburu area, which was about forty miles from the drop zone. Samburu has one of the best safari game reserves in the whole of Africa. It is teeming with wildlife: elephant, giraffe, buffalo, antelope, zebra, and the associated predators that support the eco system of Africa. Tourists pay a fortune to go there and travel around on the top of Land Rovers taking pictures of the wild animals, and here was a section of soldiers on foot walking through the game reserve.

After the soldiers had walked for about twenty-five miles it was starting to get dark, so Corporal X decided it was best to stop have a bite to eat and stay where they were for the night, get some sleep before moving on with the mission in the morning.

Kenya has one of the most beautiful night skies in the world. Out in the bush where there is no pollution or ambient light, the sky just sparkles with bright clear stars like a carpet of diamonds. The only down side with the hours of darkness is that it brings out a lot of predators who are looking to kill and eat some meat.

Corporal X organised the sentry duties for the night so that everyone had a fair rotation of sleep and protecting the group from enemy attack. He had been in his sleeping bag thirty minutes when the sentry woke him up, reporting that there was enemy close by as he could hear them moving around, circling their position. Corporal X jumped up from his sleeping bag, grabbing his rifle, and went with the sentry to investigate. When they got to the edge of their position they listened. Corporal X could also hear some movement; he was mulling it over as to what it could be when a lion let out the mightiest roar from a hundred metres away. "Shit!" cursed the corporal, and they both moved backwards to the section position facing where the roar came from – trying very hard not to run.

When they got to the section position everyone was wide awake and looking to the corporal for guidance; they all knew exactly what was out in the darkness circling them.

The corporal briefed them to close in together and form a circle facing outwards looking into the bush. Every time the lion roared it caused the circle of soldiers to squeeze tighter. The corporal told two of the soldiers to collect wood from the fallen tree that was close to them and build a fire. At this stage he thought sod the enemy and giving his position away, there were man-eating lions not a hundred metres away. The only weapon he had apart from the blank cartridges in his rifle was a pack of mini flares. A mini flare is used for signalling: it is a small phosphorous flare which can be white, red or green. When it is fired, it pops and rockets for about fifty metres, but would not be much defence against a lion in the attack.

Once the fire was lit, the corporal briefed everyone to sit in a circle shoulder to shoulder and face outwards with their rifles ready. If the lion attacked they were to fire their weapons loaded with blank ammunition and he would fire mini flares in its direction. If that failed, they were to attack it with their machetes, which they had sticking in the ground ready for use. He stressed that whatever happened nobody was to run in any direction.

For the remainder of the night the lion circled the petrified soldiers, who sat motionless staring into the darkness with eyes like saucers. They kept putting wood on the fire, which seemed to keep the lion at the edge of the darkness. Every time it roared, any of the soldiers that were starting to feel tired were soon fully alert again.

When the sun raised itself over the African plain, the lion wandered off and very tired soldiers couldn't wait to get their kit packed and get out of the area.

Corporal X reported the lion incident on the company radio and carried on with the mission to find the expat farmers. By the time the exercise was over, everyone in the battalion had heard the story of the circling lion. When Corporal X and his section came into camp they were known as the Simba section.

The platoon had been conducting live firing on the ranges in Otterburn training area in Northumberland for about a week. The weather had been horrendous as normal – it wasn't uncommon to experience the four British seasons all in the one day. Rain that attacked you from the vertical, horizontal, swirling, and it would even appear from underneath, drenched the soldiers to the skin, regardless of the most expensive Gortex jackets being worn.

The platoon was a very professional group of soldiers who had all passed a physically demanding internal battalion cadre in order to serve in the platoon. Their task was to find the enemy, conduct route recces and provide as much information about the ground or enemy to the Battle Group Commander so he could plan accordingly. They were largely self-sufficient and were able to operate on their own for longer periods of time than normal Rifle Companies. They manned the battalion's forward observation screen for long periods of time, watching and reporting. They were all trained to call in mortar and artillery fire. Every patrol also had the ability to call in air-delivered munitions from aircraft.

Each patrol consisted of four soldiers: a lead scout, Patrol Commander, signaller and a trained medic. When the platoon found the time to conduct its own live firing, it concentrated on four-man contact drills, camp attacks and ambushing. When operating in four-man groups it was not equipped to fight. Over the years the patrols had developed contact drills, which were designed to return maximum firepower at the enemy so the patrol could extract and escape if they were spotted. The platoon had the ability to be called in and grouped together to conduct platoon-sized camp attacks or raids. Ambushing was practised in platoon-size area ambushes and much smaller patrol-size ambushes, which were very effective with the aid of Claymore anti-personnel mines and were called mechanical ambushes.

The soldiers that served in the platoon were older and more mature (allegedly) than the normal Rifle Company soldiers because they had all served for two or three years in the companies before they were posted into the platoon after they had passed the cadre.

At the rear of the rifle range, where the soldiers had been practising their four-man contact drills all day, there was an old rusting bus that a few of the soldiers had squeezed into to escape the incessant rain. Here they caught up on some sleep, cooked their rations and generally relaxed while they waited their turn back on the firing range.

Later in the day the rain stopped and the sun came out, which was marvellous for the soldiers' morale after twenty-four hours of continuous rain. The lads came out of the bus and took any wet clothing they had from their bergans and draped it over bushes and the branches of trees so it would dry in the sun. One of the junior members of the platoon noticed that the old bus still had inflated tyres and decided that he would pop them with his Army-issue clasp knife – must have been bored. He decided that he would make slow cuts along the outside of the tyre so that it would eventually slowly let the air out. He obviously didn't realise the Pounds per Square Inch (PSI) that a bus tyre is inflated to. As he sat there slowly drawing his knife along the same cut,

Corporal X asked him what he was doing. When he explained, the corporal said, "That's not how you burst a tyre," and came over with his own knife in his hand and plunged it into the tyre.

The tyre exploded and blasted out, sounding as if a bomb had gone off; there was smoke and debris in the air. When the other platoon members rushed over to see what had happened, imagining that someone had set off a grenade or a Claymore mine by accident, they couldn't believe their eyes. The two soldiers were staggering around in a daze rubbing their eyes: they had lost their eyebrows, the front of their hair was blown off, they coughed uncontrollably, the pockets on their smocks had been blown off, and they were groaning. The soldiers kept asking them if they were all right, but could not get an answer from either of them as they had temporarily lost their hearing.

They were both very lucky soldiers not to have lost their sight, hearing or even worse. Unsupervised soldiers with free time are very dangerous beasts, to themselves and anyone else in the vicinity.

49   PETRIFIED.COM

The majority of soldiers are petrified of snakes and the Belizean jungle in Central America is full of some of the most poisonous snakes in the world. The patterns on some of the snakes are so good that you can't see them until you are about to stand on them or the snake gives an audible warning when you get too close to it.

Sergeant Major X had been living in the jungle for six weeks. For the first few weeks he was part of the training team that was teaching the companies how to live and operate in the jungle. The hardest part about living in the jungle is learning to understand the environment and accept it for what it is – a large, warm wood. Soldiers who come into it for the first time believe there are snakes, spiders, animals and plants just waiting to pounce and give them a lethal injection or poison them. Once they quell their fears, the vast majority learn to love the jungle and discover what it can do for them.

The *Jungle is Neutral* is a great book by Spencer Chapman, who was a British Army officer who lived and operated in the Malaysian jungle as a guerilla for two years fighting against the Japanese in the Second World War. This is a must-read for anyone contemplating spending time in a jungle.

Once the teaching four weeks of the exercise was complete and everyone in the company was jungle experienced, the final part of the training was a test exercise where the company would operate as a unit. They were ordered to deploy into an area and set up a patrol base to operate from, locate the enemy and mount an attack against it.

When you are trying to find enemy in the jungle, your senses are used in a different order; in the European theatre you would likely find the enemy using sight, noise and lastly smell. In the jungle you find the enemy by using your senses in a different order: noise, smell and lastly using sight.

The sergeant major deployed into the exercising area to build an enemy camp and operate it with soldiers from the Belizean Defence Force, who would act as enemy forces. The idea was for the Belizean soldiers to make and operate from a fully functional camp in the jungle against the company, who should react against them and track them back to their base.

The company was inserted into an area on foot about ten kilometres from the enemy camp to set up their own patrol base. From here they would look for and hopefully find the enemy camp where the sergeant major was, monitor it, report enemy movements and draw sketch maps of the enemy dispositions so an attack could be mounted against it. The company would then be getting tested in jungle navigation, living and operating in the jungle against an enemy.

After a few days of searching the jungle, the company recce patrols found the enemy camp and then organised small groups to observe and monitor the enemy's, routine, entry, exit routes, water supply points, camp layout, sentry positions and command post. Once all the information was gathered, it was passed by radio to company headquarters so they could plan an attack.

On the last night of the exercise the company was withdrawn to an area a few kilometres away, where all the training blank ammunition was taken off them and they were issued with live ammunition. Once the sergeant major was informed that the company had withdrawn, he replaced all of the Belizean soldiers with wooden targets. When the live firing attack came in the morning the bunkers and positions which previously had living enemy soldiers, would now have a wooden target for the assaulting soldiers to fire at.

As the exercise transitioned from a blank firing exercise into a live firing exercise, the safety supervisors that would oversee the company attack moved into the enemy camp, where they would spend the night. The sergeant major would lead all safety supervisors to an arranged meeting place in the morning, where they would meet the company that were about to attack the camp. All the supervisors were nominated down to section groupings so that the right amount of safety staff was allocated and no one would shoot each other in the confusion and noise of a live firing attack – a peace-time requirement.

The safety supervisors were largely support soldiers that hadn't been in the jungle throughout the exercise and had spent their time in Airport Camp near Belize City. They felt a little uncomfortable spending a night in the jungle. When you are in the jungle hygiene is paramount – if you fall ill there is no doctor nearby, so you suffer in silence. Bodily functions are catered for by a communal hole in the ground for body waste and a piss tree is nominated for everyone to urinate against. The reason for this is so that all waste is kept in two places to help keep the camp clean and easier to control. There have also been occasions when soldiers decide to go elsewhere for privacy and end up getting lost and wandering in the jungle until they are found.

Corporal Y was standing at the piss tree going about his business when he called out to his mate, telling him there was a snake hiding in the roots of a tree a few feet away. His mate came over and had a look to where he was pointing with his finger and there was a 'Fer-de-Lance' coiled up under the tree roots at the base of a tree. This particular snake is very nasty and one of the most aggressive snakes in the world. It will attack and keep biting you until you either move away from its territory or it feels you are no longer a threat. It is easily recognisable by its yellow throat and its bite can kill you in minutes if not treated in time with anti-venom.

Other soldiers started to gather and point at the snake, which was not the cleverest thing to do because someone would eventually get brave and start prodding it with a stick. The sergeant major went over and saw the snake and told them all to move back slowly and not to agitate it. He briefed the soldiers as to what kind of snake it was, which made them all think twice – they had all heard of the Fer-de-Lance, which was the one snake none of them wanted to meet. They were all told to go to where they had hung their hammocks and get some sleep for tomorrow morning's attack.

When it was dark and all the soldiers were in their hammocks trying to get some sleep, a small terrified voice called out in the night that said, "Help, help, the snake is at my hammock." One of the soldiers lying on his hammock reading a book with his head torch noticed that the snake had risen up and was looking at him face-to-face from two feet away – he was absolutely petrified. It had slithered through the camp, passing many soldiers before being attracted by his torch and had risen up to have a look at the soldier. Trying not to upset the snake or make any sudden movements in case it went for him, he called out quietly in a shaking voice, "What do I do?" The sergeant major told everyone to turn on their torches; the snake turned its head around to the new lights looking as if it owned the place, then dropped down to the jungle floor and slithered off. The young soldier sighed with relief and had to change his underpants.

Next morning the live attack went through the camp and the snake wasn't seen. If it had been one hundred soldiers would have fired a ton of ammunition at it.

During the week spent in the enemy camp, the sergeant major had killed a few small snakes and hadn't given it a thought. It would appear that mummy snake had made an appearance. Thankfully no one was bitten; if they had been, they would most likely have died due to the remote location they were exercising in and the time it would take to get the casualty winched out of the jungle by helicopter and to a hospital.

50   THE PHANTOM STRIPPER

The majority of units in the British Army have some unusual characters within their ranks that do behave strangely, which the normal civilian population will find difficult to understand – one of these is stripping naked once drunk. Why they do this no one really knows – they are certainly not ordered to do so; the astounding thing is that no one bats an eyelid. When abroad in company locations, it isn't unusual for the whole company to be naked in a bar – chatting, drinking, playing pool, as if it is the most natural thing on God's earth.

This particular unit was heading to Norway for an exercise aboard a cross-channel ferry which was delivering them to their location. On board these ships there is very little to do, so at night time the boats do become quite boisterous due to heavy drinking to pass the evenings.

On this particular night a fight had broken out in the bar area between rival units and the ship was in turmoil: broken tables, chairs, etc. The duty staff were separating fighting soldiers (some naked) and sending them to their beds. At this point, a naked person with a mask on ran through the chaos and sprinted off around the ship, which shocked the Swedish crew more than the fighting in the bar.

The ship's captain called for the senior commanding officer and complained to him that the behaviour of his men on the ship was an outrage: fighting, damage and naked men running around the ship shocking his female crew, was totally unacceptable and not what he expected. The ship's captain informed the Army colonel that the ship would be turning round and heading back to the UK because he was not happy to transport such an undisciplined and unruly bunch.

The Army colonel was now flapping because he saw his career fluttering in front of his very eyes – this could finish his career in an instant if the ship returned to UK and he and his troops missed the exercise due to this incident. He pleaded with the ship's captain to continue onwards, promising that he would confine his men to their bunks for the remainder of the journey. After much pleading, the ship's captain finally agreed and the journey continued onwards to Norway.

Next morning, the colonel had all troops mustered on the ship, where he issued the biggest and best bollocking that an officer is capable of. All were warned that any future lapses in discipline and he would personally see that individual drummed out of the Army within a week. He also mentioned that if he ever found out who it was that was running around the ship naked terrorising the ship's crew, he would personally see them discharged that night. All soldiers were confined to their bunks and no more alcohol was sold for the rest of the journey.

The naked runner was never found or discharged from the Army. However, a select few do know the identity of this individual. Loyalty – you never grass on one of your bosses from the officers' mess.

51   THIRSTY ON THE AFRICAN PLAIN

During the final live firing phase of an exercise in Kenya, the battalion was required to complete an insertion march of around fifty miles to reach a forming-up point prior to attacking the enemy camp —in reality a wooden camp occupied by wooden targets representing enemy soldiers.

The route march was through thick African bush and was physically challenging and hard going for all concerned. This area was called 'Archers Post' and had been christened 'Archers Toast' by the soldiers. The ground is very hilly, arid, and covered in bushes that could rip the shirt from your back – the temperature could reach 48 degrees at the height of the day. In this type of terrain no one can operate without water and without it you would die. The route had been selected along known areas where there were waterholes at which the soldiers could replenish their water bottles. On average each soldier would drink around ten pints of water a day, which also added weight to his already heavy equipment and ammunition that he was carrying in his webbing pouches.

The Assault Engineers had deployed ahead of the marching troops to set up water purification plants at the watering holes along the way. This was necessary as the watering hole water was unclean and brown; it was frequented by the African wildlife that drank from it, and it was full of all sorts of bugs and germs which could prove fatal if consumed untreated.

The water purification site consisted of water pumps to extract the water and a series of large S tanks, which can best be described as black rubberised dip tanks about five feet deep and ten feet in diameter. Once the water had been extracted and filtered, it went into the S tanks to settle and be treated with a certain amount of cleaning agents like chlorine, etc. After a set period of time and various tests, the water was deemed ready to drink and fit for human consumption.

As the thirsty troops filled their water bottles from the S tank they could smell the chlorine and when they tasted it, it was horrible – just like water from an indoor swimming pool in the UK. However, it was all they had, so they filled all their water bottles and carried on with the march.

After about twenty minutes of marching through the bush, Sergeant X noticed that some of his soldiers had started to throw up. When he got to Private Z he asked him what the problem was and he replied, "I just can't keep the water down." Within another ten minutes the majority of the platoon were retching and throwing up the water they had just drunk. It got so bad that some of the soldiers had to be evacuated because they had become dangerously dehydrated through loss of fluids.

Along the whole battalion route soldiers were collapsing and being evacuated by helicopter. The helicopter was flying up and down the route collecting the weakest soldiers to fly them out for treatment. The exercise was halted until fresh water could be flown in and distributed to the soldiers before they continued the march and the attack.

Once the exercise was finished, the commanding officer demanded to know what had happened with the water supply that had poisoned his men. It turned out that the person in charge of adding the water-cleaning chemicals had done so and unbeknown to him so had another Assault Engineer – causing a double dose.

The water had been well and truly spoilt by too many engineers.

52   LAID-BACK EMPLOYEES

Belize is a former British colony – British Honduras. It sits on the edge of the Caribbean and up until the early nineties it was garrisoned by the British Army to deter invasion from neighbouring Guatemala.

All the menial work that needed to be completed in the camps was carried out by locally employed civilians – minor works, maintenance, gardening, tree trimming, painting, etc. This was a way of putting more money into the local economy and it saved thousands of pounds by not having to import the workforce from outside the former colony. The majority of the workers were either Mayan Indians or African descendants whose great, great, great grandparents ended up in Belize as a direct result of the slave trade that had thankfully been abolished many years before.

Private X had been on guard duty for four days and had been watching one of the local workers that had been tasked by the colour sergeant with painting the door beside the guardroom; he had been painting for the same period of time that he had been on duty, which seemed a little excessive. Each day he would turn up with his tin of paint, brush, apply paint to a small area of the door and then relax, clearly not in a rush to complete the job.

Painting such a small area would take a normal worker about two minutes, but this worker was using long slow brush strokes which took about twenty minutes per square metre of the door. Once he had completed his metre square area, he would close the paint tin and wash his brush. Then he would remove his T-shirt, step back and admire his handiwork for a few minutes before lying down in the sun for thirty minutes. After an hour, the process would start again and another metre of the door would get painted.

Private X was getting frustrated just by watching this long drawn out process and decided to have a word with the local worker about his work rate before he reported it to the colour sergeant. He approached the prone figure lying out in the midday sun that now had a straw hat covering his face; reggae music beat out rhythmically from an old battered radio that nestled beside him.

The young soldier nudged the worker's elbow to wake him up. He responded by raising the hat from his face and, looking up into the sunlight, he squinted through narrowed eyes and asked Private X, "What you want, soldier boy?" He told the worker that he had been watching him every day and thought he was taking a very long time to paint a door and was wondering why it was taking him so long. The local worker replied, "Don't rush de brush, man," and replaced the hat over his face and lay his head back down on the grass again.

The soldier could only raise his eyebrows and get back to his sentry post; there was no way the painter was going to finish the job in a hurry for anyone.

53   DEMOLITION GAMES

The battalion was exercising on the Brecon live firing ranges in Wales on a field-firing exercise for a few days. From the start of the exercise until the end of the live firing package only live ammunition was used – artillery, mortars, Milan missiles, heavy machine guns, fast air jets dropping bombs, grenades, and rifle fire. This training area is open countryside where only the hardiest of sheep can survive the harsh Welsh weather. Nature has unconsciously developed an outstanding testing area to prepare soldiers for operations around the world. If you can survive and operate in the extreme Brecon winter weather, you can survive and operate anywhere in the world.

The British Army is one of the few armies in the world that conducts live firing attacks to such a level that is as real as it can be, apart from the targets not firing back. When the battalion is practising live firing attacks there can be as many as seven hundred men loaded up with live ammunition and grenades and the scope for accidents is monumental. Unfortunately, over the years there have been quite a number of soldiers shot and killed during these types of exercises, due to accidents caused by tired soldiers or bad planning. There are companies firing vast amounts of ammunition at targets on a hill as another company manoeuvres around to assault the enemy (targets); at the same time the enemy is being pounded by artillery, mortar fire and heavy machine guns.

However, this training is essential so that soldiers can be trained in as realistic an environment as possible, so that when they go and do it for real they are practised in what to do. The noise and manoeuvring with live ammunition is second nature, which will save lives in the long term.

Captain X was nominated by the battalion second-in-command to plan and conduct the battalion live night attack and the commanding officer wanted all weapons to be used in the attack. The amount of planning that goes into these attacks before the soldiers put a foot on the ground takes days of planning and rehearsals. The targets have to be dug in and arcs of fire worked out so that soldiers can continue to fire until the last minute before it becomes unsafe under peacetime rules. Every section, platoon, company that is manoeuvring around the area is escorted by safety staff that have walked the range many times before in rehearsals, so they know exactly when the soldiers in their charge can fire and when they cannot. If any soldier attempts to fire out of arc, it is their job to stop them, because a kilometre or so away there could be other soldiers where the bullets might land and cause injury or worse.

The heavier weapon controllers, like artillery and mortars that fire on the enemy positions, are given lines to draw on their maps when they must stop firing to avoid troops getting too close to the exploding munitions. Every weapon system is checked for bearing and elevation by the safety staff before the shells are fired. An artillery shell landing in a group of troops would certainly result in death and injury.

The night attack was finally planned and Captain X decided that Milan missiles (anti-tank rockets) would be fired into the first enemy positions, artillery and mortars would pound the hill with high-explosive shells and white phosphorous shells to create smoke as the first company moved up the valley to get into position. Another company would fire into the enemy position as the first company went underneath their rifle fire. Once the first company was on their objective, the next company would move along the valley under their covering fire plus artillery and mortar fire. This would continue until the three companies had supported a company in the attack and assaulted an enemy position using support weapons. The night attack went without a hitch and all of the companies and soldiers achieved their goals.

As the officer in charge of the night attack, Captain X was also responsible in ensuring that the night range was clear of soldiers and any blind ammunition (not exploded), before he handed it back to the civilian range warden in the morning.

The Mortar Platoon commander informed him by radio that one of their bombs had misfired but left the barrel of the mortar and had landed two hundred metres in front of their position, but hadn't exploded. They had to pack up and move position for the next phase of the exercise and did not have time to deal with the faulty mortar round. They sent the grid reference of the unexploded bomb and had marked the position with white tape for him to find before they left the area.

Captain X was driven over to the position by the company sergeant major, who was his second-in-command for the night attack. When they got to the grid reference there was a large white arrow marked out on the ground, approximately ten metres in length, pointing to the unexploded bomb lying on top of the ground. Captain X got out of the vehicle and walked up to the unexploded munition to ensure it was the mortar bomb. Once he confirmed it was, he returned to the company sergeant major and briefed him.

The plan was simple – Captain X would walk the thirty metres from the vehicle with the demolition equipment and lay a plastic explosive charge with a long fuse beside the unexploded bomb. Once he was content the charge was laid correctly, he would give the thumbs-up to the company sergeant major, who would start the vehicle. He would then light the fuse, which had a three-minute delay, and walk back to the vehicle, get in and drive down the range track. All being well, they would be a good distance down the track and around the corner out of harm's way before the unexploded bomb was vaporised. When doing this, you always walk calmly away from the lit charge – if you run in a panic you might make a mistake or fall over and injure yourself.

Once Captain X was happy that he had laid the explosive charge correctly, he gave the thumbs-up to the company sergeant major, who started up the vehicle engine. He then lit the fuse and walked back to the vehicle. When he put his hand on the vehicle door handle, the company sergeant major pulled forward about ten feet. Captain X kept calm and walked along the track to the vehicle. Again the sergeant major pulled the vehicle forward ten feet when he got close to the vehicle. From inside the vehicle all Captain X could hear was laughter from the chuckling comedian of a company sergeant major. After the fourth attempt he managed to get into the vehicle and they sped off down the track around the corner before the bomb was destroyed by the explosive charge.

Both of them giggled as they sped down the track, having played this trick on their own children many times in the past.

The smile quickly disappeared when the elephant charged –
you don't need to be the quickest, just not the slowest.

Ninja turtles spotted in West German forest.

Hear no evil, speak no evil, and see no evil firing the 81mm mortar on Salisbury Plain.

After three weeks living in the Brunei jungle, one soldier needed helicopter evacuation after being hit by a falling tree branch. By the time he was on the helicopter his rations had been scoffed by the other starving patrol members.

CHAPTER 4

ON OPERATIONS

Soldiers enjoy going on operations because it is the pinnacle of what they have been training for and where they will have a chance to put into practice what they have learnt. Before every operational deployment, soldiers spend a few months on training exercises practising the skills they will likely use during the operation they are going to undertake. This isn't always the case. When a high-readiness unit deployed to Sierra Leone in 2000, they were deployed within days with very little extra training. Many ended up with malaria because the Army issued anti malaria tablets, which never had the time to take effect and make the soldiers immune to mosquito bites.

The British Army has just been through one of its busiest operational periods for a very long time over the last twenty years – Northern Ireland, United Nations tours, Bosnia, Sierra Leone, Kosovo, Macedonia, Afghanistan, Iraq and Libya.

When soldiers go on operations they all know and understand the risks that they might face. During the tour their thoughts are always focused on the mission and thoughts of home are put to the back of their minds. This is the way it has to be so that everyone is concentrated on the job in hand and everyone is fully alert so that mistakes are kept to a minimum. Soldiers bleating about missing their girlfriends or wives can lower frontline morale very quickly.

Operations are generally long days of boredom interspersed with a few hours of extreme terror and excitement when the enemy shows his teeth. Quite often soldiers will giggle when under enemy fire through nervousness. The giggles generally stop when someone gets wounded or worse.

The operational experience of the British Army can now be seen quite clearly on Remembrance Sunday, when the soldiers parade dressed in their best uniforms and wear their shiny campaign medals. Nowadays it isn't uncommon for soldiers to have earned between six and twelve medals, which is a lot considering the soldiers in the 1970s and 1980s normally only had one – the General Service Medal for serving in Northern Ireland during the Troubles.

Every soldier gets the same operational medal for serving in the same theatre – normally more than twenty-eight days of continual service is the qualifying period. This has always been a contentious subject because the soldier that is sat in a nice base every day drinking coffee, does not face the same dangers or hardship as a soldier who is tip-toeing through minefields and fighting the enemy on a daily basis. Every soldier earns his medals under very different circumstances and experiences during an operational tour.

54   SNIPER SKILLS UNDER FIRE

Private X was the lead soldier in a team of four soldiers patrolling through a particularly bad area of Belfast where British troops were not welcome. Recently there had been a lot of violence in the area and there was tension in the air which made the soldiers nervous but more alert. Army Intelligence was briefing all patrols that there was an IRA unit in the area who were trying very hard to kill British soldiers, because they had suffered their own losses to the British Army. Intelligence was not sure whether the IRA would try an ambush shoot or a bomb against the soldiers. The company had increased its patrolling activity to ensure they couldn't plant a bomb in their area – the increased patrolling exposed them to more danger against a sniper shoot.

Before the soldiers had deployed on the tour, they had completed a four-week training package in the south of England. The platoon sergeant in charge of their training had worked them hard on the ranges so that they could all hit targets comfortably out to three hundred metres. They practised shooting in the standing, kneeling, sitting and prone position, firing from doorways, vehicles, roof tops, windows and even from the kerbside.

The sergeant had served on numerous tours with the battalion in Belfast and was adamant that all his soldiers would survive and return home at the end of the tour. He trained them as best he could and passed on all of his experience and knowledge from previous tours.

They were taught to gauge the atmosphere on the streets. If there were no children running around in the middle of the day then that was a bad sign, as the IRA tried to avoid injuring children in shootings in their own areas. If the windows in every house in a street were open that was a sign that an explosion was about to happen – leaving windows open reduces shock and some windows would escape destruction. If you saw a vehicle sitting heavy on its axle you avoided it in case it was loaded with explosives – there were many indicators which saved many lives.

When Private X was leading his patrol back to the security base, he noticed a large crowd had gathered at the community centre which was near their base – in the past RPG rockets had been fired from there against the base.

The crowd started to throw stones and chant songs as the soldiers came down the street towards them. This was the middle of the afternoon and you never saw crowds of adults and youths gathered in this area at that time of the day – not good atmospherics.

The soldiers kept walking towards the crowd of around forty people until they reached the edge of the effective range of the stones being thrown at them. They started to memorise the faces of the stone-throwers so they could arrest them at a later date when they weren't hiding in the safety of a crowd.

As the soldiers stood observing the crowd, it suddenly parted and there stood in the middle of them was a man dressed in a black trench coat wearing a black balaclava over his head concealing his face. In his arms he held an AK assault rifle, which he levelled at the patrol and fired at the soldiers.

Private X was the first to see the terrorist and moved forward into a firing position and returned fire at the gunman. As quickly as the terrorist had sprayed his magazine of thirty rounds at the patrol the crowd closed in around him; he was now hidden from view, which stopped the soldiers from returning fire at the gunman.

The patrol all ran forward to try and shoot or arrest the gunman, who was spotted running towards the nearby houses. The crowd tried to hinder the patrol so the gunman could escape. Private X and the rest of the patrol gave chase; they started searching the houses and gardens for the gunman – they knew he couldn't be far away. Eventually they found and arrested the terrorist, who was hiding under a bed in one of the houses; his weapon was recovered from a shed in the garden of a neighbouring house.

After the many hours spent on the rifle ranges during the pre-deployment training, the platoon sergeant was not best pleased with Private X for shooting at the terrorist and not hitting him. Private X replied, "Shooting on a range is easy enough, but shooting whilst receiving incoming fire changes the rules." He was also a trained sniper and never lived down missing the terrorist – the terrorist had been approximately one hundred metres away. When he walked round the battalion lines, he would be followed with sarcastic comments of "cracking sniper".

Private X was awarded a Mentioned in Dispatches (MID) for his part in the capture of the terrorist and the recovery of an illegal weapon.

55   THE SAFWAN FRIDGE

Lieutenant X was new to his unit and was serving in Iraq on his first operational tour; he was very keen to impress his soldiers and fellow officers. He noticed when he was out on patrol that the village of Safwan near the border crossing point between Iraq and Kuwait had a small market that sold many items, including second-hand fridges.

In the base camp that his platoon lived and operated from there was a severe shortage of fridges and consequently no cold water available most of the time to help ease the extreme heat. Lieutenant X thought it would be a good idea if he purchased a fridge for use by his platoon when they were back in camp. It would show he cared for his men's morale and it would gain him respect from his soldiers. He decided that, on his next patrol to the Kuwaiti border, he would purchase a fridge on the return journey at the market.

On arrival at the market, the platoon sergeant didn't like the place one bit, too many dodgy characters for his liking. Unperturbed, the young officer walked over to the street trader to select a fridge; the first fridge he came upon was priced at $500. The gallant officer quickly agreed and handed over his $500, which was about two months' salary for the trader and ten times the fridge's true value.

When he returned to the vehicle, the platoon sergeant asked him how much he paid for the fridge; when he told him $500 the sergeant started crying with laughter. The sergeant asked him if he bartered to get the price down. The officer had not bothered to barter as he thought it was a good price compared to the UK. When the patrol drove off in their vehicles, the platoon sergeant looked in his rear-view mirror and watched the Iraqi trader that had sold the officer the fridge hurriedly packing up his stall – he had just won the lottery and was off to celebrate.

Once safely back in camp, Lieutenant X couldn't wait to get his new fridge installed and filled with water bottles to produce cooled water for his soldiers. After a fortnight the fridge had still not produced one single bottle of cold water and it began to dawn on the young officer that he had been ripped off.

For the remainder of the tour the fridge sat beside the officer's bed with the door open and became an excellent bedside light for reading.

56 DRIVING IN THE DUST

The battalion had been living and fighting in the Green Zone to the south of Kajaki Dam for about three weeks and finally the operation was coming to an end. The aim of the operation was to deliver a huge electrical turbine that would be fitted to the existing turbines, which produced hydro-electrical power at the dam. The new configuration of turbines should provide enough power for the surrounding areas and Kandahar City, which was about three hundred kilometres away.

The operation incorporated the majority of the troops in the British brigade plus extra soldiers from the Afghanistan battalions; this was the main effort for the unit's six-month operational tour – providing power should win the hearts and minds of the local population in Southern Afghanistan. The brigade was responsible for moving the turbine from Kandahar along Route One, thread its way through the desert and rendezvous with the battalion south of Kajaki, avoiding all enemy action if possible so that it wasn't damaged or destroyed on the way.

3 Para was ordered to deploy into Kajaki to clear and secure the last ten kilometres of the route south of Kajaki to the brigade meeting point. This was to allow the convoy carrying the turbine to travel along a safe and protected corridor to deliver the turbine and drive back out to the safety of the desert when they had finished.

The task for the battalion was colossal: it had to in load over twelve hundred troops for the task by helicopter, clear and search every inch of the route for bombs that may have been planted, search all nearby buildings along the route for bombs and clear the Green Zone of any Taliban either side of the road so they could not interfere with the convoy.

The troops started deploying into Kajaki about ten days before the convoy had even left Kandahar because the time it would take to clear and secure the route wasn't known. The more bombs found and Taliban action against the soldiers would delay the clearance of the route. At the same time the brigade didn't want the battalion to clear too quickly and get to the meeting point and have to wait a week for them to arrive.

Once the orders to move south were received from the brigade, the battalion moved forward and from the outset it became very kinetic. The Taliban did not want these troops in their back yard and were willing to fight for it. The outcome was only ever going to go one way – the battalion used artillery, multi-launch rocket systems, aircraft bombs, mortars, rifle, machine guns, rocket launchers and grenades to push the Taliban back from the route. At the same time the troops were clearing through the thick vegetation of the Green Zone, the engineers were walking the route searching for bombs planted in the road, beside the road, in buildings and trees close to the road. Once the areas were cleared, companies were given stretches of the route to picket and protect so the Taliban couldn't slip behind them and place more bombs into the road which had been declared clear.

Above the route being cleared there were very high mountains which towered over the valley below; the commanding officer had placed his mortar and artillery observers there. Throughout the first week the crash of exploding artillery and mortar shells could be heard up and down the route as the soldiers sitting in their eagle's nest looked through binoculars and rained death down on the Taliban. The engineers clearing the route found numerous bombs buried under the road, due to time, these were all blown in place and the hole quickly filled in with soil. The battalion fighting through the Green Zone was having great success as they fought against the Taliban, bringing in mortar fire onto the enemy before moving forward and clearing up with rifles and grenades.

Finally, the battalion had fought its way along the route and reached the brigade meeting point and completed its first part of its task – the route was clear. The next part of the task, to escort and secure the route, went unhindered by the Taliban and the convoy slipped in one night and delivered the turbine before it disappeared back into the desert the next night.

The final part of the operation was to withdraw the battalion back up the route and into the safety of Kajaki camp before extraction by helicopter and home to base for some rest before the next mission.

Throughout the operation a convoy of British vehicles that belonged to the battalion had been driving up and down the secure corridor, supplying ammunition, food, water, rations and moving soldiers and equipment to new locations to support the commanding officer's plan. The withdrawal plan was simple – the Afghanistan battalions who were nearest Kajaki would stay in their location until all of the British companies had moved through their part of the route and into the base. Once all the British were through, the Afghanistan soldiers, who had less distance to travel, would come into the camp last.

For some reason, when it came to the withdrawal, the Afghanistan soldiers packed up and were the first into Kajaki base, which meant the British battalion was walking up a route in the Green Zone with no protection where the Afghanistan soldiers should have been securing. They were requested a few times to stay put, but the message was either not understood or ignored – their soldiers were packed up and gone.

It ended up that the battalion's vehicles were the furthest troops from Kajaki because they had been picking up soldiers – beyond that was once again territory that belonged to the Taliban, as they reasserted themselves back along the route. It was now night time and very dark; visibility was reduced even further by dust that was kicked up by the vehicles as they crept and bounced along the pitted road. The night-vision goggles the drivers wore were not much good for night driving when the dust was kicked up. One of the commanders decided that they needed to get a move on as the Taliban would not be far behind. He told the drivers to put their side lights on, to see if that would help them to speed up.

They had only driven about fifty metres when the first enemy machine gun opened up and the green tracer bullets from the Taliban arched their way towards the vehicle convoy. Everyone in the vehicles hissed out in unison, "Turn out those f**king lights." Thankfully, no one was shot or injured and the convoy slowly made its way along the route – through the darkness and the dust into the relative safety of Kajaki camp.

57   INTERVIEWS IN THE MOUNTAINS

The battalion was recalled from leave early to deploy to Macedonia, where it was to organise and collect weapons from the rebels that had been fighting against the government troops. A ceasefire was put in place so 2 Para and other NATO soldiers could go up into the mountains to agreed locations where the rebels would hand over their weapons hidden away from government eyes.

At the time there was great public interest in this NATO intervention because the world was relatively quiet and it was the first major operation for British troops for about two years. Macedonia bordered onto Kosovo and there was a fear that if the fighting wasn't curtailed it could spread and embroil the West in another Balkan War – so the task was taken seriously.

Once the weapon collection sites were organised and nominated, the battalion deployed a few days ahead of the collection point opening times so they could check and clear the area – each operation lasted about four or five days. Three of the weapon collections were in the villages of Redusa and Brodec, which is located above the Tetovo valley near the Kosovan border. A very beautiful part of the country, set high in the mountains to the west of the capital city, Skopje – very similar to the lower French Alps.

When the battalion was given the orders to deploy and set up a weapons collection site, there were always two parts – ground convoy and a helicopter force. The helicopter force would deploy first to clear the ground for the vehicles to arrive with the heavier equipment and support weapons like mortars and heavy machine guns. Although the battalion was invited and allowed into the rebel-held territory, there was a fear that it could have been a trap and the soldiers would end up having to fight back out of the mountains to safety.

Once the soldiers were on the ground, the commander organised all-round defence of the collection site so that the rebels could come in and drop off their weapons with no outside interference from the government troops. In effect, when the rebels entered into the collection site they were under the protection of the British troops.

The sites were open for a specific period of time, which was passed to the rebels so they could organise bringing in all their weapons and ammunition. On the first collection, no rebels appeared until the site had been opened for about an hour. In the distance a mule train of about twenty donkeys was spotted coming down the high mountains by one of the deployed companies. When the mules got closer they were laden with ammunition boxes, heavy machine guns, surface-to air-missiles, rifles, anti-tank mines, rocket launchers, grenades and many more weapon systems.

There were lots of national press journalists at the weapon collection site who had been invited and briefed on what they could and could not photograph by the battalion press officer. The sight of the donkeys bristling with a vast array of weapons got them excited and scrambling all over the place to get the best pictures for their paper. In the area there were minefields, plus the majority of the rebels did not want to be photographed. This media frenzy almost halted the first weapons from being handed in. The commander had to quickly organise his soldiers to grab the journalists and get them back to the area where they were supposed to be and couldn't cause any interference to the operation – and for their own safety: journalists being killed in minefields whilst under a unit's protection is not good.

Journalists can be very stubborn when they are trying to get the best photographs and interviews to enhance their own careers. Soldiers can be just as stubborn when ordered to get them back into an area where they were supposed to be. The end result – some of the soldiers got a little heavy-handed with the journalists when herding them back to where they should have been located all along. Subsequently, some of the journalists wrote unflattering things about the soldiers in the national papers – heavy-handed, hiding the truth and uneducated thugs.

Once the weapon collection was complete and all the weapons had been flown out for destruction at a designated site, the battalion withdrew back to barracks to await their next operation. The commanding officer debriefed the commanders on how the operation went. He was content, apart from the media running amok, almost scaring the rebels from handing in their weapons and blowing themselves up in the nearby minefields. He briefed the media officer and the regimental sergeant major that he wanted the media cordoned in an area where they could not move from, for their own safety, and so they couldn't interfere with the operation, and he wanted intelligent soldiers nearest to the journalists who could be interviewed.

The next weapon collection operation was back up in the mountains above Skopje and was based on the same principles as the first operation. This time the media were flown in by Chinook helicopter and landed in an area that had been cordoned off by six-foot pickets and orange mine tape, so they couldn't wander off anywhere they weren't supposed to be. The area was also picketed with soldiers at five-pace intervals so the media couldn't break through and run amok again.

When they disembarked from the helicopter, they were briefed by the media officer that they had to stay in the cordoned area due to operational constraints and their own safety. They were also welcome to interview any of the nearby soldiers as they wished.

Once the operation was finished and the battalion had returned to barracks, the next morning's daily newspapers mentioned the new operation. It commented on the smoothness of the weapon collection and the very bright soldiers that were operating in difficult circumstances, and how impressed they were with the open relationship they had between the media and the soldiers and commanders during the operation.

What the media didn't know was that the commander of the company responsible for cordoning the journalists' area had hand-picked every soldier within earshot of the journalists for their intelligence. So when the media were told they could interview any soldier they liked, they were in fact calling over the most intelligent soldiers in the company. It was hardly surprising that they went away with an impression that all the soldiers were very bright and articulate.

On return to barracks near Skopje, the battalion witnessed the second airliner slamming into one of the Twin Towers in New York – three hundred soldiers crammed around a small TV, watching incredulously as the full story unfolded before their eyes. This was to signal the start of the busiest period for the British Army for many years.

58   FIRE-FIGHTING IN BELIZE

The company stood on the edge of the helicopter-landing site (HLS) at their new Belizean camp. They were at the start of a six-month operational tour in this Central American country and had only just arrived in the camp. The helicopter-landing site had been etched out of the jungle; it was identified as the only place suitable to demonstrate to the whole company the different types of fire extinguishers and which type of fire each one should be used against.

The company sergeant major bellowed out at the men to keep quiet and listen in to the instructor, stressing how important it was to learn how to use the equipment as it could save lives. The demonstration was taking place at midday under the full blast of the sun; everyone had been travelling for about three days from the UK and had very little sleep. To say no one was really interested would be an understatement.

Corporal X was the company clerk and would also double-up as the duty fire non-commissioned officer for the six-month tour. He wasn't a very confident instructor; he held little respect from the men due to the fact that he often mucked up their pay and administration. He started off his lesson by stating that the period of instruction would last about an hour. This was not well received by the audience of tired and grumpy paratroopers and needed the company sergeant major to get the men into order again so the lesson could continue.

He started by showing six different types of fire extinguisher and the types of fire that each one could fight. Clearly he had listened and learnt about fire fighting on his week-long course at Deepcut, where all Army fire training courses take place. Once all the theory was out of the way, he asked if there were any questions before he moved on to the practical part of the instruction. Funnily enough, there were no questions at this stage!

For the practical part of the lesson Corporal X poured a little petrol onto the grass from an old jerrycan and stood back before lighting it. He then proceeded to explain again the type of fire extinguisher and the coverage of fire that it could put out, before he extinguished the fire in front of the audience. He was feeling quite proud of himself and how the lesson was progressing so far. The finale was going to be the large cream-coloured foam fire extinguisher, which is used in the case of a helicopter crash or a fuel fire. For this he had a few extra jerrycans of petrol and started to sprinkle the fuel liberally around the demonstration area.

At this point the company started to wake up and watch with interest, because he was liberally pouring petrol everywhere on one side of the cleared area. Twenty metres away on the other side there was a small flicker of a flame from a previous demonstration which he hadn't extinguished properly. The members of the company that were sitting on the grass started to move back slowly, all nudging their mates to make sure they were fully awake in case they had to leg it backwards into the jungle.

Corporal X and the company sergeant major were now the only two people in the entire company who were oblivious to the naked flame and impending disaster. When Corporal X was still ten metres away from the small flickering flame, the petrol fumes reached it and ignited. There was an almighty flash and fireball which lit up the whole of the helicopter-landing site. The company all ran backwards into the jungle, giggling in hysterics at this spectacle. The company sergeant major ran forward into a scene straight out of *Apocalypse Now* and grabbed Corporal X by the scruff of the neck and pulled him out of the flames. The other corporals in the company started to grab the soldiers and organise putting the fire out properly, once the gravity of the situation was fully realised.

Fortunately, Corporal X never received any significant burns, but the company had to use all of its allocated fire-fighting equipment to put out the fire before the jungle caught fire, which would have been a major disaster. Not a good start to a six-month tour a few thousand miles from home. The company sergeant major put Corporal X on extra duties for the next few weeks for embarrassing him in front of the company.

Many years later, the company sergeant major was made a Member of the Most Excellent Order of the British Empire (MBE) in the rank of major for his work during an operational tour of Northern Ireland

59   ON STAG IN CYPRUS

Lance Corporal X and Private Y were serving with their battalion on a United Nations tour on the 'Green Line' in Cyprus. The Green Line is a line on a map that separates the Turkish from the Greeks after the invasion of the Cypriot Island in 1974.

Cyprus was a fantastic place to be stationed on a six-month tour, particularly for two young Scotsmen that had not really been abroad before they joined the Army. Their normal working days consisted of eight-hour shifts standing on a tower looking across the Nicosia plain and reporting any Turkish troop movement to HQ. Not very exciting, but what made the tour fantastic was when they had time off they could discover the rest of the magical island of Cyprus and the towns of Limassol, Larnaca, Paphos, Ayia Napa, etc. Tourists paid a fortune to do this and they got paid to be here – outstanding. There were some members of the battalion that had such a good six months they were still paying off their credit card bills that they racked up in Cyprus four years later on a tour of Northern Ireland.

On this particular weekend, these two young paratroopers found themselves heading to the tourist town of Ayia Napa for a weekend of partying and drinking. Ayia Napa was a fantastic town in the middle eighties – not overly crowded as it is today, and it was mainly full of Scandinavian tourists who were very keen to party just as much as these two youngsters.

After a fantastic weekend of drunken partying and debauchery, Sunday night arrived and it was time to head back to base in time for Monday morning's parade. Lance Corporal X was packing his kit and Private Y was still rollicking around the bed with a young Scandinavian chick. The young lance corporal told him to get his kit together as it was time to get the taxi. The private soldier wasn't having any of it and had decided he was staying for a while yet and refused to get the taxi. So the newly promoted lance corporal headed back to base on his own, knowing that the company sergeant major would be going mental if Private Y wasn't there on Monday parade.

The 0700 hours Monday morning parade was always fitness training to blow away the cobwebs from the weekend of partying. The company sergeant major noticed straight away that the soldier was missing and had still not returned. He called for Lance Corporal X to explain where the missing soldier was. The young lance corporal tried to bluff the company sergeant major by saying he thought he was in camp, but was not sure where, at which the company sergeant major exploded in a rage. "I know he isn't in this camp because he didn't sign back in with you last night," screamed the company sergeant major. "I need to know now, is he in jail or hospital?" Lance Corporal X had no way out and had to tell the company sergeant major that he was all right and was with a couple of girls in a hotel in Ayia Napa. "OK," said the company sergeant major, "off you go with your platoon on morning fitness."

Four days later, Private Y returned to camp and got out of a taxi, unshaven and still half-pissed. The company sergeant major was sitting on the veranda of the building reading a book when he saw the taxi roll in and the young private get out. As he walked towards the company sergeant major, he became instantly sober before he had moved ten metres from the taxi door. The company sergeant major had a mean reputation for being very hard and thinking first with his fists.

When he reached the company sergeant major, he stood firmly to attention, not knowing what to expect from this volatile character. The company sergeant major calmly told him, "You do realise that you have been absent without leave for four days and should be charged?"

The young soldier replied, "Yes sir." The company sergeant major told him to go and get changed into uniform and to be back in five minutes – he sprinted to his room to get his uniform on.

He returned dressed in uniform as instructed by the company sergeant major and was told to get up onto the observation tower and relieve the current soldier on duty. When Private Y got to the top of the tower, he called down to the company sergeant major, "How long am I up here for?" to which the company sergeant major called up, "How long were you absent without leave?"

The young private shouted back down, "Four days, sir," to which the company sergeant major called back, "You will be up there for four days then."

For the next four days and nights Private Y stayed up the tower in the baking Cyprus heat and cool nights without sleep. Strangely enough, no one else turned up late again after they saw the young soldier crawling down from the tower days later.

Private Y was still unrepentant; the two girls from Sweden were worth every minute spent up the tower.

The battalion was halfway through its summer leave when it was recalled at short notice so that it could deploy to the former Yugoslavian Republic of Macedonia. The Albanians and Macedonians had been having skirmishes with each other and Western Europe did not want it to escalate any further. A peace deal had been struck and a multi-national force from NATO was assembled to go and disarm the rebels in the mountains that surrounded the towns around Skopje, south of the Kosovo border.

Once the troops arrived in the country there was very little infrastructure to support them, so the battalion had to be self-sufficient in supporting most of its needs. The battalion was split into two groups and accommodated in separate factories. One was a factory that used to pack fruit and the other stored nuts – this was not lost on the soldiers. The commanding officer named the camps, Arnhem and Normandy, but they were always known as the Fruit and Nut factories by the soldiers.

Each factory held over three hundred and fifty squashed-in soldiers and officers; both were an open space of approximately one hundred metres by one hundred metres. Everyone slept on camp cots and kept their equipment and personal belongings underneath. Outside the factory were portaloos and showers made out of wood and piping for the soldiers to administer themselves. The chefs had set up a field kitchen where everyone ate fresh food that was purchased locally.

Having so many soldiers living in such close proximity to each other was going to cause hygienic problems at some point. After living like this for a few weeks, some of the soldiers were affected by a severe bout of diarrhoea and vomiting. This quickly spread through the factories and caused an epidemic. The bug was clearly transferred by air and affected the majority of the battalion. The factories were emptied, swept, mopped on a continual basis and disinfected but the bug was never defeated. The sickness was more prevalent at night time: you could be standing chatting to someone and they would visibly start to go pale in front of your eyes. They would then need to dash to the portaloo before they made a mess of themselves. When they came back into the factory they were made to collect all of their belongings and sleep outside. When they walked out of the factory carrying their possessions, this was known as the "walk of shame" and they were subjected to verbal abuse from the unaffected soldiers as they went past. The bug was so quick and effective that the soldiers christened it the 'shit sniper'.

When the sickness was at its worst it was mentioned daily at meetings and the number of soldiers 'shot by the shit sniper' was accumulated across the battalion for the medical report. At its height there were as many as one hundred soldiers bedded down at the same time – an operation was nearly cancelled due to a lack of manpower. Once the sniper struck the soldier or officer, they were off the road and bedded down for three to four days. They were all lined up outside the factory on their camp cots in quarantine away from the healthy soldiers to try and contain the sickness bug, which was the best that could be done at the time. Many of the soldiers were so bad that they had to be given intravenous drips so that enough fluid could be administered into them.

Many soldiers and officers had theories on the cause of the sickness, but none were ever factually proven – chefs cooking with dirty fingers, rotting vegetables, meat that was off, lack of hygiene, something in the dust from the factory floor – the list of theories was endless.

One company sergeant major paraded his company and ripped into them after quite a few of his soldiers fell sick. He blamed it on poor hygiene and threatened to charge the next soldier in his company that went sick with diarrhoea and vomiting. The next day he was shot by the shit sniper and bedded down for four days – he never lived it down.

61   HOW TO DEFEAT BOREDOM

In the regiment it has been said on a number of occasions that the most dangerous creature on the planet is a bored private soldier. I am inclined to agree with the statement.

On a late afternoon out in the desert area of Southern Iraq, Major X was sitting in the shade beside his vehicle, resting his eyes. He was enjoying the last of the day's sun as it started to cool, which is an awesome experience, particularly as a respite to the 50-degree heat they had endured throughout the day. The patrol had been out in the desert for the last two weeks, checking on the Iraqi border police forts dotted along the Iraq/Iran border. Not the most interesting of work, as it was quite clear from the beginning that the border guard officers were not in the least interested and the standard expected at Dover customs would never be emulated in this part of the world.

So the scene was set for keen soldiers trying hard to pass their levels of professionalism onto an unwilling work force. Eventually, after a few weeks, the soldiers lost interest in training the border guards who did not want to be trained – they were on the most part only interested in getting bribes for illegal activities. It then became an endurance test for the soldiers between living in the desert and getting back to camp as quickly as possible so time would pass quickly on the tour and they could get back home.

Every few minutes, Major X could hear a stifled grimace and laughter coming from an area about twenty metres away behind his vehicle. After about thirty minutes of listening to the noise and laughter, curiosity got the better of him and he thought it best to investigate.

He approaching the semi-circle of seated soldiers where the merriment was coming from and noticed that a soldier would jump back, "curse" and all the others would howl with laughter at the soldier.

When he approached them, he asked, "What are you up to?"

A young signaller replied, "We are playing a game of dare." The young private explained that the game was done on the flick of a coin and the loser had to complete the dare.

"OK," said the major, "what's the dare?" The young signaller then elaborated that they had discovered that the new high frequency (HF) radios recently purchased by the British Army at vast expense of billions of pounds to the UK taxpayer gave off an electric shock if you touched the antenna when someone was pressing the send button. This was quite painful and the dare was:

every time someone held the antenna another would press the send button and shock the soldier holding the antenna. Each time the number of shocks was increased to the individual and the most anyone had managed to hold on for was three shocks. This explained the noises that the major had heard whilst resting – grimace noises as the soldier was shocked and laughter from the others as he pulled his hand away from the antenna and the electric shock.

The major, being a very competitive bloke, decided to join in and managed to set a new record of four shocks. This helped with morale and also kept boredom at bay for a few more hours in the dry dusty desert of Iraq.

62   PADDLING POOLS ON THE NICOSIAN PLAIN

The box factory was an old fruit-packing factory in Cyprus that got its name because it used to make boxes for the orange harvest that took place each year on the central plain of Nicosia in Cyprus. Turkish forces invaded Cyprus in 1974, reclaiming land they believe to be theirs and pushed the Greek Cypriots south across the island. After the eventual cessation of hostilities, the box factory found itself located in the middle of the Green Line – and it was converted into accommodation for United Nation peacekeeping troops.

The Green Line is a line that is drawn through the length of Cyprus separating Greek forces from Turkish forces. It is called the Green Line simply because the officer that drew up the line marking the demilitarised zone used a green chinagraph pencil – green line.

There are now many foreign armies that man the Green Line twenty-four hours a day three hundred and sixty-five days a year to stop any border disputes between both countries – a situation not commonly known by the partygoers and tourists that visit Cyprus each year on holiday.

All troops employed on the Green Line are there under the United Nations mandate and all soldiers must wear the famous blue beret and cap badge of the United Nations when on duty.

The troops are there purely to report any troop movements, border disputes or incursions that either side commit. For Private X it meant spending many hours up an observation tower with a huge pair of binoculars attached to his head, staring at either Greeks or Turks and reporting anything unusual, which there rarely was. The lads were all getting bored and the daily fitness programme was the main escape route for frustration and boredom.

Private X had a company sergeant major who was a very keen volleyball player and most days a game would be organised, which was great fun in the cool Cypriot evenings. The company sergeant major decided that the company should put out a challenge to all the other nations that were serving along the Green Line and host an international volleyball competition at the factory.

Great idea – so all the other nations were asked and all agreed: Danish, Swedish and Canadians. It was going to be a great competition and the company sergeant major was going to make sure it was all organised properly so that the foreign nationals that attended had a great day and would think the Brits were excellent hosts and good fun.

Nothing is simple in the British Army; for the next two weeks, every hour of the day prior to the competition saw all of Support Company soldiers stationed in the factory working late evenings. They painted anything that didn't move from top to bottom, cleaning up years of dereliction around the surrounding box factory, which did cause concern as there was a minefield nearby! However, the company persevered and got on with the reconstruction and refurbishment of an old run-down and dilapidated camp, to make it look as good as possible in order to impress the other nations on competition day.

The day before the competition the company sergeant major got hold of Privates X and Y and said, "Right, young fellows, I have just the job for you two to finish off and it needs to be ready for tomorrow – follow me." He led the young soldiers to an area behind the ops room, where the company sergeant major pointed out what must have been an old paddling pool. How he spotted it is miraculous because all the soldiers could see was a concrete rim sticking up a few inches out of the hard Cypriot ground. It was about four metres long, three metres in width and oval in shape – covered in mud and years of dead mulch leaves piling up on top. Only later did the soldiers find out that the company sergeant major knew it was there because fourteen years earlier he had paddled in it on a previous UN tour when he himself was a private soldier and had always remembered it. Over the years it had obviously fallen into disrepair.

Pointing at the ground, the company sergeant major said, "Right, lads, that is a paddling pool and I want that all cleaned out of all mud and debris, washed, repainted in United Nations blue and once dry refilled with fresh clean water. You have got about six hours to get it done, so stop gawping and get on with it," and off he marched.

Once the company sergeant major had gone the two soldiers were not best pleased, but got on with the job in hand. After removing about five tons of mud and debris from the concrete basin and having spent six hours doing as requested, the company sergeant major came back to inspect the work. He was very impressed: the two lads had worked hard and there was now a gleaming paddling pool about two feet deep filled with water.

"Excellent job, well done, lads. I knew you would do a good job. There is now only one thing missing," stated the company sergeant major. "You two stay here, I will be back in five minutes," before he strode off in the direction of the cookhouse.

He returned as promised. "Right, lads, the only thing that is missing from that pool is fish and I want some in it tonight."

The soldiers looked at each other and in unison said, "Fish."

"Yes, lads, fish and I know how to make them." The company sergeant major produced a bag of carrots and two potato peelers from behind his back. "Right, get carving and I want a shoal of at least thirty lifelike goldfish in that pool."

The company sergeant major walked off and the two private soldiers took their clothes off and sat in the pool, carving goldfish out of carrots for the next hour, thinking the company sergeant major had lost his marbles. The company sergeant major was in the sergeants' mess that night giggling and telling his mates, "You will never guess what I had two soldiers doing today."

The volleyball competition was a great success and everyone enjoyed the BBQ by the paddling pool. Every time a foreigner commented about goldfish in the paddling pool, the company sergeant major would giggle under his breath.

63   TEMPER TEMPER

The battalion had been exercising in Kenya for about six weeks when it was warned off for an 'Emergency Tour' of Northern Ireland during the last week of the exercise, whilst sunning themselves on the African plain. Instead of a nice long period of leave (cancelled) after Kenya, the battalion spent the time packing and training for another operational tour before the soldiers found themselves once again in Northern Ireland. There had been an upsurge in mindless violence in the Northern Irish Province and Her Majesty's Government requested more soldiers to be deployed as soon as possible. So the soldiers found themselves patrolling the hills and valleys of East Tyrone – the towns and villages of Dungannon, Coalisland, Cappah, Moy, Benburb, Pomeroy and Cookstown, as their tans slowly faded from their faces in the rain.

Tensions at this time in the early 1990s between the local population and the security services in Northern Ireland were running very high. A lot of murders were taking place, plus the security forces were being very successful against the terrorists. The British soldier, as normal, was piggy in the middle of this maelstrom of havoc and mudslinging between loyalists, republicans, and politicians – his only concern was doing his duty and getting home with all of his mates intact.

As all sides of the divided people tried to score points against the security forces with photographs or complaints, it was becoming a political nightmare that even rested on the shoulders of the youngest private soldier. If he said or was photographed appearing to be doing something wrong – however innocently – it could be quickly turned into a propaganda coup for one side or the other, with repercussions that would likely end up on the prime minister's desk in London.

For Sergeant X this was his fourth tour of duty in Northern Ireland; his main responsibility was to play his part to the full in the defeat of terrorism and ensure the twenty-six men under his command all returned home at the end of the tour.

One Sunday morning, he was at his desk writing out a patrol report, having just returned from a two-day patrol. Sitting at his desk, tired, hungry and dripping wet from the typically Irish weather, he had camouflage cream ingrained into his face and hands. He fought to keep his eyes open and finish the report so that he could get into bed and catch a few hours' sleep before going back out on another patrol.

The company sergeant major popped his head into the office and told him that the company commander, Major Y, wanted a word with him before he went to bed. He finished off the patrol report and walked across to the company headquarters to find Major Y. Sergeant X knocked on his door and was called in. Major Y asked him how the platoon was doing and how their morale was during this very busy period of continuous patrolling. He replied, "All men in my platoon are doing a fantastic job, even the newest lads on their first tour have now become seasoned in the arts of the Northern Irish campaign."

Major Y replied, "That is good to hear. I expected nothing less from 5 Platoon." Major Y informed the sergeant that he had a bit of an issue, which had been highlighted to him by the Royal Ulster Constabulary regarding complaints from the public.

The sergeant asked him, "And how does this affect my platoon?" The major quickly pointed out that his platoon had been identified by the time, date, and location from his patrol reports, which put his soldiers in the specific area and time of the complaint. Sergeant X asked for the complaints report so he could see what it was all about. Major Y passed them across the table for him to read; once he had finished reading them, he passed them back and said, "It is a load of old tripe." The main complaint was to do with rough handling whilst suspects were being searched and bad language to the public. Sergeant X knew this wasn't happening as the soldiers under his command had been drilled hard on how to deal with the public, particularly when dealing directly with them whilst searching – no cheap propaganda coup would come from them.

Major Y accepted the sergeant's explanation and asked if it was all right for him to accompany him on his next patrol so he could see first-hand how his soldiers interacted and operated with the locals. Sergeant X replied, "Not a problem, sir; be on the helipad in four hours' time and be prepared for a twelve-hour patrol."

The area of the next patrol was a very dangerous place: only a week before one of the soldiers in another platoon within the company had stood on a homemade improvised explosive device (IED) and lost both of his legs from the thigh downwards. There had been numerous weapon and explosive finds – this was an area where there were known terrorists who blended in as innocent civilians in the blink of an eye. At the pre-patrol briefing, Sergeant X told the major that he would accompany him and to stay by his side throughout the patrol. The main aim of this patrol was to intercept vehicles travelling along a certain road and to search an area of farmland for weapons, ammunition, explosives or any other terrorist equipment.

Once on the ground, the patrol headed down a hill to set up a snap vehicle checkpoint on the road and search every passing vehicle. In this area, a security checkpoint would only stay on the road for approximately twenty minutes because the terrorists in this area had ambushed checkpoints before that had stayed too long in the one spot. So the idea was to set up for a short period of time, melt away into the terrain, and then appear somewhere else to keep the locals and terrorists guessing where the patrol actually was. It was well known that terrorists would not attack unless they held all the cards and they could escape unscathed after an attack. It was unlikely they would try and hit the patrol unless they knew exactly where every soldier was. Major Y was starting to physically tire a little after the fifth vehicle checkpoint. Each time they finished a search, Sergeant X made the patrol climb high into the wood line along the ridge to disappear, before reappearing at another snap vehicle checkpoint in a different location.

So far the public had been all right and were not being bothersome with any of their normal back-chat trying to rile the soldiers. On the next checkpoint, the major said he would do the talking to the drivers for a change. By now it was raining heavily, everyone had wet feet, they were all getting physically tired due to the terrain, being continually alert, moving in and out of fire positions, watching for potential snipers in the hedgerows and wooded areas.

The next car drove into the checkpoint and the major approached it; he knocked on the window and in his best Oxford accent asked the young fellow inside to lower his window. The driver sat in his seat looking straight ahead, not even acknowledging the existence of the officer at his car window. He lent forward and turned his car radio up and stared straight ahead whilst the officer stood outside with rain dripping off the end of his nose. The major, who was known for being quick-tempered on the rugby pitch, was starting to get irate at the driver – the harder he knocked the driver's side window, the more the driver turned up the music and stared straight ahead.

By now the major had steam coming out of his ears with frustration and near braking point. He then started to shout at the driver of the vehicle. "If you don't open this window I am going to smash it in."

Sergeant X, realising that a disaster would unfold if the major did break the driver's window without a proper warning, rushed over to the officer and grabbed his elbow just as he was raising his rifle to strike the window. Sergeant X said, "No, sir, this is how we do it." He took his notebook out of his pocket and wrote in it – *can you open your window so we can have a chat?* – placing the open notebook on the windscreen so the driver could read it. The driver leaned forward in his seat, making a point of taking his time reading what was written on the paper. Once the driver had read the note a few times, he wound down his window. "Sorry, lads, I never saw you stood in the rain. How can I help you in this God-awful weather?"

At this the officer nearly blew a gasket at the impudence of the driver. Sergeant X ushered the officer away to the sentry cut-off position so he could cool down whilst he searched the car. After a very thorough inspection of the vehicle and the driver, he was allowed to continue on his journey.

Throughout the remainder of the patrol Major Y never said a single word until they were safely back inside the security base at the end of the patrol. When they had finished the debriefing, the major took Sergeant X to one side and thanked him for taking control at the checkpoint and apologised for his unacceptable and naive behaviour. He had forgotten how some of the local people enjoyed playing games to wind soldiers up, to get a reaction for compensation through the police and courts.

Many years later, Major X was made an Officer of the Most Excellent Order of the British Empire (OBE) in the rank of colonel.

64   OFFICER SPORT

When young officers join the battalion after passing out of Sandhurst on completion of their officer training, it is normally good sport to play pranks on them in their first week in the battalion.

After commissioning, Second Lieutenant X was fortunate to have joined his unit just before it started a two-year residential tour in Northern Ireland. He was sent on the battalion recce to Belfast, where they would operate in for the next twenty-four months.

The unit currently in Belfast was looking forward to their sister battalion taking over responsibility for the city so they could then go back to Aldershot at the end of their own twenty-four-month tour.

Second Lieutenant X arrived in RUC Woodburn in West Belfast with the rest of his unit's recce party and attended a lecture being given by a warrant officer from the unit currently operating in the area. They were briefed on the area that they would be responsible for – terrorist threat, location, suspected terrorists in the area, etc.

The company sergeant major giving the brief had an old mate in the audience from the new unit who had told him that Second Lieutenant X was a brand-new officer and this was his first week in the battalion.

The company sergeant major didn't want to miss a trick and briefed the new unit members that they would be split up and go out on patrol with his guys to get to know the area. He explained that there had been a recent upsurge in petrol bombings in the area and all patrols were to take counter-measures. From behind the desk, the company sergeant major produced an old bergen frame that had two red and very large water fire extinguishers tied to the frame so that they could be carried by someone – approximately 60kgs in weight.

The older members of the new unit that had served in Northern Ireland before were listening to the company sergeant major and thinking – you must be joking; we are not carrying that weight around all night. He asked for a volunteer and pointed to a young officer. "What about you, sir, how about you leading by example and volunteering to carry the improvised fire-fighting kit on tonight's patrol?" The young officer couldn't really refuse in front of his fellow officers and soldiers.

The company sergeant major concluded his brief with a warning that there was currently a high sniper threat in Belfast. This meant hard targeting was to be carried out on the night's patrol and all patrol members were to run everywhere to present a moving target and make it harder for the sniper to acquire an easy shot.

At this point the older soldiers realised that the company sergeant major was setting the young officer up for a wind-up.

Second Lieutenant X spent his first night on operations in Northern Ireland sprinting around West Belfast carrying two very large and heavy fire extinguishers on his back for four hours. By the time he came back in from patrol, he hardly had the strength to get the fire extinguishers off his back.

Once all the patrols were safely back inside the camp, the company sergeant major gathered the patrol together and briefed them. "We used to use the fire extinguishers carried by the young officer, but we found they were far too heavy to be practicable, so we requested these ones." From his day sack he produced a very small green fire extinguisher which weighed approximately 2kg.

The young officer looked aghast as he lay on the floor in a pool of sweat. The company sergeant major looked at the young officer and said, "Welcome to the regiment – as an officer, speak up when you know things are not right," as the rest of the soldiers howled with laughter at the very tired young officer.

65   HUNGRY TROOPS

Troops who live in poor conditions and close proximity to each other spread germs quickly; if you have everyone eating centrally there will probably be an extreme outbreak of diarrhoea and vomiting. The battalion was fortunate or unfortunate enough to learn this lesson during operations in Macedonia a few months before it deployed to Afghanistan.

The battalion had been in Kabul, Afghanistan, for two months and were still eating from Army ration packs and not centrally feeding or eating nice fresh rations lovingly prepared by the chefs. The new commanding officer had taken command of the battalion just prior to the Afghanistan deployment. He had not been in Macedonia or witnessed the level of sickness that the battalion had experienced there four months previously.

Army ration packs are very good and nutritious; there are about six or seven different menus that contain – Lancashire hotpot, treacle pudding, sausage and beans, beef stew and dumplings and a many more delightful dishes. A very good variety for short periods of time, but a little monotonous after a few months. The food comes in a 'boil in the bag', which is very convenient, hygienic and easy to heat up in an issued mess tin.

The commanding officer was getting tired and bored with the same rations that hardly varied from day to day; he wanted the battalion to go onto field kitchen and fresh rations as soon as possible. The quartermaster and regimental sergeant major had both served on the Macedonian deployment and seen first-hand the sickness that was caused there by eating fresh food and were totally against the idea.

Together they went to talk to the commanding officer to explain what would happen if they changed from Army rations to fresh food and cooking. Thankfully he listened to the senior officer and soldier, so the battalion remained on ration packs for the remainder of the four-month deployment. As they were leaving his office, the commanding officer requested the quartermaster to see if he could at least find local bread, so that it would offer a slight variety from the standard-issue rations.

The next day each company was handed a black plastic bin bag full of naan bread, which had been made in the local bakery near the camp. The soldiers and officers were grateful for this slight change in their normal diet of Army rations and happily scoffed the bread down daily.

After a few weeks the regimental sergeant major was sitting with the quartermaster having a spot of lunch and he mentioned that he had never seen him eating the naan bread. The quartermaster replied, "There is absolutely no way I am eating any of that bread. I have seen how they make it." He explained that he had watched them making the bread in the local bakery and they used their feet to mix and roll the dough on the floor of the shop. He then posed the question, "Have you noticed the five long lines that are on top of the bread? Have you any idea how they got there?"

The regimental sergeant major replied, "I haven't a clue." The quartermaster then explained, "The lines are put there when they stretch the bread flat for the last time and the lines are made when the bakers scratch their toes through the dough."

The regimental sergeant major never touched the naan bread again, but did laugh to himself every time the commanding officer did.

More importantly, by staying on Army ration packs the battalion didn't suffer any cases of diarrhoea and vomiting – unlike the echelon troops at Kabul airport who went for the easy option and switched to fresh-cooked food as soon as they could and suffered the consequences.

The commanding officer was made an Officer of the Most Excellent Order of the British Empire (OBE) for his leadership and command during this operational tour of Afghanistan.

66   SHOCKING BEHAVIOUR

The British Army spent many years in Northern Ireland patrolling the towns and fields across the six counties, trying hard to keep the warring factions apart and defeat terrorism. It was a thankless job and one that had very few exciting moments; mainly it was boring days spent on either sentry duty, eating, sleeping, or on endless foot patrols.

Soldiers being soldiers don't really like being bored and when they are, they generally play games and pranks on each other when on or off duty. When new guys join the battalion in the middle of a tour they are generally an open target for the first few months and the brunt of most practical jokes.

Private X had only just joined the battalion straight from training and found himself in his new company patrolling the towns and countryside of East Tyrone. East Tyrone is a very scenic part of the Emerald Isle, but was also a very dangerous place in the eighties and early nineties. Many a shooting and bombing caused terrible deaths and injuries there courtesy of the Irish Republican Army (IRA).

Sergeant X decided it was time to play a trick on the new private soldier to give the others in the platoon a bit of a laugh at his expense and cheer them all up on the long and wet foot patrols. The area that they were patrolling was very rural, and being in Ireland the lads were always fighting through blackthorn hedges, jumping ditches, fighting with barbed wire and getting zapped by electric fences that were used to keep cattle and horses in the farmers' fields.

The sergeant called Private Y in for a brief at the next patrol stop, which was in the middle of a thick blackthorn hedge. "Right, young lad, you will have noticed that a lot of the guys keep getting zapped by these bloody electric fences that keep the cattle in the fields," said the sergeant.

"Yes, Sergeant, I have noticed," replied Private Y. The sergeant briefed him that to save all the guys getting zapped by the electric fences it made sense for one member of the patrol to volunteer and to lie on the fence while the others ran over the top of him – only one guy would then get zapped. As a new member to the platoon and eager to please, he quickly volunteered for the job.

As the patrol moved off through the fields and another electric fence was encountered, the young soldier was called forward and told to go and lie on the fence. When Private Y reached the electric fence he jumped forward and lay down so that the fence was flattened by his body and he was lying flat on the ground in the mud. Every few seconds his body would give an involuntary twitch, as he was shocked by the electric impulse coursing through the wire fence. After about five minutes and all members of the patrol had run over his back, giggling as they went, the patrol continued on.

About two hours later the patrol was having a water stop at the side of a hedgerow and the sergeant asked Private Y how he was coping with the electric fences. The young soldier replied, "I have now laid down on ten fences and it is starting to get a little painful; perhaps we could swap over and someone else could lie on the fences." The whole patrol burst out laughing at this reply. It took the young lad a few minutes to realise that they were all laughing at him and he had been played along as a practical joke. All he could say was "you bastards", before he also joined in the laugher with the rest of the patrol on a cold and wet rainy day in Northern Ireland.

67   BLIND PEW

During the turbulent years in Northern Ireland, danger not only came in the shape of a bullet or a bomb. There were other hazards that were extremely dangerous – it seemed as though some of the worst drivers in the world lived in Ireland, bogs that took you up to your waist or further, hedges that you had to fight through, or animals that were inquisitive and gave your position away or chased you through the fields.

Private X found himself on another tour in Northern Ireland. This time his unit was in County Tyrone and not the city of Belfast, which made a nice change from the usual urban environment that he was used to. The countryside of East Tyrone is very beautiful but physically very difficult for soldiers to operate in because of the continual fences, hedges, bogs, streams and rivers that need to be crossed. It is also very easy for the local terrorists to operate in, as they know the land like the back of their hands.

He had already served in the battalion for about three years – the majority of which had been in Northern Ireland and Belfast in particular. He was a bit of a fitness freak and heavily into body-building, which made him a little vain. Unfortunately, he was also as blind as a bat and should have been wearing spectacles, but he wouldn't wear them in front of his mates. Absolutely no use for spotting and returning fire onto potential terrorists' positions.

Private X was lead man in the patrol as it wandered through the beautiful countryside; he fought his way through a blackthorn hedge and moved across the open ground, not paying any attention to the grazing cattle. The rest of his patrol saw the huge bull that was standing in the field amongst the cattle looking at the lone figure walking through its territory – they stopped and stayed at the fence.

Corporal Y was about to shout a warning to Private X, but decided that he would see what would happen regarding the huge bull. The bull decided that he wasn't having any of this and started to paw the ground before he charged headlong towards the moving shape – Private X.

Private X was straining his eyes to see where the rest of the patrol was when he felt the ground shake and heard the bull thundering towards him before he even saw it. As he turned to see what he thought was a cow, he realised that it was in fact a huge bull. He knew that he was too far into the field to out-run it and get to the fence before the bull caught him.

The rest of the lads in the field thought the sight of this huge bull charging down on him was hilarious and some shouted out encouragement for him to run. They were all shocked and stunned when he dropped to his knee, cocked his weapon, took aim and shot the bull, which dropped dead at his feet – laughter instantly ceased.

Corporal Y was furious and saw his career flash in front of his eyes. To make matters worse, when the investigation was over it turned out that the bull was in fact a prize bull worth at least £20,000.

Thereafter, Private X was always teased about scoring a bull's eye – even with his eyesight.

68   FIREMAN SAM

The battalion was recalled early from Christmas leave in 2001 to deploy to Afghanistan. In fact, one of the companies celebrated New Year on the bus en route to RAF Brize Norton to catch their flight out to Kabul. Over the next month the battalion trickled out of the UK and into Kabul in small section- and platoon-size groups.

The reason for the slowness of the deployment was that the only route into Afghanistan at that time was by air and the only aircraft that could land at Kabul airport was the Mark 1 C130 Hercules flying at night piloted by Special Forces aircrews. Due to the distance from the forward mounting airfield in Oman and the height above sea level that Kabul is situated, the aircraft could not carry full loads.

Each aircraft could carry a maximum of forty-five troops or equipment. Every time an extra piece of equipment was put on the aircraft, soldiers were taken off the manifest to await the next flight. Weight being a premium, all soldiers could only deploy with their fighting kit and a Bergen; all luxuries were left in baggage in Oman which would follow on later (allegedly).

Once in Kabul there was absolutely no infrastructure, as it had been ruined by the fleeing Taliban, who were being chased by the

Northern Alliance. Kabul could best be described as a ghost town at that time and what the soldiers brought with them was all they had.

The majority of the battalion arrived in January, right in the middle of an Afghan winter, which can best be described as Arctic conditions with thin air. The soldiers had been issued a winter clothing enhancement pack, which consisted of a pair of windproof trousers, Arctic issue mittens, gloves and a mosquito net. If you were tall like the commanding officer and the regimental sergeant major, then you had to sew a four-inch strip of material around the bottom of the trousers in order to get the right length – Army procurement at its best!

Eventually, all the battalion arrived into Kabul with very little equipment, absolutely no home comforts, but enough to survive the cold weather. Patrols around the city were started to reassure the locals that had started to appear from hiding knowing that the Taliban had in fact gone. Being mostly white-faced and using large Russian Antonov aircraft to bring in the heaviest equipment in daylight, it was hardly surprising that a lot of the population thought the Russians had returned!

The Battalion was now living in an old Telecom complex behind a wall for security; it had lots of rooms that between six and eight soldiers were squashed into. There were no glass windows, so the engineers rigged plastic sheeting over the window frames to try and keep the chilly wind and snow out (called winterised). All soldiers slept on the cold concrete floors at night wearing every stitch of clothing they possessed to stave off the cold winter nights.

There wasn't a huge amount of land inside the compound to stack and store the tons of ammunition and fuel that was now starting to arrive for the battalion. All the stores were stacked and separated by their explosive or hazardous content away from living accommodation and not mixed together in case of enemy attack. The soldiers in charge were doing their best with the limited space to secure, separate and keep the munitions as safe as possible under the difficult circumstances. The anti-tank rockets used at this time by the Army were called 94mms, which could knock out a tank or a bunker quite easily. They were the first weapons to be issued out to the soldiers in case any Taliban still lurking in the area were still feeling brave. These weapons were now located in almost every room in the building where the soldiers slept.

The quartermaster at the time who was in charge of equipping and supporting the battalion in any way he could to make the soldiers' lives comfier, had his guys out looking for ways to warm up the rooms where the guys slept. The best they could find was a diesel heater made from tin that slowly dripped diesel into a basin inside the heater, where it ignited and gave off great heat and kept everyone in the room warm. The problem with the heater was the slightest bit of wind outside would snuff the flames out and the diesel would continue dripping until it combusted and the heater exploded in the room. The diesel heater needed to have a tin chimney about six inches in diameter and four feet long burned out through the plastic, winterised window to operate, or the diesel fumes choked the soldiers inside the room and made them all oily and covered them in soot.

At around this time the regimental sergeant major, who also becomes the unit fire officer on operations, received a call from the brigade regimental sergeant major that his unit was about to receive a fire inspection. He laughed down the phone at his opposite number, thinking that it had to be some kind of a joke at this stage of the operation.

Normally in the UK a unit fire inspection is a big affair and every Army camp complies rigidly with civilian legislation for the storage of ammunition and explosives, as you would expect. It turned out that a Ministry of Defence fire service inspector had indeed somehow got himself on to a military flight to Kabul and was hell-bent on inspecting all units to ensure they complied with the correct fire regulations. Brigade headquarters had already failed their fire inspection and the battalion was next on the list to be inspected. Apparently, the inspector had turned up at brigade in his black uniform with the red stripe down the trousers and a peaked cap on his head, expecting the same standard as UK. He had walked around the brigade, who were extremely busy trying to in-load a few thousand troops, tons of stores and ammunition for the campaign, with his clip board and proudly presented them with a very thorough debrief – they had FAILED the fire inspection.

The regimental sergeant major briefed the commanding officer that they were being fire inspected the next morning – he thought it was a joke as well. That night buckets were bought from the market and filled with sand or snow and placed in the accommodation to at least make some kind of an effort. The regimental sergeant major briefed the company sergeant major that the 94mms needed to be outside the rooms for the inspection. If the fire inspector saw the dangerous tin diesel heaters in the rooms, which keep exploding beside weapons that have a high explosive content, he would go through the roof as they would be breaking every fire regulation known to man.

The next morning the fire inspector arrived and was met at the camp gate by the regimental sergeant major, who welcomed him into the camp. The inspector looked straight out of fire school – wire-rimmed glasses, shiny black shoes, black uniform, shirt, tie, peak cap on his head and a clipboard under his arm. He clearly wasn't a fighting soldier and never had been.

From the outset this character thought that fire safety was the Holy Grail to all purpose of life on the planet. He gave the regimental sergeant major a one-way brief on what was expected, to which he replied, "You do know there is very limited fire-fighting equipment in the country because other war-fighting equipment is more important. However, the correct fire-fighting equipment has been ordered and will arrive eventually." That statement went down like a lead balloon with the inspector. He was shown around the outside area where all the ammunition and fuel was stored – lots of pacing, huffing and puffing, teeth whistling and pencil scribbling ensued.

When they eventually entered the building, he commented on the fire buckets with snow and sand in them – at least this unit had made some kind of an effort, unlike the other one. The inspection on the whole wasn't going too badly until he entered Support Company accommodation and the anti-tank platoon floor. On entering the first room, there were eight soldiers gathered around a tin heater trying to keep warm. The heater was going full blast and the soldiers were sitting on top of the 94mm anti-tank rockets, using them as chairs.

At this spectacle and blatant disregard for fire regulations, the inspector broke his pencil and threw up his hands in disbelief and stormed out of the room and down the stairs. He thrust a report into the hands of the regimental sergeant major, stating, "Obviously your unit has failed the fire inspection."

The regimental sergeant major replied, "What do you expect in a war zone, you pencil-pushing twat," and threw him off the camp.

Afterwards, the commanding officer and regimental sergeant major laughed into the night at the fireman's expense, which at least kept them warm for a little while. Next morning, the commanding officer wrote a letter up the chain of command asking the question: "How was it possible that valuable space on an aircraft could have been wasted on such a pompous fire inspector when the battalion was still short of essential war-fighting equipment?"

No response ever came back from higher command, who would have been as annoyed as the soldiers trying to survive the harsh Afghan winter.

69   JACK IN THE BOX

During a residential tour of Belfast the battalion lived in and operated from Palace Barracks just outside of the city; because it was a residential tour this meant that the battalion plus families lived in Northern Ireland as they would in any other garrison town in the UK.

The battalion's main area of responsibility was RUC Woodburn, a police station that was located in West Belfast. This part of the city was designated as a strong green area, which meant that it was very active with IRA members and sympathisers. When on patrol in this area, soldiers remained very alert as they treated every person as suspicious; every dark shadow a potential sniper position; every parked car could be a potential bomb waiting to vaporise them in an instant. Every company that rotated through RUC Woodburn experienced shootings, bombings, hostile civilians and riots – truth be known, the young soldiers found this quite exhilarating in a strange sort of way. They also all believed they were standing up for democracy on the streets of the UK. Normally, companies would rotate through the police station for six to eight weeks at a time.

After a tour of RUC Woodburn, the companies normally took a period of leave to bring them back down to normality after living and operating in such conditions. This meant that the married soldiers would stay in barracks and spend time with their families or go to the mainland if they still had travelling tickets remaining from their allowance. For the single guys it meant a huge piss-up in the camp bar the night they got back from RUC Woodburn, to release pressure before flying out on leave the next morning nursing a huge hangover.

Prior to getting the morning transport to Aldergrove airport outside Belfast, the commanding officer and his regimental sergeant major would always inspect the company's accommodation to make sure all was in order. The main reason was for the commanding officer to get around and see the troops, to see how they were after weeks of high tension before standing them down for some well-deserved leave. For these inspections all bedding and mattresses were packed away, so all the commanding officer would see when he entered the room was the young soldier stood beside his bed and his luggage sitting on the bed springs. The commanding officer would always ask questions like, "How was Woodburn? Where are you going on leave?" The regimental sergeant major would try and dig into corners to see what he could uncover in the way of hygiene, etc.

On entering the room that belonged to Privates W, X, Y, and Z, the regimental sergeant major noticed that there was a locked cupboard that should be open for inspections. He looked at the platoon sergeant who was accompanying them and asked him to open it so he could have a look inside. The sergeant knew what was in the cupboard and wasn't very keen to open it – he explained that it was just bedding. The regimental sergeant major replied, "I am not after an explanation, open the cupboard." The platoon sergeant looked at Private X and told him to get the key and open the door.

Private X approached the cupboard in terror, as he knew that behind the door were four mattresses, which had been squashed in and were soaking wet from the previous night's drinking. Quite a lot of soldiers urinate in their sleep after they have had a few too many beers. I once asked my civilian brothers if they knew of anyone that wet the bed after drinking and they looked at me as if I had two heads – both in total denial. I suspect a large part of the population participate in this sport when they drink enough.

When the young private got to the door, he fitted the key and announced that the key was stuck and it wouldn't open. The regimental sergeant major stepped forward, pushing the young soldier out of the way and turned the key and handle. As soon as the handle was down, the four mattresses inside the cupboard expanded back to their full size, which catapulted the door open into the regimental sergeant major. He was pushed back with such force that he was knocked over and was lying on the floor covered in four urine-sodden mattresses. He quickly got to his feet and noticed that he was now wet – knowing full well what it was from. At this point the four young private soldiers couldn't hold it in any longer and got a fit of the giggles, which grew into loud hysterical laughter. The regimental sergeant major exploded into a rage and threatened to jail everyone in the company.

Once the regimental sergeant major calmed down, the young privates were sent to the guardroom for some extra physical training to sober them up for their morning flight back to the UK mainland. By the time they got to the airport that morning they were totally sober and dripping wet from the morning's extra fitness lesson, courtesy of their wet mattresses.

70   SCREAMS IN THE NIGHT

In the early days of the Afghanistan campaign which started in 2001, for some soldiers in Kabul there was a lack of real life support and the battalion was living in an expeditionary warfare setting. As more soldiers arrived into the battalion area, the normal things that are associated with large numbers of soldiers came to the fore – the provision of food, which turns into rubbish and human waste.

Getting food is easy, as it will come through the Army system – eventually.

Getting rid of rubbish is not an issue as most of it can be burnt – easily enough.

The only issue is human waste, which no one likes to handle – understandable.

To get over the human waste issue, the engineers attached to the battalion were tasked with digging a pit about three feet wide, twelve feet deep and twenty feet long. On top of the hole they placed a row of wooden toilet boxes, which the soldiers could sit on and their waste would drop away into the abyss below. Once a fortnight this would be filled with petrol and burned to stop it overflowing and the need to dig a new pit.

Due to the ground being frozen solid, it was taking the engineers longer to dig the pit than normal, plus there was a shortage of suitable wood to make the toilet boxes. As the days passed, the hole slowly got longer until it was eventually finished, then the wooden toilet boxes were placed over the top of the hole ready for use. Unfortunately, they ran out of wood and never had enough to cover the last three feet of the hole, so it was decided by the engineers to put hessian material over it to help keep the smell in.

Private X awoke in the night bursting for the toilet and needed to get to the toilet quickly before he made a mess of his trousers and sleeping bag. He got out of bed and put his warm smock on and headed out into the snowy Afghan night to find the toilet. He was in such a rush that when he approached the toilet block he cut the corner and stepped on the thin hessian material. Falling through it, he ended up waist deep in the excrement of the battalion twelve feet below.

Fortunately for him, a passing soldier heard his screams and had seen him fall into the toilet trench. Looking down into the hole, he told the very unfortunate soldier who stared back in sheer terror from the bottom of the filthy pit, that he would go and fetch help. About five minutes later, Private X looked up from the hole and could see a few heads looking down at him and cameras started to flash. Private X yelled out, "You bastards, get me out of here!" which caused much laughter from above until a ladder was put down for him to climb out.

When he climbed out he was made to strip down totally, all his clothing was burnt and he was scrubbed with ice-cold water to get the filth off him.

The next day the quartermaster, who was not known for his humour or charity towards the human race, allowed the soldier to get another set of clothing without charging him for the privilege. The regimental sergeant major commented to the quartermaster that he was being unusually charitable, to which he replied, "I looked into the hole this morning where he fell in. I saw the fingernail marks scraped down both sides of the wall where he had tried to stop himself from falling all the way to the bottom. Even the coldest heart would have to be a little sympathetic!"

71   KEEP YOUR HAIR ON, COLONEL

During a tour of duty in East Tyrone in Northern Ireland, the battalion was split – two of the companies were attached to an Ulster Defence Regiment (UDR) battalion and found themselves in Dungannon, whilst the rest of the battalion operated from the town of Cookstown about thirty miles away.

When the two companies arrived in Dungannon, the commanding officer from the UDR unit met them on the helicopter pad; from the very outset it was clear that he was not keen to have them in his camp. Instead of embracing them, as they were there to help his soldiers who were struggling with the current level of violence, he was rather frosty in his approach. This is very unusual, as most commanders in these positions can see the bigger picture: they understand the concept of what is to be achieved and they will support all operations to the best of their ability. His quiet backwater posting was now being invaded by paratroopers that were very keen to get out into the villages, fields and hedgerows of East Tyrone and find the terrorists and their weapon hides.

The camp they were now living in was extremely cramped with too many soldiers living on top of each other – understandably, frictions were to occur. The camp normally held one UDR company plus a headquarters. It now had two UDR companies, a battalion headquarters, two extra companies and two extra company headquarters all squashed inside its perimeter. Originally built to house and support around 150 soldiers, it now accommodated approximately 600 soldiers.

The tour was deemed as an emergency tour, which meant – get the troops into the area quickly, the administration and infrastructure would follow at a later date. Some units are very good at this and can do so at the drop of a hat – some cannot. The battalion had only returned from Kenya on the Tuesday and was now in Northern Ireland on the Saturday, having had its leave cancelled.

Once the Companies had been flown in, a few hours and days later Chinook helicopters began dropping off portacabins into any space that could be found inside the camp perimeter, so that the soldiers would have somewhere to live when not out on patrol. The cynics did comment that the UDR were accommodated in hardened rocket-proof accommodation and the new companies were sleeping in gyms, cupboards, corridors, portacabins, and any space that could be utilised. In a short space of time the normally neat little camp was turned into a hive of activity, with all units fighting for real estate and building contractors building temporary walls for segregation. The life support for these numbers quickly started to creak at the seams. The kitchen couldn't cope so the standard of food went downhill; not enough washing machines; too much litter; not enough toilets: the list was endless.

The UDR battalion commander was less than impressed, to say the least, so he kept badgering the company commanders on a daily basis regarding trivial issues – why weren't the soldiers saluting him when he passed them in the camp, rubbish, hygiene, his cooks being threatened, soldiers eating too much, untidy camp, stores lying in the open, etc. The company commanders would pass these points down the chain of command to the lowest ranks so all knew the points briefed from the UDR commander.

Private soldiers are a strange beast and generally they do not like being continually harangued with routine camp administration trivia – as they see it. After spending days out on patrol in the soaking wet countryside – enduring lack of sleep – patrolling for miles with heavy kit – continually scanning through weapon sights for potential snipers – falling into streams and fighting through the blackthorn hedges. When they did get back into camp for a short period before heading back out on patrol again, all they wanted was a hot shower, food, sleep and they were ready to go again. They had no time for picking up litter, administration tasks, etc.

The other thing about private soldiers is they are very perceptive and intuitive to what is going on around them. Very quickly they could sense that the officers and sergeants were getting really pissed off with the continual trivia that was being forced upon them from the UDR commanding officer. The officers and sergeants were busy planning and conducting operations themselves and had very little spare time to harangue the soldiers on unnecessary bullshit, as they saw it. The soldiers at the bottom of the food chain were even less impressed and now saw the UDR commanding officer as the enemy and it was time to play a trick on him.

Private X, from one of the companies, had noticed that the commanding officer was always accompanied on his camp walkabouts by his black Labrador dog. He also noticed that the dog was badly trained and would often run off into the buildings where the soldiers were living. The dog would root through the soldiers' belongings and be a nuisance in general; quite often it would defecate outside the accommodation and tired soldiers back from patrol would tread in the dog muck, spreading it through their bedrooms on the bottom of their boots, so no one was overly impressed with his dog either.

The plan was hatched that the next time the dog came into the accommodation they would trap it and Private X would shave the top of its head.

A few days later the dog appeared and was captured, barber's clippers appeared and the top part of the dog's head was shaved. Once it was released, it happily bounded back to its owner sporting the latest fashion in dog haircuts. It looked like a seal pup with a grey patch where the black fur had once been between its ears.

The officer nearly had a heart attack and went berserk trying to find out who had committed this heinous crime against his dog. The accommodation was searched for dog hair that would incriminate the barber – but to no avail.

This, of course, did even less to help relations in a camp with an unhappy chain of command, but the private soldiers thought they had won a little payback for all the mucking around they felt they were receiving whilst in camp and chuckled contentedly.

Thereafter, when the commanding officer was on his camp walkabouts the dog was on a lead and no more poo parcels were left lying around for soldiers to tread in.

72   SUITED AND BOOTED IN THE JUNGLE

The battalion was halfway through a six-month operational tour of Belize and had been very successful in carrying out its patrolling tasks and manning of observation posts along the Guatemala border to deter any aggression from its neighbour – Guatemala.

For the majority of the soldiers they were on a work rotation of approximately one week patrolling, one week in an observation post, one week training, and one week in base camp carrying out fatigues and guard duty. A good rotational system which incorporates variety is essential for soldiers to keep them interested in the tasks. It also shares the good and bad tasks equally across all of the platoons so that some soldiers don't feel as though they are always getting the unpopular jobs.

All the soldiers loved the patrolling as they were out in the deepest jungle that Central America had to offer and it was soldiering at its best. The jungle is a place that is never quiet; the vast majority of soldiers grasp the opportunity of being in this warm green environment, constantly wet through from rain or sweat, heavy packs, physically exhausting, potentially deadly animals, flora and fauna that is awesome, and very testing navigation. I am quite sure many British soldiers crossed and re-crossed the Guatemalan border many times over and were never truly aware, due to the difficulty in map reading. The difficulty in navigating is caused by the lack of accurate maps and the inability to see further than twenty or thirty metres due to the thick vegetation, so the only way to navigate is by pacing and compass bearings.

Observation posts along the border were set up to look across into Guatemala to ensure they weren't going to invade along the obvious roads and tracks through the jungle. The days spent in an observation post were quite dull, particularly as there was rarely anything to report. Each morning and night clearance patrols were sent out around the local area to ensure the Guatemalans weren't going to assault the position. When the Puma helicopter arrived to drop off the relieving soldiers for their stint, it collected the off-going soldiers and returned them to base camp, which was a relief for many.

The week in camp doing training and administration was spent doing fitness, weapon handling, classroom work and getting air around the bodies that had been sweating continuously for at least two weeks in the jungle and observation posts. The human body is like a machine and isn't designed to sweat profusely for days on end; it will eventually breakdown if not treated correctly. Getting fresh air around the body clears up the sweat rashes, crotch rot, and allows your mate to check your body for any bugs that have decided to bury into your skin and make it home.

The week on fatigues and camp guard was the week everyone disliked the most – washing cooking pots in the kitchen, sweeping the camp, camp maintenance, painting, and guard duty. This was a long week to endure before the soldiers could get back out and into the jungle.

Some soldiers never left the camp during the six-month tour as their job was to support the troops deploying backwards and forwards to the border areas. They were called 'base rats' and were employed in administration, logistics, chefs, mechanics, drivers and storeman-type jobs.

The base the soldiers lived in and operated from was called Salamanca Camp, which was in the southern part of Belize and located in thick jungle. The camp had been built in a jungle clearing and was on its own; the nearest local population was about ten miles away down a long and twisting road, and only one road passed the camp.

For the 'base rats' the tour must have been a little bit like a six-month prison sentence, because they never left the camp and only had the NAAFI shop and a small dip tank to swim in outside of their work and bed space. Every morning they would go running and their choice was left or right out of the camp along the track. When you turned right out of camp there was an old rusting and abandoned bus at the side of the road about two miles out, which was normally used as the turnaround marker.

The company sergeant major would usually lead the morning run with all the base rats – they comprised about fifteen soldiers. This particular morning they left the camp and turned right, heading down the ragged uneven track towards the old bus as normal. Corporal X was the company clerk; he had a lot on his mind at this time due to his own domestic affairs back in the UK, plus constantly living in the small camp was starting to play on his nerves.

He was the most unfit guy in the small band of base rats, which had been noticed by the company sergeant major, who continually harangued him to catch up and stay with the other troops during the run. As the troops sprinted down the track, Corporal X would fall behind, carry on jogging and catch up with them again when they slowed down. On this particular day, the company sergeant major wanted him to work harder and put more effort in to keep up. By the time they got to the old bus and the turnaround point, Corporal X was flagging and just about all in physically. The last thing he needed was getting bawled out by the company sergeant major every few minutes, so he decided enough was enough and started to walk.

Well, walking without being told to was a big NO, NO during fitness, unless told to by the person in charge. The company sergeant major went ballistic and started ripping into him to get a move on. At this, Corporal X told him to get lost and leave him alone as he had had enough and was walking back to camp. This added fuel to the fire and the company sergeant major was now blue in the face with rage. However, he was just not getting through to Corporal X. So he left him there and told him to get back to camp and be in his office in tray at 0800 hours after breakfast to be charged, and to make sure he was wearing his best kit.

Later that morning, when everyone was back in the camp and had breakfast, the company sergeant major went to his office to charge Corporal X for his disobedience.

When the company sergeant major entered his office, Corporal X was standing on his desk in the position of attention with his arms by his side, dressed in a civilian suit and standing in his in tray. "What the hell are you playing at, Corporal X, have you gone mad?" bellowed the company sergeant major.

Corporal X replied, "No sir, you told me to be in your in tray and in my best kit."

The company sergeant major started to laugh particularly when he noticed Corporal X had his own charge sheet for insubordination in his hand, which he must have typed himself.

73   AN EYE FOR AN EYE, A STONE FOR A STONE

In Northern Ireland a lot of the locals liked to throw bricks and stones at soldiers when they were out on foot or vehicle patrols. One of the worst places for this very disrespectful treatment of British soldiers was in the republican estates of West Belfast.

During a handover between units, the new unit could not believe the amount of stoning and bricks that the off-going unit was accepting from the locals. The unit was even starting to avoid areas because they knew they would get stoned. This was unacceptable, as a unit must be able to operate freely in all of its operational area. There can be no NO GO AREAS in your sphere of responsibility, for the simple reason that when troops are not patrolling that area the terrorists can be planting bombs in preparation for when they allow the security forces back into the area. There was a lack of strong leadership in this regiment and they were just ticking the days off the calendar until they went home.

The new unit had a reputation for being hard but fair with all terrorists and locals on both sides of the warring factions – republican or loyalist. The sergeants and officers that had been on many tours of Belfast before couldn't belief the way the other unit operated. They were certainly not going to accept the same treatment from the locals and all of the area would be patrolled to the best of their ability.

Once the off-going unit had finished their handover and tour, they returned back to their barracks in Germany, and the new unit hatched a plan so it would be noticed very quickly that there was a new battalion in the area. The areas where the heaviest stone and brick throwing took place were the first targets: the vehicles would drive straight in and see what happened with the locals.

When nightfall started, the troops all loaded up into the vehicles and drove into the area; sure enough, the locals appeared and started throwing stones and hurling bricks to damage the soldiers and vehicles. The soldiers standing up in the vehicles had sacks full of their own missiles and threw them back at the locals. At the same time troops hiding inside the vehicles rushed out after they had come to a shuddering halt, and arrested the stone throwers who were caught red-handed in the act. By the end of the night all areas where stoning had been taking place were being patrolled again and were very quiet.

The faces on the stone throwers was a picture as the soldiers threw bricks back at them. There was complaints of "you lot aren't allowed to do that" as they were arrested and taken away by the police. The troops giggled – an eye for an eye or a stone for a stone.

Normality had returned and the unit never received any casualties during their tour from brick or stone thrown injuries – unlike the previous unit.

74   FUN IN A SANDSTORM

The soldiers were serving in Southern Iraq in an area to the west of Basra city and were living in sixteen-man tents. They were back in camp, while normally they were out on patrols along the Iraq/Iran border. The platoon had a day off, which is when the lads would normally have time to sort out their personal administration: clean weapons, get their laundry done, write a letter, visit a coffee shop and send e-mails.

On this particular day a severe sandstorm had hit the area and the soldiers couldn't really get much done as the sand was flying everywhere, getting into all nooks and crannies – it was a day best spent inside their tents sleeping and chilling out. Experiencing a full-blown sandstorm is not pleasant: the skies darken, sand lashes you at fifty/sixty miles an hour winds, and the only defence is to stay inside or wrap up totally and wear goggles to escape injury. Visibility can be reduced to an arm's length. Soldiers can only sleep or chill out for so long before they get bored and start to play pranks on each other.

Captain X was the company second-in-command who ran the company operations from the ops room on the other end of the camp. He worked very long hours and only left the ops room at night for about six hours, for sleep and meals throughout the day. On this particular day he was making slow progress by following the edge of the road to get to the cookhouse for lunch; the visibility was so bad his eyes were nearly clenched shut to avoid losing his sight as the wind and sand whiplashed him. En route to the cookhouse, he passed the accommodation area where all his company soldiers were accommodated; he knew they were inside the tented accommodation due to the bad weather.

As he neared the accommodation he caught a glimpse of what he thought was a naked soldier wearing a respirator (gas mask) run into the first tent, and then he heard the roar of laughter from soldiers inside. A few seconds later he saw another naked soldier wearing a respirator come out of the tent, run around it, before disappearing back inside to more applause, cheering, and chicken noises from the soldiers inside.

Captain X was thinking what the hell is going on here and thought it best to get in there quick and investigate before any local nationals or soldiers from another unit spotted this, and complained to the higher command about naked soldiers running around the camp.

On entering the tent, Captain X shouted, "What the hell is going on in here?" As he looked around the tent, he noticed there was a group of at least a dozen soldiers naked with sand clinging to their wet bodies. On hearing Captain X shouting, all the soldiers ceased chattering, stood to attention and looked towards the captain. He spotted Corporal X in the crowd, who was clearly the ringleader, and asked him to explain what the hell was going on: why were naked soldiers running around outside the tent wearing respirators?

Corporal X started to explain that they had a day off and couldn't do much due to the hideous sandstorm outside, so they decided to play a game. The game they were playing was highest card – everyone picked a card from a splayed deck: the soldiers with the higher cards were safe, but whoever held the lowest scoring card was the loser and he had to carry out the challenge. The challenge was to be carried out naked, only wearing flip-flops and a respirator. Prior to leaving the tent the loser was soaked in water, he then had to run around the tent as quickly as he could so that he didn't get too much sandblasting from the storm outside. When they returned, they were deemed to have been Kentucky Fried Chickened as the sand stuck to their wet skin, and cheered back into the tent.

And so another afternoon during a six-month tour was ticked off the calendar in Southern Iraq. Captain X told them to stop it and explained that nudity in a Muslim country was not allowed. When he left the tent and continued on his way to the cookhouse, he could only shake his head in amusement at the antics of his soldiers.

75   GRAVEYARD CAPERS

The platoon sergeant was called into the Intelligence Section office in Dungannon and briefed that a member of the public had telephoned to say there was an assault rifle in his local church grounds lying half-hidden under a broken headstone. He wanted the Army to come and collect it before a terrorist retrieved it and committed more gruesome murders in his local area of Northern Ireland. The telephone call came late at night, and intelligence were not sure if it was a trap to lure soldiers into the area and a well-prepared ambush or hidden bomb.

The company commander briefed the sergeant that a helicopter would be there for him and his platoon in thirty minutes, and he wanted the paratroopers briefed fully and to be on full alert just in case it was a trap. The helicopter would drop them off one mile from the churchyard so that the platoon could patrol into the area and get a feel for the place, before they moved into the graveyard and confirmed if a weapon was hidden there or not.

Sergeant X was very experienced and briefed all of his soldiers and team commanders that they would approach the area and circle around the church when they were one thousand metres away. This way they could check for any command wires that might lead to a bomb or a terrorist crouching behind a hedge waiting to explode the hidden device when they approached. The IRA was very good at concealing command wires at the bottom of fences or digging and burying them into the ground. Later, when it suited them, they would attach the bomb at one end and the firing pack at the other – instant death and destruction for many poor souls. As the soldiers crossed every fence, hedgerow, stream and culvert, they got down on their hands and knees and searched with tools and fingertips for buried command wires.

After they had completed a circle loop at one thousand metres out, they would get closer and do it at five hundred metres, two hundred metres and finally one hundred metres, before the sergeant would have to go in and have a look to confirm the presence of a weapon or not.

The platoon was made up of three teams; to keep the platoon fresh, the sergeant kept changing the order of the teams so there was always an alert team at the front searching and digging for command wires. This puts stress on soldiers and fresh troops are a necessity so a command wire does not get missed.

Corporal Y was at the front of the platoon with his team, about one hundred metres from the churchyard wall, and they had been briefed to go through the car park and check the wooden fence for command wires before everyone else crossed. Off he went with his team; when they reached the wooden fence, Corporal Y leapt over and two seconds later leapt back over the fence and sprinted back to the sergeant's position, trailing his men behind him. When he got there he was gasping for air, but managed to blurt out, "There's a grey-coloured command wire at the bottom of the fence which runs along it towards the church."

The sergeant asked, "Are you sure?" The corporal briefed him again about what he had seen and pointed out the exact place where he had stepped over the wire.

The sergeant had to go forward to confirm there was a command wire before he called in the bomb disposal squad. He briefed all the soldiers to stay put and he would go and investigate – he set off on the lonely walk. When he got to the fence where the corporal had crossed, he looked down and there was a command wire: he could see about four metres of it threading through the grass. He stepped back and walked ten metres along the fence, got down on his hands and knees and searched for more of the command wire – nothing. He walked back down the fence in the other direction and did the same again on his hands and knees – nothing. He stood back up and walked back to where he had seen the wire and followed it for a few metres, where he found the end – good sign, no command pack or bomb on the end. He followed the wire in the other direction and found a hand-held car vacuum cleaner attached to the other end. Relief flooded through his nervous body and he started to giggle – more through nerves than anything else. He called the others over to the fence and they all had a good chuckle; someone had obviously thrown the vacuum over the fence, and the lead looked as though it was threaded through the grass. It had been there for such a long time the grass had grown around it, making it look as though it was running along the fence bottom.

Once they were content that no command wires were leading into the church area or hidden in any other likely approaches that a terrorist might place a bomb to kill or maim soldiers, the sergeant made another lonely walk – this time into the churchyard. After five minutes of searching, he spotted the butt of a rifle sticking out from a broken headstone that had fallen over. He radioed back to HQ and confirmed that he had eyes on a weapon that looked like an assault rifle.

In the morning the weapon technicians and the bomb disposal team came to clear the weapon before it could be moved. They confirmed and secured the weapon, which had a magazine of thirty rounds attached, ready to commit murder in a lovely part of Northern Ireland.

76 NIKI LAUDA ON OPERATIONS

Private X had only recently passed the training and been posted to his new unit when he was deployed on operations during the first Gulf War of 1991. He had been living and training in Saudi Arabia for a few weeks with his unit, awaiting orders to cross the border into Iraq to play a part in the liberation of Kuwait, which had recently been invaded by the Iraqis for their oil.

When the orders were issued, it required them to be flown deep behind enemy lines to find and report any SCUD missiles and report on enemy activity in their allocated area. His patrol decided and agreed that they would load their vehicles inside a Chinook helicopter and fly into enemy territory. That way they would be mobile and able to cover more ground and have the ability to escape if they were compromised by the enemy. This was a very important mission, as SCUD missiles were being fired at British and American forces building up in neighbouring countries preparing for the invasion – it was causing havoc and lowering morale. The missiles were also being fired at and landing in Israel; the Western governments did not want Israel to retaliate or enter the war, as it would likely fracture the Arab support for the removal of Iraqi forces from Kuwait.

Private X was the driver of the vehicle, responsible for reversing the vehicle into the helicopter and driving it off when they landed in enemy territory. When vehicles are loaded into helicopters they are secured to the aircraft by chains and shackles to stop them moving around inside. If the vehicle is not secured properly it can cause major damage inside the aircraft and if it broke loose, causing the weight to shift, it could make the aircraft unstable and cause it to crash. The landing drills were practised so that the rest of the patrol knew when and how to unchain the vehicle so that Private X could drive it off the helicopter and get on with their mission.

They practised with the RAF crew until each man knew which chain he would undo and the order in which they would be undone and unloaded from the aircraft – this was to be done at night. Once the chains were undone, the RAF loadmaster, who was responsible for the safety and storage of all equipment inside the helicopter, would go to the rear of the aircraft, pull down and place the two ramps for the vehicle to drive off. Once the ramps were in position, he would flash a red torch back to Private X, which was the signal that the ramps were in place and he was safe to drive off. This seems very easy, but when you add in the darkness of night, the down-draft from the helicopter's rotor blades, dust and sand being blown everywhere and the noise, it can be very confusing.

The night of the helicopter insertion operation finally arrived; all the vehicles, troops, equipment were loaded into the helicopters, and once the final orders were issued the patrol flew off into the night. After flying for a period of time, all was going to plan: the loadmaster briefed them that they were a few minutes out from the drop-off point and the soldiers went to work. The chains were released. Private X was sitting ready in his driver's seat watching for the red torchlight, which he knew would shortly be flashed at him. The tension amongst the troops at this point was electric; they all knew they were now a very long way behind enemy lines and fully aware that there was no help nearby for them if anything went wrong. As the helicopter touched down on its wheels, the loadmaster went to the ramp of the aircraft, pulled the two ramps down and placed them on the desert floor for the vehicle to drive over. Private X sat revving his vehicle engine in case he stalled it; he was straining his eyes through the swirling dust and sand that was being kicked up by the helicopters downwash. He was ready and raring to go: when he saw the red flash of torchlight he would be straight out of the aircraft as fast as he could.

When he finally saw the red flash of torchlight from the loadmaster, he put his foot on the accelerator and the vehicle leapt forward – he left the ramp of the aircraft too quickly and ran over the loadmaster. When he turned and looked back in his seat, he could see some of his mates picking him up by his arms and legs and throwing him back onto the helicopter ramp before it lifted off and disappeared into the night. The invasion of Iraq had begun.

In later years, Private X became a very successful businessman and multi-millionaire when he left the Army at the end of his twenty-two years' service to the Crown.

77   JOE 90

Lance Corporal X was one of life's naturally funny characters who always looked on the bright side of life – great for morale and cheering soldiers up regardless of the situation. Once again, the battalion and soldiers found themselves in Northern Ireland patrolling the streets of West Belfast. So far on this particular tour it had rained continually; patrolling in this weather was getting all the soldiers down, plus there had been a lot of terrorist activity in the shape of shootings and bombings in the area.

The ever-joker decided that he would play tricks on the local population to cheer up his soldiers and keep them alert. He was the patrol commander of a four-man team and should have been more worried about suspected terrorists and looking out for potential snipers and hidden bombs. His view was: if he was surrounded by locals then the chances were that the IRA wouldn't try and shoot for fear of hitting a local child or person.

In Northern Ireland there were many laws, rules and regulations which governed the way soldiers could operate whilst serving there on operations. One of the laws was the right of every soldier to stop and search any person they deemed to be suspicious. You could ask the suspect their name, date of birth, address, where they had been and where they were going to. If they didn't reply with answers to the questions, they could be arrested by the police.

In Lance Corporal X's smock pocket he had a pair of wire-rimmed spectacles with glass lenses about an inch thick, which looked like a milk bottle's bottom. When he called on one of his team to stop a person he wanted to chat to, he quickly turned around, facing away from the suspect, and pulled the thick-glassed spectacles from his pocket and put them on before he approached the suspect for questioning. When he approached the suspect he pretended to be almost blind; during the body search he would touch and read their faces with his fingers as if he was reading Braille. When it came to the questioning, he would make a point of standing at an angle, looking away from the suspect as if he was talking to a shadow. Throughout the search the suspect would be looking totally bewildered, not believing that the British Army would employ someone who was clearly lacking in the visual department – more worryingly, let him carry a gun!

Once they had finished searching the suspect he would walk away in total disbelief at what had just happened. The patrol would go the other way chuckling to themselves, looking for the next victim to play the prank on – morale enhanced, if only for a few minutes.

It's amazing what you find lying about – collecting weapons from the rebels in Macedonia, 2001.

Moments before the football riot in Kabul Olympic Stadium – not exactly the Premier League.

Kabul meals on wheels – no wonder the battalion wanted to stay on army rations for four months.

Always pay attention to the signs – the commanding officer, adjutant and regimental sergeant major guarding the front gate of Bessbrook Mill, Northern Ireland, on Christmas Day so private soldiers could have a few hours off duty.

"Army Procurement: Be The Best"-issued desert boots for an Afghan winter, which went well with mosquito nets.

CHAPTER 5

OFF DUTY

Just like in any employment, soldiers are free to do whatever they want to once the work for the day is finished and they are stood down. Soldiers are quite fortunate because they travel the world and go to some very interesting places and countries that tourists would pay a lot of money to visit. Sitting in Hemingway's bar near Mombasa, Kenya, overlooking the beach, gazing out over the Indian Ocean was very nice, particularly as it was free and nearby tourists had paid a fortune for a once-in-a-lifetime holiday.

Soldiers are generally in their early twenties and like to have a drink and to party wherever they are, just like their civilian counterparts of the same age. Off duty is where the soldiers let their hair down and can get into trouble, normally due to alcohol consumption.

It has to be admitted that soldiers in their prime of life can drink to capacity when they get the chance; there is no logical or proven reason for this. The old adage of 'work hard, play hard' is very true. I believe it is because the soldiers live under military restrictions and some of them are put into a lot of high-pressure situations and locations where they could be killed or maimed. A lot of front-line soldiers that do the fighting live for today, as they may not be here tomorrow, so they like to make hay while the sun shines.

Thanks to the modern airliner, the soldiers of today can be partying in Colchester one day and fighting for their survival against a heavily armed Taliban attack a few days later many miles from home.

78   PILSNER

At the Royal Military Academy Sandhurst (RMAS) the officer instructors that train the cadets have an awards ceremony of their own at the end of each teaching term. They all gather together every three months for a lunch that is called the 'louts' lunch'. This gives them the chance to get together as an officers' mess and let their hair down whilst the cadets get away for some well-earned leave.

At this ceremony the floppy cane gets presented to the officer that has made the biggest and embarrassing mistake during the last term. The floppy cane is in reference to the official bamboo cane that they carry with them as they walk around the Academy whilst on duty. The floppy cane is about two feet long, made from black garden hose piping, brass caps on both ends and is set on a wooden plinth. Once awarded the officer keeps the cane for three months until the next louts' lunch, where it will be presented to the next reluctant winner.

On this particular occasion Captain X had been selected for this unwanted honour. She was very embarrassed due to the reason why she had been unanimously awarded the trophy.

Three weeks earlier, the cadets had been on their final exercise in Germany near the Luxemburg border, next to the town of Bitteburg, which is world famous for making 'Bitteburg Pilsner'. Captain X had been asked to organise a trip to the brewery so that the cadets could visit, see how they make German beer, relax for the day and see a bit of their culture. The officer had the brewery trip all sewn up: all of the cadets had paid their thirty euros for the visit, packed lunches ordered, transport booked, visit booklets issued to the cadets, etc.

The day of the visit arrived, a lovely sunny day just perfect for sinking a few cold beers at the brewery after the walk around. All the cadets were dressed in their best civilian clothing, sitting on the bus and ready to go for their day out. After thirty minutes travelling time the coach arrived at the brewery. Captain X stepped off the bus and walked across to the reception, only to discover that the brewery was closed on this particular day.

Captain X was awarded the floppy cane for not being able to organise a piss-up in a brewery.

79   ALDERSHOT: HOME OF THE BRITISH ARMY

In the early eighties the pubs in the centre of Aldershot were always packed with off-duty soldiers at the weekends – The George, Queens, Exchange, Globetrotter, and the Trafalgar. Two of these pubs are now closed and one has changed its name. The pay wasn't very good in those days, so the majority of soldiers stayed the weekends instead of going home because they couldn't afford to purchase a car and rail travel was still very expensive – even with an Armed Forces rail discount card.

The good side of all the soldiers staying the weekend was the friendship and unit cohesion that was forged amongst the young soldiers in the battalions and brigade during many hours of socialising and merriment in the pubs. When the soldiers were on operations or on exercise, the friendships between these soldiers in the same brigade paid off in dividends ten times over. The bad side was the excessive drinking that led to fights and boisterous behaviour that some normal civilians would find strange. How often do you see men dressed as women in a pub? It was guaranteed every weekend in Aldershot in those days.

When soldiers are together and drink is taken, games and pranks are never far away, one of the games that made me giggle was the squash ball trick. One soldier would tell the listening soldiers who hadn't seen the trick that they had to be very physically fit to undertake the challenge. It was a very dangerous trick which could lead to fainting, collapsing on the floor or brain damage if the soldier taking part wasn't fit enough.

It was explained that the half squash ball is licked and then squashed onto the centre of the forehead. The suction will hold the ball in place, but the constant pressure caused by the ball on the front of the head can cause some weaker guys to collapse due to the pain on the front of the skull. A good time to keep the squash ball on your head was two minutes; after three minute you risked collapsing and no one had ever reached five minutes without blacking out.

All soldiers love a challenge and the unsuspecting volunteer stepped forward to take part in the challenge – what could possibly be difficult about suctioning a squash ball to the front of your head? The soldier selling the pitch would egg him on by saying asking him if he was sure he wanted to take part in this and if he collapsed it was his own responsibility. Eventually, the volunteer would say, "No problem, let's get on with it."

With the crowd listening and cheering, the soldier would lick the inside of the squash ball and press it onto the volunteer's forehead with the palm of his hand until it was flat and suction would take over. He would then stare at his watch, checking the time and egging him on. The unsuspecting soldier would stand there with no obvious side effects from the squash ball on his head and the controlling soldier would call out two minutes, three minutes and when he neared five minutes he would ask if he was sure he wanted to go for the five-minute record. Eventually, when they got to the five-minute point, the soldier told him to take the squash ball off his forehead to cheers from the crowd, telling him he must be very fit to have lasted that long.

Later when the victim went to the toilet and looked into the mirror, he would see that there was now a large, round, black bruise, the size of a squash ball in the centre of his forehead. He then realised that he had been the willing volunteer in a prank. On the Monday morning after the game was first introduced to Aldershot, half of the brigade soldiers were standing on parade with embarrassing, round, and black bruises hidden under their berets.

Corporal X was one of the battalion characters who possessed a fantastic sense of humour and appreciated a good laugh. He was a veteran of the Falklands War of 1982 where sadly he had stood on an anti-personnel mine and had lost one of his legs, amputated above the knee.

After the Falklands campaign he wanted to remain in the Army despite his injuries and continued on to have a full twenty-two-year career, reaching the rank of warrant officer. Considering a lot of guys with two legs complete twenty-two years' service and don't reach warrant officer rank is testimony to the type of guy he was.

Nowadays there are so many service personnel that lost limbs during the recent Iraq and Afghan campaigns that it would be difficult for all of them to continue to serve in a frontline battalion without affecting its future deployability. Although recently a young non-commissioned officer that stepped on a mine in 2006 and lost one of his limbs deployed back into Afghanistan in 2008 with 3 Para and served throughout the six-month tour.

Corporal X was in Cyprus with his battalion on an exercise – Ex Lion Sun. The exercise is normally six weeks long, where you do Army field work for about five weeks and then have a week off at the end to do adventure training – canoeing, windsurfing, diving, water-skiing and a few days off to rest and recuperate. The costs for the exercise, including the week off, are all courtesy of the taxpayer and very popular with the soldiers who were fortunate enough to be in Cyprus during the summer tourist season.

On the rest and recuperation phase of the exercise, Corporal X went to Ayia Napa with his mates to sample the best that Cyprus could offer. Ayia Napa has a fantastic beach with white sand, turquoise water, cheap beer, and loads of half-naked tourists – bliss after working and living in and around the woods of the Troodos Mountains on an exercise for five weeks.

After a few beers they decided to go for a swim in the nice warm Mediterranean Sea. Once in the water, Corporal X decided to play a trick on the tourist population that were all languishing in and around the beach – couples, children, young, old people, all having a great time in the cool water. He slipped his false leg off and jumped up from the water and started hopping towards the beach; when he got there, he stood on his good leg with the stump of his other leg on show for everyone to see. As he was hopping along the beach he was shouting "Shark, Shark, Shark" at the top of his voice.

There was utter and complete devastation as mothers ran to grab their children that were playing in the surf, people sprinting through the water, knocking people over as they desperately tried to get to dry land, children crying, and spectators standing on the beach pointing out to sea.

Corporal X and his mates found this hilarious. Once all the tourists calmed down and realised that there wasn't a man-eating shark in the water, some of them saw the funny side. However, the majority wanted to string him up for nearly giving them a heart attack.

I suppose there are some things that are just not funny – being eaten by a shark is obviously one of them.

Corporal X was made a Member of the Most Excellent Order of the British Empire (MBE) a few years later for his hard work and dedication to the regiment.

81   BULLIES NEVER WIN

The Globetrotter pub in Aldershot was a fantastic place to learn drinking and fighting skills, where many a soldier honed his boxing style; by sheer coincidence it could have been described as the British Army's premier unregulated unarmed fighting school. Lots of scores were settled and grudges started within its walls; even the DJ took refuge behind the chicken wire that surrounded his spinning decks.

In life, some people just cannot get along with each other and even if they were left in an empty room they would still end up fighting. Corporal X and Private Y were prime examples of this trait of human nature.

Corporal X was a short beefy individual who had clearly done weight training at some time or other but was at the stage of life where he was getting chubbier rather than muscular. He had a reputation as a fighter but wasn't really; he just knew how to pick fights with soldiers that had imbibed too much to drink and earn himself a reputation as a hard man.

Private Y was the opposite: a new lad to the battalion, keen as mustard, fit as a fiddle and a bit of a scrapper from near Glasgow – an unknown quantity at that time. The people who did know him properly said he would face the Devil himself if provoked.

These two individuals were in the same platoon and would never be friends. Corporal X liked to take the mickey and give lots of shitty jobs to Private Y – often unfairly, as no other private soldiers were getting the same amount of jobs to complete. All the time Private Y was quietly simmering away inside, biting his lip. How could a new soldier straight from training stand up to a corporal with eight years' service in the battalion?

Corporal X had noticed the defiant look that Private Y sometimes gave him when he was given more tasks to complete and had decided he would bide his time and get him some night in the town when he was drunk.

The Globetrotter pub was packed one Saturday night and Private Y and Private Z were stood at the bar having a chin-wag and a few beers, when in walked Corporal X with some of his old cronies. The corporal spotted Private Y at the bar and thought to himself that, seeing as it was nearing closing time, the young soldier must have had a few beers inside him by now and was probably drunk and not able to put up a good fight.

Corporal X spoke to his old sweat cronies and made his way across the room to where the young soldiers stood at the bar. Both soldiers were facing across the bar and never saw him sneaking quietly through the crowd behind them. Corporal X took a great swing of a punch that landed squarely on the back of Private Y's head, which knocked him to the floor. Realising what had just happened, he quickly got to his feet, looked at Corporal X and his cronies in the eye and stated, "If that's the best you can do, I suggest you keep your hands in your pockets."

Corporal X gulped and quickly scuttled away before disappearing into the bar crowd and out the door. On Monday morning Private Y's job list was considerably shorter than the previous week.

82   SPACE EXPLORATION

Private X and a few of the lads had just finished a six-week exercise with the US Rangers in the Seattle area of Washington State. They had worked hard throughout the exercising period, which included, parachuting, survival training, assaults, live firing, fitness training, long marches and short exercises practising various other military skills.

As is customary at the end of a military exchange exercise, there is always a period of rest and recuperation in whatever country the soldiers are fortunate enough to be in. They get stood down from all military duties for five or six days and get the chance to go and see a bit of the country, sightsee, watch a baseball game, relax, whatever they fancy doing.

This was early 1986 and the first of a few space shuttles had sadly exploded during take-off from Cape Canaveral and was all the talk at the time.

The lads had decided to visit Seattle and spend their time seeing the sites, watch the Seattle Mariners play a baseball game, visit the Space Needle, take photographs, and generally have a good time, as young fellows do.

On this particular day they decided that they had had enough of traipsing around the city and fancied chilling out in a downtown bar for the afternoon. They found a bar which was so typically American and met their needs nicely – long wooden bar,

bar stools, chips in bowls, cool beer, shots and a jukebox in the corner.

The guys arrived at lunchtime and by early evening all of them were very merry, having a great time after drinking tall cool beers and the odd Wild Turkey shots. They were having such a good time telling stories and jokes that even the locals and the bartender had been joining in the fun with them as well.

Private X, who was the loudest in the bunch and liked to tell jokes, stood up and asked everyone in the bar to quieten down. He yelled and flapped his arms to get everyone's attention, telling everyone present in the bar that he had a joke to tell. Once he was content that he had all of their attention and they were listening, he started to tell his joke.

He started off by saying, "I hear that President Reagan is going to win the next election."

The bartender asked, "How do you know that because the elections haven't even started yet?"

Private X replied, "Because he doesn't have a Challenger." Private X and his fellow Brits laughed their heads off at the punch line. As they looked around the bar, not one single American was even smiling never mind laughing. The bartender reached forward across the bar and grabbed the beers back from the Brits and threw them out of the bar and called the cops.

It was very clear that the space shuttle called 'Challenger' which sadly blew up at its launch a few weeks earlier was still very raw with the Americans in the bar. Who said Americans don't have a sense of humour! If a country can't laugh at itself in times of tragedy then that speaks volumes.

83   PERCY PONGO

The Royal Air Force, Royal Navy and Royal Marines have a nickname for soldiers in the British Army – Percy Pongos. Apparently, wherever the Army goes, the pong follows them.

Corporal X and a few of his mates were lucky enough to get sent on a two-week adventure training sailing course in Portsmouth, which is the home of the Royal Navy. At the time the majority of the Royal Navy ships that were normally based there were out at sea on training exercises or deployed on operations somewhere around the globe.

On nights off from sailing, the guys went to the local clubs and pubs of Portsmouth, where they noticed that they were always full of females. It transpired that the majority of these females were sailors' wives, partners or girlfriends and their menfolk were at sea – and in a lot of cases had been for a long time.

Corporal X was very fortunate in attracting females and managed to be taken home by one of these women. It turned out that the female that took him home to bed was the girlfriend of a petty officer who had been on an operational cruise for the past four months and still had another two months until he returned to Portsmouth. She explained that she was feeling lonely and missed adult company – what would be the harm in it if the boyfriend never found out?

In the morning the lovely lady went downstairs to make Corporal X some breakfast, and as he looked round the bedroom he noticed a photograph of salty Sam the petty officer who was presumably her boyfriend. He looked every inch the Navy man in his peaked cap, white shirt and full beard.

Corporal X had a flash of inspiration which he thought funny and a good story that he could tell his mates later that night in the bar, who would certainly giggle at it. He picked up the framed photograph and removed its back; reaching over, he retrieved a pen from his jacket pocket on the chair next to the bed. He then wrote on the back of the photograph – *Percy Pongo was here*, dated and signed it, before carefully putting the photograph and frame back together. Once he was finished, he placed it back on the bedside cabinet before his girlfriend for the night came back up the stairs with his breakfast on a tray.

When she got back into the bed she asked him what he had been up to. He told her he had gotten a pen from his jacket pocket so that he could finish the crossword that was sitting on the bedside cabinet; she said that was very sweet of him. Perhaps this story is not a good example of inter-service cooperation.

84   FIGHTING IN THE USA

The soldiers were having a few days in camp between exercises so they could recharge, check kit and administer themselves before going back out on to another exercise with the American soldiers they were working with. The American base they were currently living on was gigantic compared to what the young soldiers were used to back in the UK. There were car sales garages, swimming pools, fitness centres, shops, bars, restaurants, and clubs all within walking distance of the accommodation. It was the opposite of the barracks in Aldershot that they were used to: it only had a NAAFI shop that was best known for selling Ginsters pies and porn magazines.

Once all the administration was done for the day, the soldiers were stood down so they could get cleaned up before dinner and a night off. As all young men do when abroad, they were quickly showered, changed, dressed and were off out looking for a bar and some excitement.

The first bar they came across was called 'The Hub Bar', which was small but quite a lively bar with good music. It had a long wooden bar along one side, a few pool tables at the far end, loud music, a linoleum floor that smelled of bleach and spilled alcohol. A lot of the US servicemen had finished for the day as well and were converging on the same bar as the British paratroopers. These servicemen were American rangers, who are a cut above normal infantry, generally quite professional and skilled in the art of warfare. They are instantly recognisable by their haircuts; they shave all around the sides of their heads and leave a small hair growth on top of their heads about an inch high. They seem to think it suits their macho image, so who are we to disagree – each to their own, I suppose.

As the drinks started to flow and the night got later, the Americans became louder and louder and seemed to like yelling out "whooaa ahh or RECCONNNNN" from the top of their voices and thumping their chests. Brits just aren't programmed that way and are definitely more reserved. Private X and his mates were happily playing pool and staying out of the way of the loud alcohol-fuelled Americans. As the bar filled up, the pool area started to get infringed upon as the servicemen spread out across the room. One of the rangers noticed that there were Brits playing pool at the table and came over to interrupt them. He was clearly drunk and seemed to have a bit of an issue with them, and started to accuse one of them of shagging his girlfriend as he had been dumped for a Brit. The lads knew nothing about it and explained that they had been out training all week and not in camp and never even knew who his girlfriend was. He wandered off to the bar for a beer.

Ten minutes later the accuser came back to the pool table where the Brits were with three of his mates, which made it quite clear where this was going. The American went up to Private X and took a telegraphed swing at him with his fist before another word had been exchanged. At this development the remaining Brits head-butted the other Americans, who fell to the floor. As they scrambled back to their feet clutching their noses, with blood pouring through their fingers, one of them shouted, "Goddam, I can't believe this guy hit me with his face; these guys are street fighters," before they made a quick exit through the crowd and out of the bar into the night.

That night, as the Brits were staggering back to their accommodation, they kept giggling to themselves and mimicking the American serviceman. "Goddam, I can't believe this guy hit me with his face and we're street fighters." Private X's hard upbringing in Glasgow had not been wasted after all.

85   MAINTAINING PUBLIC RELATIONS

Private X came home on leave from Germany to discover that his younger brother had been getting hard times from the owner of the local corner shop. His brother had told him that he and his mates would hang around the shop after school, just hanging around and not causing any bother. On occasion the owner of the shop had been quite abusive to his younger brother and had even chased him and his mates down the street, waving a brush at them.

The local corner shop was owned by an elderly gentleman who was quite grumpy and set in his ways; he had run the shop for about forty years. He was in his sixties and did not appreciate kids hanging around the shop, making noise and disrupting his customers. The shop sold papers, sweets, washing-up liquid, and anything that you may have forgotten from your weekly shop at the superstore.

Private X had always been protective of his kid brother and was not impressed when he heard about the old shopkeeper. Who did the shop owner think he was, shouting at kids, chasing them down the street and treating them badly?

The young soldier thought it was time the shop owner was taught a lesson and he was just the man for the job. He had brought a thunderflash back from Germany, where he was currently based with his county regiment, to show to his kid brother. A thunderflash is a pyrotechnic designed to simulate a grenade blast whilst on training exercises. It is made of hard compressed cardboard and has a gunpowder filling; once lit it has a three to five second fuse. It is quite powerful and could take your hand clean off if it exploded whilst still being held. When they explode in a confined space they could easily be mistaken for a small bomb being detonated.

The soldier should not have had a thunderflash in his possession, never mind on leave with him. They are normally tightly controlled and handed back in at the end of a field exercise if not used. All soldiers give a declaration at the end of training exercises stating that they have no ammunition or pyrotechnics in their possession. Private X had committed a military offence by stealing a thunderflash.

The lesson to be taught was simple: he would walk along to the corner shop and ignite the thunderflash and throw it through the open door into the shop. He would then walk away giggling and between three and five seconds later there would be a big bang. The shop owner would get a fright and learn a lesson.

WRONG. Private X, in his naivety, forgot how powerful a thunderflash could be in an enclosed space and instead of a big bang and a giggle he received quite a shock. On hearing the explosion, Private X turned around and was totally aghast: his eyes were like saucers as he viewed the carnage he had caused. The whole shop front had been blown out. There were cabbages blasted across the pavement, shards of window glass tinkling in the road, tins of beans rolling along the street and shoppers in a complete panic at the devastation. Within minutes police sirens could be heard in the distance, getting closer by the second. Once they arrived, mine tape was soon being erected as the shop was cordoned off by the police officers and a crowd began to gather.

The young soldier was in shock and so flabbergasted at the devastation he had caused that he admitted it straight away to a policeman standing on the cordon. He told the officer that there were no terrorists involved, and he had caused the explosion, which was meant to be a prank that had clearly backfired.

Eventually, Private X was court marshalled through the Army legal system for stealing military property (thunderflash), causing an explosion in a public place, being a threat to the public, endangering life and causing criminal damage. He was sentenced to six months in Colchester Military Prison.

86 DRINKING AND DIVING

San Pedro is a small, beautiful Caribbean island just off the coast of Belize that nestles on the edge of the barrier reef, which is second only to the Great Barrier Reef of Australia. The white sand, palm trees, clear turquoise waters, and laid-back style of living was an idyllic place to relax and have some fun after spending six weeks sweating and working hard in the Central American jungle on exercise.

Sergeant X and five of his mates decided for their five days' rest and recuperation period, they would get the water taxi from Belize City and head out to San Pedro and spend their time there, relaxing on the beach before flying back to the UK on conclusion of the exercise.

When they arrived on the island one of them suggested that they should all do a sub-aqua diving course and get qualified as open-water divers on the Professional Association of Diving Instructors (PADI) course that he had seen advertised on the hotel notice board. The course would qualify them to dive down to thirty metres in open water; all of the course dives were along the barrier reef – what a great way to see it, so they all agreed.

The next morning they went down to the dive shop, paid their money, booked in and enrolled on the four-day training course, which consisted of six dives, lots of theory and progress tests. The instructor briefed them that the course was a pass or fail course.

If any of them didn't pass the theory, exams or the training exercise dives, he could not pass them as qualified divers for their own safety. Once they were qualified they could turn up at any dive shop around the world and produce their PADI identity card and dive. He had to sign off every dive qualification certificate, which was the reason that the instructor wouldn't pass them unless they were capable and competent divers at the end of the course.

The first few days it was going fantastically well and all the soldiers were enjoying the course immensely. The barrier reef was beautiful, clear warm water with visibility out to fifty metres, pretty coral, awesome fish in all shapes and sizes, fish brightly coloured like a rainbow, moray eels peeking out of the rocks, turtles, and crayfish hiding in the crevices of the reef. All the dives and training exercises went very well; they all learnt how to share oxygen with a buddy in an emergency, mask-clearing drills, control their buoyancy, how to replace a mask that had been knocked off, and decompression stops on the way to the surface, etc.

The third night of the course was a Friday night and the instructor told them that drinking and diving doesn't really mix very well – by all means have a couple of beers, but not a heavy drinking session.

The soldiers were sat on the balcony of a beach bar enjoying a meal and drinking a few quiet beers when they heard music beating out rhythmically from the hotel along the beach from where they were sitting. They decided to go along and investigate. Remembering what the dive instructor had told them about drinking and diving, before they went inside they all agreed to have one more beer at the hotel before heading to bed in preparation for the next morning's dive. When they entered, it was packed with tourists dancing on the sand and in the bar. There was a live band in the corner beating out calypso music, everyone was drinking cocktails and having a great time. They all ended up partying until the early hours of the morning and getting smashed in the process.

When they woke in the morning all of them had hangovers that would have killed a conventional ground troop. They just had enough time for a shower and a shave before rushing down to the beach to meet the dive boat. The weather was a little windier than normal and the sea was a bit choppy. They collected their dive kit, air bottles, loaded the equipment and got into the boat before heading out to the first dive site of the morning. The crashing waves, which were battering against the boat, were starting to make some of them feel a bit queasy. When they dropped anchor at the dive site, they managed to get their dive kit on without too many mishaps in the rolling boat; it was a relief to get into and under the water to escape the swells, which were making them feel seasick.

Sergeant X was feeling particularly fragile and commented, "The tequila shooters we drank last night were probably not the best idea we have ever had," before he placed his regulator into his mouth and rolled backwards into the water. This particular dive was the soldier's first dive at a depth of thirty metres. The scenery was breathtaking as they descended the wall of the barrier reef to get to the correct dive depth. As they were swimming along the bottom, Sergeant X broke out into a cold sweat that you only ever get when you are about to be sick. He was starting to panic as he looked up towards the silvery surface that shimmered some thirty metres above his head: knowing that he couldn't swim up there quick enough to be sick, which he knew he was about to be. Before he could think too much, nature took over and he spewed out through his air regulator. He continued to retch by taking his air regulator out of his mouth and spew his sick into the water, before replacing the air regulator back in his mouth for a gasp of air before repeating the process until his stomach was empty. The other soldiers who witnessed this couldn't help but laugh through their own air regulators as Sergeant X went through his potentially drowning experience. He was surrounded by a cloud of his own sick, which quickly became a maelstrom of brightly coloured fish fighting and darting around to scoop up the biggest lumps of his sick.

None of the soldiers wanted to be in the same predicament that Sergeant X had found himself in during the day's dive. That night they all drank Coca-Cola with their meals in preparation for their final dive the next morning.

87   DOCTOR FINLAY

The three soldiers had just finished a weekend leave and were driving the long journey back to Aldershot from their homes in the west of Scotland. They came from the same town and shared a car so they could split the petrol money between them, and get home and back to barracks at a cheaper cost than getting the train.

A few weeks previously two of them had been on the same two-week Patrol Medic Course where they were taught medicine and minor surgery. They were taught these skills so that when they were in some far-off jungle on behalf of Her Majesty's government they could use them in an emergency situation to save life. What they were taught was quite advanced and very interesting to learn and understand. They received no civilian qualifications from the course – some of the subjects they had been taught could only be practised in the UK by qualified paramedics and registered doctors.

Most frontline soldiers are never too far from proper medical support – company medic, Regimental Aid Post or a Field Dressing Station. These soldiers are taught the basics of first aid with an aim to save life and stop the condition worsening; remove the casualty from danger; make sure he was breathing; stop any bleeding and get him to the nearest medical station as soon as possible. To achieve this they carried plastic airways, bandages, first field dressings and a stretcher.

The Patrols Platoon was trained to operate independently at great distance from the battalion and needed to be able to medically support itself. If a member of a patrol became unwell or was injured and couldn't be extracted because of the enemy or lack of helicopters, then the patrol medic would need to identify the symptoms and administer the correct drug to treat the injured soldier. The medical pack carried by the patrol medic would have kept a junkie happy for a few weeks and NHS-qualified paramedics content with the toys inside for a long time.

The corporal instructors that taught on the course were very well qualified and had spent weeks on civilian hospital attachments at inner cities up and down the UK, observing and working in Accident and Emergency departments to gain more medical knowledge and skills.

Everyone on the course was taught the mechanics of which drug or tablet was the best to cure certain illnesses and what symptoms to look for to identify the ailment. Once the illness was identified, what dosage should be administered needed to be decided – ibuprofen, codeine phosphate, cicatrin powder, laudanum, Imodium, salt sachets and many more. They were taught how to suture (stitch) open wounds and to administer injections to dull the pain – they practised on pig skin. The administration of intravenous drugs and the insertion of cannulas into arms and legs were practised until they could do it second nature. They were taught how to do a tracheostomy – cutting through the neck into the trachea to make a new airway if the casualty's airway is damaged and blocked, plus advanced treatment of gunshot and shrapnel wounds.

The three soldiers had been travelling south on the M6 for about five hours and were starting to feel a little hungry, so they decided to pull into a service station for a burger and chips, and have a rest before continuing with the journey.

Just as they walked through the sliding doors into the shopping area of the services, an elderly gentleman started to have a fit and collapsed onto the floor in front of them. He started to shake uncontrollably, arms thrashing around, feet kicking, eyes rolled back, so only the whites of his eyes were visible, swallowed his tongue, growling, spittle flying, and gnashing his teeth – clearly some kind of epileptic seizure.

Private X quickly stepped forward and raised his arms and shouted out to the gathering crowd, "Stand back, I am a medic." The crowd stood gathered around a few feet away as he then knelt down beside the fitting gentleman and pushed his fingers straight into the man's mouth to pull his tongue forward and clear his airway to stop him from choking. The patient had different ideas and bit down as hard as he could onto Private X's fingers, which were knuckle-deep in his mouth. Once he was locked on to the soldier's fingers he wasn't for letting go. After struggling for a few minutes to get his fingers back out, Private X had to punch the man on the chin and pull hard to get them released. He now had teeth marks in his fingers, blood running down his hand and the old man was still in the middle of his seizure.

Fortunately, there was a medical crew in the services who rushed to the man and cleared his airway using a wooden spatula, before taking him to hospital.

For the rest of the journey back to Aldershot two of the soldiers kept laughing their heads off, mimicking Private X's, "Stand back, I am a medic." Private X sat in the back of the car nursing his bleeding and painful hand, refusing to see the funny side of it. However, he had learnt a very painful lesson which he would remember when dealing with casualties in the future.

The next time you are in an Accident and Emergency ward in your local hospital, it might be worth checking to see if any of the staff wearing white coats are from the Army – if they are you might just be a guinea pig.

As the years passed and the soldiers' careers progressed, one became a warrant officer, one an officer, and the other became a member of the Special Air Service (SAS).

88   FLYING LIKE AN EAGLE

Some six-month overseas tours are not very dangerous but are extremely good fun; sadly for the young officers and soldiers of today's Army they don't seem to get the same easy tours that were available in the early 1970s and 1980s. The United Nations six-month tour in Cyprus was one of these classic easy tours looked forward to and enjoyed by soldiers fortunate enough to get on the tour. A fantastic experience, the only danger might have been falling off an observation tower, cutting your finger on a paper clip or getting into trouble with tourists in one of the Cypriot towns of Limassol or Ayia Napa.

On these tours a lot of the officers would bring out their wives or girlfriends for a two-week holiday instead of returning home to UK for their rest and recuperation – compulsory two-week leave period during the tour.

Whenever there were girlfriends visiting or dignitaries to be impressed, then dinner and cocktail parties would be organised in the officers' mess. At the rear of the officers' mess in Dhekelia, where the battalion HQ was located, there was a large swimming pool that was very popular during these parties.

Occasionally, the pool had to be emptied for routine maintenance, repainted and refilled, which normally took around four days from start to finish. Not everyone always knew when the pool was due for repair, empty and closed.

On this particular evening a dinner party had been organised to welcome a few of the wives and girlfriends who were out visiting their husbands or boyfriends. Captain X had a party trick of swallow-diving into the pool fully clothed dressed in his dinner jacket, which he thought impressed the girls – he didn't know the pool was empty on this occasion.

At the end of a late dinner all the officers and guests left the dining table and came out on to the patio to get some cool air, stretch their legs or have a cigarette. The young gallant captain was already heading straight for the pool, calling behind him, "Last in the pool is a rotten egg."

The young mess steward called out, "Sir, sir, wait…" but before he could shout any further warnings the quartermaster kicked him in the shin and told him to keep quiet. "But, sir, the pool it's empty," replied the steward.

To which the quartermaster replied, "Keep quiet, I won't tell you again."

The young steward didn't know that Captain X had recently posed a question to the quartermaster at the commanding officer's weekly meeting, knowing full well that he never knew the answer so it would put him on the spot and embarrass him in front of the colonel.

The gallant captain was now in mid-flight over the swimming pool, flying like an eagle in a marvellous swallow-dive position, with a "look at me, I am fantastic" grin on his face, when he suddenly realised, "Shit! There is no water in the pool." He just had enough time to change his position into a tight parachute-landing roll as best he could. Thump – he landed in a heap on the bottom of the concrete pool 2.5m below, and there were gasps of concern from the ladies and laughter from the men. He stood shakily to his feet and dusted himself off; he had holes in both knees and elbows of his dinner jacket and blood streaming down the side of his face. "Someone could have told me," he blurted out through quivering lips, as he staggered towards the shallow end to climb out.

The young steward looked at the quartermaster and said, "Sir, I was only trying to warn him," to which the quartermaster replied, "Sonny, that will be a little secret between you and I." The steward didn't understand that the price for embarrassing the quartermaster in front of the commanding officer had now been paid in full by the gallant captain, as the old officer chuckled away to himself in between dragging on his cigar.

89   ON YOUR BIKE

Private X had just been released from the battalion jail after spending fourteen days incarcerated for a crime that he did not commit. According to him, it wasn't quite the way the evidence was presented at his trial and he was provoked. Whether he did or not is open for debate – the witnesses who gave evidence at his trial had observed the assault and were adamant that he did commit the crime as per the statements.

He felt so strongly about his innocence that he wanted to give the commanding officer a bit of payback or revenge for his miscarriage of justice.

On the first Friday night after his release from jail, he headed down town into Aldershot and got blind drunk. On his way back to camp he was still thinking on how best to exact revenge on the commanding officer for his miscarriage of justice. As he was going through the battalion lines, he noticed that there was a motorbike sitting under the covered way and an idea just popped into his head.

The covered way to the door that leads up the stairs that take you to the commanding officer's office is in the shadows and it would be very easy to place something in his office as a prank.

So for the next hour or so Private X struggled, sweated, pushed, and pulled the motorcycle up the two flights of stairs and wheeled it along the corridor into the office. Not content with that, he manoeuvred it so that the machine was placed on top of the desk, on its stand.

When the commanding officer walked into his office on Monday morning, he couldn't believe his eyes. How did a motorcycle end up on his desk? He was totally bewildered as to why anyone would want to go to the effort of such a task. Behind his desk on the whiteboard was a scrawled message: *A miscarriage of justice – now you can carry it.* Instantly he knew who it was and called the regimental sergeant major.

Private X was called for by the regimental sergeant major and made to carry the motorcycle back down the way he had brought it in. He denied all knowledge of how it could have ended up in the office. He was called back for interview with the commanding officer, who explained that he had no time or the inclination to try and prove one way or the other if he had brought the machine into his office. Private X was told to grow up and get on with his military service; if he felt he was tried unjustly, he should have said so at his trial and not try any childish pranks as a way to get back at the system.

The regimental sergeant major took Private X aside and tore a strip off him for wasting his time; he also gave him praise for having the patience and willpower to drag a motorcycle such a distance upstairs and into an office. The regimental sergeant major explained that if he could be so determined in such a petty issue he should channel all of his energies into his military career and he might go far – which he then did over the next twenty years.

Corporal X and Y had just completed a seven-week Jungle Warfare Instructors Course in Brunei and were transiting back through Hong Kong to the UK. They were staying in Osbourne Barracks on Kowloon Tong for two days before catching their flight home. Having spent long weeks in the jungle, they were glad to see people, relax, sightsee, shop, try the local food, hit the local bars and generally chill out.

Hong Kong is a fantastic city with so much to see and do that the two corporals planned to make the most of the forty-eight hours they were there. As soon as they landed and stowed their kit, they were showered, changed and out of the barracks exploring the city. They crossed from Hong Kong Island to the mainland on the 'Star Ferry' because they had seen it in a James Bond movie. They found a tailor's shop so they could get some shirts and a suit made; the shop promised made-to-measure garments within the hour. If you weren't pleased with the product, then you didn't have to take the suit or pay – both were very pleased with their purchases. They watched local Chinese people in the street paying a snake trader to kill one of his snakes so they could drink its blood, which was just fascinating; apparently, it can bring luck or make you very virile – neither of them tried it.

Even walking around the fish market down by the harbour was an education; there were all sorts of fish and shellfish that they had never seen before. They both stood and stared in astonishment when they watched a woman talking to the fishmonger. It was clear from her hand actions as she pointed into the fish tank that she wanted about twelve inches of the live fish that was swimming around minding its own business. The fish looked like an orange-coloured carp or goldfish about four feet long. The fish seller gaffed the fish in the gills and hauled it up onto the wooden chopping block, where he confirmed how much she wanted by placing his metal chopper twelve inches along its spine from the tail. The woman confirmed that was how much of the fish she wanted and he raised the metal chopper above his head before bringing it down hard to chop the lump from the fish. The fish flipped and flopped all over the place, wriggling as he chopped the remainder of it up into portions and threw it into a basket beside his table. The last they saw of the fish was its head sitting at the top of the basket on a pile of fish pieces; its gills were still working away trying to breathe life into its mutilated body. The woman certainly bought the freshest of fish, although a bit gruesome by Western standards.

They sat at a street stall for lunch and were presented with some of the best shellfish that they had ever tasted. They had never seen the likes of it before and didn't have a clue what they had just eaten. Hong Kong is a bustling city which never stops and it can get very humid; it was time to get back to barracks for a shower and change into new clothes before hitting the town.

At the time karaoke singing was very big in the Far East and in particular Hong Kong, but it hadn't reached the UK at that time. After a few hours of visiting different bars, drinking the local alcohol, the two corporals stumbled upon a karaoke bar by chance and wandered in. They thought the singers were fantastic and never realised until later on that they were all willing volunteers and not professional singers. The place was packed and every time a singer finished belting out a fantastic song the whole bar erupted and went mad with applause.

The corporals both decided that, seeing as though they had been entertained so wonderfully by the local Chinese, they thought the least they could do was sing a song on behalf of Britain. They put their names on the list to sing a song. By the time they were called up to the stage to sing, a few hours had passed and they were both pissed and could hardly string a sentence together, never mind sing a greatest hit.

They both staggered up onto the stage clinging to each other for support as they started to sing the hit 'Green Grass of Home' by the legendary Tom Jones – both of them gave it their best shot. Bearing in mind that they had been on the beer for about six hours, when they tried a bit of hip rolling they nearly fell off the stage, all the words were slurred and they were just awful. They were very enthusiastic and tried their hardest to impress the Chinese audience with their double act. They built up the song to the last chorus and belted it out into a crescendo, anticipating huge applause and thanks from the audience.

When they finished the song there was total silence in the bar; there was not one single set of clapping hands, just staring wide-eyed Chinese – how embarrassing. The singing duo had no option but to scurry out of the bar to save themselves from any further embarrassment and find somewhere else that might appreciate them. I am not sure if this had anything to do with the Chinese not extending the ninety-nine-year lease on Hong Kong to the British for another ninety-nine years, but I am sure it didn't help.

Support Company had recently finished three months of duty serving on the United Nations Green Line near Nicosia in Cyprus and moved to Ayios Nikolias, where a British Army signal unit was based. There were many stories surrounding this unit and what they actually did, but no one in the company had any real idea. They allegedly eavesdropped on the Russians and Arab countries, recording information and trying to glean any secrets that could prove useful.

The company was sent to the base to provide static security and mobile patrols around the perimeter of the camp; they would spend a month there before the next company would rotate with them. A few months previously the US had bombed Libya using American aircraft that were based and flown from the UK. This subsequently raised the security threat against British bases on Cyprus from the Libyans due to its close proximity in the Mediterranean. The signal unit had recently appeared in the national media and become infamous after a member of the unit had been 'honey trapped' in a bar in Limassol and pictures taken of him in compromising positions. He was then blackmailed and allegedly gave secrets away. Eventually, he was caught and court-martialled.

Soldiers do not really enjoy guarding bases because it can be very dull and mind-numbingly boring, particularly in the Cypriot heat, where days were measured in hourly shifts. However, the task had to be done so the company commander split his three platoons – Anti-tank, Machine Guns and Mortar Platoon – into a rotation of static guard, mobile patrols and training weeks. The stronger platoons could organise their shifts so that the soldiers could have more time off, as long as the guard shifts were all covered.

On the camp there was a bar which the soldiers could use whenever they had some time off to relax. The bar was quite popular because the signal unit had a lot of female soldiers that used the bar when they were off duty as well. One night a fight broke out in the bar, which was most probably over one of the girl soldiers. The manager of the bar intervened to stop the fight before his bar was wrecked, but unfortunately he was 'knocked out' by a flying punch from one of the soldiers from Support Company in the confusion of the bar brawl.

The next morning the company commander was called before the base commander and thoroughly debriefed on the outrageous behaviour of his men in the bar the previous night and the damage that was caused. He left the office feeling a little let down and called his platoon commanders into his office, where he debriefed them about the behaviour and how it had let the company's reputation down. The Mortar Platoon was on the training week, so it had to be some of them that had caused the trouble in the bar.

The Mortar Platoon commander was a sergeant major and he was told quite firmly by the company commander to get a grip of his platoon or he would find someone else who could. This embarrassed the sergeant major, who had served twenty years in the company.

The sergeant major went straight across to his platoon, who were already formed up in three ranks outside their accommodation, and asked them, "Whoever dropped the bar manager and wrecked his bar last night step forward." No one replied. The sergeant major then said, "OK, if that's the way it's going to be, go and get your bergans and make sure they weigh fifty pounds, collect your weapons from the armoury, bring your helmets, and be back here at 1000 hours." All the soldiers scurried away to get their equipment.

At 1000 hours the platoon was formed up again in uniform, wearing helmets, bergans weighing fifty pounds and carrying weapons. The sergeant major demanded once again, "Whoever dropped the bar manager and wrecked the bar last night step forward." Again, no reply came from the soldiers in the platoon. The sergeant major briefed them that until the culprits stepped forward and owned up to their crime he would march the platoon day and night around the base.

The distance around Ayios Nikolias base was almost exactly ten miles when you started and finished at the main gate. There was a track that ran around the inside of the perimeter fence that marked the route to follow. It was very flat and the ground was either sun-baked or loose sand – ideal for giving you sore feet and blisters. The platoon started off on its lap of the base just as the Cypriot sun was reaching the hottest part of the day – forty-five degrees. After an hour some of the soldiers were starting to feel uncomfortable due to the heat, bergan straps cutting into their shoulders due to the weight inside, feet starting to ache, which wasn't surprising as the sergeant major was tearing round the route at speed.

The platoon was very fit and arguably the fittest in the battalion at that time. As paratroopers they all enjoyed fitness and a challenge so they kept up with the sergeant major the whole way around. When they had completed the ten-mile lap of the camp and were back at the main gate they were told to sit on their bergans and have a water break. After five minutes the sergeant major asked again, "Can the culprits from last night step forward?" Again no one stepped forward.

The sergeant major told them to stand up and put their bergans on and off they went around again. He pushed them hard the whole way round and some of the soldiers were starting to feel the pain – because of the speed they were racing around at, everyone was feeling the pain, including the sergeant major. However, they all kept up and bit their lip, because they were not going to show weakness to the sergeant major. A few hours later they had completed a second lap and were back again sitting on their bergans, drinking water at the main gate. It was starting to get dark by now. The sergeant major asked once more, "Can the culprits from last night step forward?" Again no one said anything.

He told them to stand up and get their kit on, as they were going around again. All the soldiers stood up and got ready to move. Just as the sergeant major said, "Follow me," one of the younger private soldiers called out, "It wasn't us, it was the Anti-Tank Platoon."

The sergeant major called a halt and asked, "Is this true? Was it the Anti-Tank Platoon?" One of the corporals agreed that it was true. The sergeant major said, "Lads, why didn't you tell me that hours ago and we could have avoided all the pain?" He told them it had been a great effort on the fitness; now they should hand in their weapons to the armoury and go and get a shower.

The sergeant major was making a beeline for the company commander to clear his platoon and tell him to investigate the

Anti-Tank Platoon; he had noticed their platoon commander looking all smug when he was getting told off by the company commander.

The reason why none of the soldiers stepped forward and volunteered the information to the sergeant major was due to the fact that he never asked – he assumed and accused them of being guilty. If they had done the crime, the guilty soldiers would have stepped forward to accept their punishment.

92   CURRY HOUSE MALARKEY

There was a great curry house in Aldershot called 'The Cannon', which produced the most wonderful Indian food. It was run and owned by Omar – never knew his real name, but that's what the soldiers called him and he answered to. He had been there for several years and knew exactly how to deal with and handle drunken and troublesome soldiers. The soldiers would normally come into his establishment late at night when the pubs were either shut or closing for the night, which meant they were always boisterous and the worst for drink.

Omar knew the majority of the soldiers in the brigade by their nicknames or by their first names. A lot of the lads that came in would do a runner from his restaurant without paying, which was a bit of a joke because he knew their identity. The following week the same lads would be back in his restaurant apologising and paying up for the previous week's meal before the weekly runner cycle would start all over again. Some of the lads were so predictable and rubbish at hiding their intent, Omar would hang around the exit door so he could hold it open for them and let them do a runner. I suppose he preferred this than trying to stop running drunken troops and ending up in a fight or damage being caused to his establishment as they made their drunken and clumsy escape.

Private X and two of his mates had enjoyed a good night in the town, where they had visited a few of the local pubs and were quite sozzled due to the amount of alcohol they had already consumed. Before heading back to camp, they fancied a curry but because it was nearing the end of the month, they were a bit short of cash for a full-blown meal. They pooled their resources and worked out they still had enough for more beers and some food that they would need to share. When they got into the restaurant it was very busy, but Omar managed to squeeze them onto a table next to some other soldiers who they recognised but never knew from their own brigade.

Private X placed the order for all three soldiers with Omar. "Three bottles of beers, one chicken curry, one portion of boiled rice, three forks, make the curry the hottest you possibly can and make it snappy." Omar nodded his head and wrote the order down and disappeared into the kitchen to prepare their order.

Ten minutes later the beers and food arrived and the hungry soldiers tucked in with their forks, devouring the meagre food in just a few minutes. Once all the food was gone, they were still feeling hungry as they sat at the table sipping their beers and chatting away to each other.

The soldiers at the table beside them had obviously been drinking as well and were quite tiddly and noisy. Unlike Private X and his mates, they were clearly not short of cash, judging by the amount of food they had piled up in the centre of their table

– naan bread, various rices, curries, biryanis, chicken tikkas, prawn madras, and poppadums. The hungry soldiers just glanced across at the food beside them and quietly salivated, drooling over the food enviously.

After ten minutes the soldiers sitting beside them got up from the table laden with food, and together they walked out of the door, leaving the restaurant and abandoning the mountain of uneaten food.

After five minutes they hadn't returned to their table, so Private X said to the two other soldiers that they must have either paid up earlier or done a casual runner from the restaurant and weren't coming back. He reached across to their table and lifted all of the uneaten food onto theirs and the three soldiers quickly got stuck into the food and started to devour it like starving cavemen. In between chewing and gorging, the three soldiers burped, giggled and laughed as they ate the free food they had managed to scavenge.

A few minutes later the soldiers that had earlier left the table and stepped outside returned and found their table cleared of food. They kicked up a row and shouted on Omar, who tried to defuse the situation. When the soldiers realised that Private X and his mates were eating it, a fight broke out. In between trying to apologise and gulping down mouthfuls of food, Private X and his mates still had to throw punches and make a fighting withdrawal to the exit door to make their escape. As they walked up Hospital Hill en route back to their camp that night, they giggled like children for most of the way at the night they had just experienced.

The soldiers that had bought the large amount of food had only stepped outside for a cigarette break.

The majority of soldiers get married in the spring or summer, due to the routine Army leave pattern or prior to an operational deployment in case the worst happens and young love is cut dead.

Private X was getting married in Scotland prior to an operational tour to Belize in the mid-eighties. The stag do was organised for the night before the wedding because that was the only time all of the soldiers that were attending the wedding could get together at the same time. Nothing special was organised, apart from a pub crawl around the old town and a meal at the end – well, that was the nice simple plan.

At the start of the evening the groom's father bought a round of drinks for everyone that was there, which was about twenty-five people, including soldiers, friends, brothers and uncles. He had just left the Army having attained the rank of regimental sergeant major and served for twenty-two years in a Guards Regiment. He came round the tables asking everyone what they wanted to drink and ordered it at the bar; once everyone had a drink he proposed a toast to his son and wished him luck the following day.

Private Y was the best man and thought that he should return the favour and get everyone a drink as part of his duties. When he came around he had a notebook and pencil in his hand to ask and write down what everyone wanted to drink, which the groom's father laughed at, "Typical para, can't remember anything and needs to write it down," to which he guffawed with laughter.

Feeling slightly embarrassed in front of strangers, Private Y replied, "Perhaps if the guards had used notebook and pencils they wouldn't have left their mortar base plates sitting in Southampton docks when they left for the Falklands War." This reply did not go down well with the groom's father, but did stop his guffawing laughter in an instant.

As the night got later the numbers got thinner as the father, uncles and family friends left the pub, leaving behind the soldiers and brothers. One of Private X's brothers suggested a drinking game: he explained that you weren't allowed to use your left hand for anything, otherwise you had to drink a forfeit. A forfeit was a glass from the jug that had every spirit in the pub mixed up with lemonade and tasted vile. An hour later the rules changed and you weren't allowed to use your right hand, which confused some, who then had to have a glass of the foul forfeit. Everyone was now on the way to being pissed.

The older brother accused the groom of using his right hand, which he denied; they then had an argument about whether he did or did not use his right hand. To end the argument the brother reached across and smacked Private X on the side of the head. The blow split the corner of his eyebrow and blood poured down his face.

Private Y pulled Private X to his feet and took him around to the local hospital, where they waited a few hours in casualty before he was examined by a doctor. It was around 0400 hours in the morning when he was finally seen by the medical staff and had a few stitches put into the cut above his right eye to close it over. The medical staff were very sympathetic when they found out he was getting married in several hours' time.

When they got back to Private X's house, his father opened the door, took one look at the state of him and his eye and gave him a right telling off. He warned Private X that if his eye was black in the morning he would not allow him to get married in the Queen's uniform.

Private Y made his way back to his accommodation, which was with a neighbour of the bride-to-be. In the morning he popped in to see her before he left for the church, and she asked him if everything was all right the previous night and did they have a good stag do. He replied, "Yes, great night, thanks," whilst thinking, if the groom hadn't told her about his eye, then he wasn't going to either.

Standing at the altar the two young private soldiers looked very smart in their best uniform while they waited for the bride to make her entrance. Once the bride had walked down the aisle, she only became aware of the cut and stitched eyebrow when Private X turned to face her for the first time at the altar. Looking at the two sheepish soldiers, she could only raise her eyebrows in a silent "what happened last night?" look as the congregation looked towards them from behind and the minister watched them from the front.

They have both been very happily married now for over thirty years; a slight hiccup at the start of married life clearly never had an effect. Someone famously said a good wedding should incorporate a fight – perhaps this includes the stag do as well.

Sadly this cannot be said for a very large proportion of Army marriage, which end in bitter divorce for all sorts of reasons.

Privates X and Y both lived in Scotland and used to spend some of their leave at each other's parents' houses so they could enjoy each other's hospitality in their own home towns and get to know the different areas. Both of them had lovely parents who never showed any concern for them going out early in the evening and coming home late in the morning, having been out clubbing and partying. They were two young soldiers doing what most lads do when they finally cross the legal age of eighteen and are then allowed to legally visit bars and consume alcohol – they were enjoying the youth of their lives and having a great time.

One Friday night they had been out drinking and clubbing in Glasgow, where they had a fantastic night. They had been out since the early evening and had been drinking for about ten hours; by the time they rolled back into Private X's house in the early morning they were both totally pissed and ready for their beds, as they were wrecked. They both headed up to their bedroom where they were sleeping for the night. Private Y stripped off completely and jumped into bed and was quickly sound asleep. A few hours later he awoke in the darkness from his drunken slumber bursting for a pee and desperate to find the toilet. He got out of his bed and stumbled off nakedly to find the toilet to relieve his bladder in the unfamiliar house. Once he was finished he staggered back to bed half asleep and still in a half-drunken state.

When he returned to his bed he pulled the duvet back and jumped in, before collapsing into the mattress, but he never realised that he had taken a wrong turn and was now in the wrong bedroom – he had jumped into bed with Private X's mother and father.

Private X was awoken when he heard all of the commotion and realised that Private Y was not in the twin bed beside his, where he should have been. He leapt from his bed and rushed into his parents' bedroom to find them both sitting up, clutching the duvet to their chests. His father was trying to pull the duvet back off Private Y and push him out of the bed, while his mother giggled through nervousness and the hilarity of the situation. Private Y was asleep lying on his side, trying to curl up into the duvet, pulling it around himself as he laid his head on their pillow, still unaware that he was in the wrong room and bed. Eventually, Private X got him out of his parents' bed and dragged the naked soldier back to his own room and bed.

Sitting at the breakfast table in the morning, Private Y was now sober and nursing a slight hangover; he could only hang his head in shame as he listened to the stories being told by Private X's father. He wore the brightest red face of embarrassment and could only apologise for his outrageous behaviour earlier in the night/morning. Private X's mother had by now got over the shock and found it hilarious: she could only laugh and giggle at his expense, saying that he certainly had a fine body and was all grown up.

Dancing like an Egyptian in Mexico.

Practising camouflage on a Caribbean beach.

Fancy dress parties were all the rage in the army.

Who said there were no cowboys in the British army?

CHAPTER 6

IN GLORIOUS MEMORY

During my service in the Parachute Regiment a total of eighty-seven members of the regiment lost their lives during training or on operations around the world and more than a further three hundred were injured and wounded.

Everyone knows and understands the risks of what might happen when they join the services – no one expects it to happen to them. When someone is killed on operations it is felt by everyone in the battalion and regiment: everyone feels for the families that have lost a son, daughter or sibling. A difficult part for a soldier is sending the body of their comrade rearwards through the repatriation chain and seeing the flag-draped coffin disappearing into the aircraft hold on his final journey home.

During a tour the coffin disappears and the soldiers have to return to the ongoing operations as if nothing has happened. They grieve properly when they come home and visit their friend's parents and family.

95   PHYSICAL TRAINING FOR THE DEAD

Sixteen soldiers from the regiment were returned to the UK for burial in Aldershot Military Cemetery after the Falklands War. Sergeant Ian McKay, who won a posthumous Victoria Cross, was amongst that number. The soldiers had all been killed in action during the heavy and bloody fighting for either Goose Green and Darwin, Mount Longdon or Wireless Ridge.

The coffins containing the dead soldiers were delivered and accommodated in the battalion's gymnasium in Aldershot on the night prior to the mass burial. The gymnasium had to be guarded overnight so that its glorious contents were secure before being buried in their final resting place, the next morning. The coffins were lined up in two rows and placed a few feet apart on stands – every coffin was draped in the Union Jack flag, which was a very sobering sight.

Privates X and Y were both seventeen-year-old soldiers who had not fought in the conflict but had recently passed out of training and joined the battalion on its return from war. Being new guys, they were nominated to guard the door of the gymnasium throughout the night with orders from the company sergeant major to make sure everything inside was kept as it should be.

In the early hours of the morning darkness the two soldiers heard voices coming from the nearby battalion accommodation where the soldiers lived. About a dozen soldiers dressed in civilian clothing appeared in the night and came towards the gymnasium;

the young soldiers noticed all of them were carrying heavy plastic carrier bags and chairs.

When they reached the young soldiers they asked them if they could go into the gymnasium to say a final farewell to their mates resting inside. Privates X and Y were in no position to deny the soldiers their request, but they were also aware that they had been briefed by the company sergeant major that no one was to tamper or muck about with the coffins inside.

They allowed the soldiers to pass and go inside the gymnasium and left them to their mourning. Ten minutes later they looked inside to make sure everything was still okay and nothing untoward was going on. The soldiers inside had arranged the chairs they had brought with them around a coffin in a semi-circle. From the carrier bags they had produced candles standing on saucers, which were now alight, casting an eerie glow, and bottles of whisky and glasses were resting on the Union Jack-draped coffin.

The soldiers sat around their friend's coffin chatting away in the candlelight as if he was still with them and part of the conversation; now and again one of them would propose a toast and they would all stand up, raise a glass and drink to their fallen comrade. This went on well into the small hours of the morning until daylight was starting to filter through the gymnasium windows.

Once they were finished, they collected all the candles, saucers, empty whisky bottles, whisky glasses, rubbish, picked up the chairs and left the gymnasium as it was. When they left the gymnasium they thanked Privates X and Y for allowing them in to say their last farewell to their friend and disappeared back to the accommodation.

Privates X and Y could only marvel at the sight, closeness, comradeship and affection they had just witnessed by the dead soldier's friends – they wondered what type of unit they had joined. As the years passed and some of their own friends lay down their lives for their comrades in the regiment, they both knew that they had joined one of the finest battalions and regiments that the British Army could ever muster.

96   THE DOVES OF PEACE

When the battalion first arrived in Kabul, Afghanistan, at the end of 2001 and early 2002 it was to a very quiet, desolate and empty city. Kabul had been systematically destroyed and reduced to rubble during the years of fighting between the Russians and the Mujahideen. More recently the fighting between the Taliban and Northern Alliance had dragged the city to its knees. Large areas of the city were strewn with the debris of devastation and wilful destruction, collapsed buildings, rubble, no electrical power, no lighting at night, and the smell of death hung in the air. A large amount of the population still lived in the ruins of their former homes, barely surviving the harsh Afghan winter. The majority of the local inhabitants had fled the city to live in the surrounding mountains of Tora Bora or across the border into Pakistan, where they sought refuge. There was very little traffic on the roads and every street corner was manned by Afghan policemen wearing old, white-painted, Russian military steel helmets – relics from the Soviet occupation more than a decade earlier, grey greatcoats, and armed with AK assault rifles or RPG rocket launchers.

The soldiers had only been there for one month and the transformation of Kabul was astonishing; the soldiers were there to reassure the locals that the Taliban had gone and normality was returning very quickly to the battered city. The people that had fled the city returned from their refuge in the mountains of Tora Bora and Pakistan in their droves. Vehicle traffic increased daily until the sounds of beeping horns and traffic jams signalled the city's recovery; market traders returned to sell their wares of fruit, meat, clothing, and roadside food. Beggars once again appeared on street corners and started to plead for food to feed their children. Women, dressed in light blue coloured burkas, that covered their bodies from head to toe, allowing them only to see the world through a mesh window covering their faces, could be seen walking around the streets. They were going about their normal womanly duties of shopping and herding their children around the streets. The old men wore flat Afghan pakora hats on their heads and draped blankets over their shoulders, as they started to gather into small groups to drink tea, chat, observe and stare as the world passed them by.

The task for the NATO soldiers was to reassure the locals and stop any tribal fighting that might occur, now that the Taliban had been beaten from the city and neither the Northern Alliance nor government was fully in control. The tribal warlords now had the opportunity for revenge against any long-standing enemies and the chance to seize power against their rivals if they had the urge, thankfully none did. Kabul's main security was split in two: a German paratroop battalion looking after the northern sector and a British paratroop battalion (2 Para) looking after the southern sector. Both were supported by their respective brigade headquarters and one divisional headquarters that was based in the centre of Kabul. If the Taliban had returned in force, there would have been an urgent request for reinforcements to be flown into the country by both nations – there was a lack of troops to do any serious war fighting. Both units had recced and rehearsed a fighting withdrawal plan and route from Kabul to Bagram airport, just in case their intervention went horribly wrong and they had to be extracted.

Some bright spark in divisional headquarters was very keen to try and pull the locals together into some kind of celebration to commemorate the defeat of the Taliban. The football stadium in Kabul was very symbolic because it was where the Taliban had executed hundreds of people for spurious reasons. The unfortunate individuals were dragged through a baying crowd to the 'kick-off' spot in the centre of the football pitch and shot through the back of the head or neck with an assault rifle. The Taliban deliberately executed people in the football ground because they were against all kinds of sports, from football to kite flying.

It was decided that a football match would be organised between the Afghan national football team and a team of soldiers put together from the in-country NATO force. This was advertised all over Kabul and thirty thousand tickets were printed and distributed to the local population by the NATO forces.

Security for this event was monumental in anyone's eyes; thankfully in those early years the suicide bomber was yet to make his deadly appearance in Kabul – this event could not happen nowadays without months of security planning.

The security plan on the day was simple enough: the Afghan police and German soldiers would be responsible for the outer cordon and search everyone and any vehicles arriving to drop off

VIPs at the stadium entrance – no other vehicles were allowed anywhere near the event. The British soldiers were responsible for the inner cordon, which meant they searched everyone again as they came in to the stands and seated area. They also placed a ring of soldiers at the side of the football pitch facing the crowd to watch for anyone that had managed to sneak weapons into the stadium with an aim to cause mayhem and death. The soldiers were all armed and ready to respond if necessary. The Afghan president and NATO general plus other dignitaries were in attendance, which presented a juicy target for terrorists that were against the new government and NATO forces' presence.

On match day it was all going as planned until the British Army band started to play music on the pitch just like *Blackadder*: bass drum, trombone, trumpets, clarinets – but they were dressed in combat uniform wearing body armour. When they started to play their music, the Afghan locals still outside the stadium thought they were missing out and started to rush the gates to get in as quickly as possible. Not content to wait and get in through the security gates, they started to climb over the walls to get in and miss out the security checks. Afghans are some of the best counterfeiters in the world and the thirty thousand printed tickets had now become over a hundred thousand tickets, and there was simply not enough space inside the football stadium for everyone that had a ticket in their hand for the game.

The Germans and Afghan soldiers manning the outer security cordon were overwhelmed by a sea of thousands of Afghans who were all intent on getting into this football match. The security was adamant that all would be searched before being allowed in. The end result was utter mayhem. The Germans were pushing the Afghan crowd back using large German shepherd dogs, which were biting the crowd in all the excitement and noise. The Afghan police fired their assault rifles into the air and lashed the crowd with large whips and pulled them off the stadium walls. The poor Afghans that had only turned up to watch a game of football were now being bitten by dogs, beaten and shots fired over their heads. They became very pissed off and started to throw bricks and anything they could get their hands on over the walls, at the seated Afghans who were lucky enough to be inside the stadium missing the madness outside. When the bricks started to hit them, they picked them up and threw them back over the wall at the soldiers, policemen and locals that were now all mixed together in a melee outside.

Inside the stadium just before kick-off it had been decided that 'The Doves of Peace' would be released at the 'kick-off' spot that had witnessed the execution of so many Afghans. A British soldier marched onto the pitch carrying a wicker basket with a dozen doves inside to be released at the appointed time. The band played music, which built up to the poignant moment when the doves would be released. The soldier checked his watch and opened the box to release the doves and let them fly off to spread the world with peace. When the box was opened none of them flew out: the heat had got to them. The soldier had to upturn the box and dump the doves (more like pigeons) onto the ground and chase them into flight. The disorientated pigeons of peace that managed to miss the crowd as they lumbered into flight were the lucky ones. The ones that flew into the crowd were quickly caught, had their necks wrung and tucked away into an Afghan's clothing for dinner that night.

NATO won the football game 3–1; when the Afghans scored it sounded just like a world cup final as between thirty and a hundred thousand locals cheered. When NATO scored it was met by very stony-faced Afghans glaring back at them.

The gesture by NATO was well meaning, but I am not convinced it was very well thought out from the outset. The killing of the pigeons of peace sums up the Afghan way of thinking quite nicely. Western symbolism means absolutely nothing to them, but thanks for the free meal.

97   THE BEST-LAID PLANS

The battalion was coming to the end of a four-month tour, packing up and getting ready to return to the UK mainland from Northern Ireland when two soldiers tragically lost their lives on the last day of the tour. Losing soldiers at any time on a tour is bad enough, but to do it on the last day was a bitter pill to swallow for a lot of the officers and soldiers in the company and platoon that the two soldiers served in. During the last few weeks of any operational tour all soldiers are thinking about getting home and spending time with their girlfriends, wives and family – glad to have survived and making plans.

Instead of going straight on to post-tour leave, the majority of the soldiers in the company were preparing for the repatriation of their friends – coffin-bearer and firing party drill to bury and honour their fallen comrades. Those not needed on duty would make their own way to the funerals from their homes up and down the length of the UK, to pay their last respects at the funeral of their lost comrades-in-arms.

Sergeant X had drilled his soldiers in coffin-bearing and firing party drills for about five days until they were perfect and ready to move to the dead soldier's home town to carry out his burial. The soldier that Sergeant X was burying was a very popular one and the coffin-bearers who would carry the coffin to his final resting place were his mates who had served with him for a number of years in the battalion.

When Sergeant X arrived at the church where the burial would take place, he had arranged to meet the minister and funeral director so that they could go through the funeral service, work out the best way to get the coffin into the church, and where he would be buried in the graveyard.

Once the minister and funeral director were clear on what the soldiers would do, they practised a walkthrough rehearsal of every part of the funeral dressed in their civilian clothes, pretending to carry a coffin – hearse arrives, funeral director opens hearse door, soldiers step forward, pull out the coffin, place on their shoulders, turn to face forward, march to the church, enter church, place coffin on stand, sit down with congregation, stand and lift coffin, leave the church, walk coffin to the grave and finally lower their friend into his grave.

Everyone, including the minister and the funeral director, were all happy with the rehearsal and understood what part they had to play in the funeral the following morning.

Next morning all the soldiers in the burial party were standing outside the church dressed in their best uniforms, polished boots and medals on display, waiting on their deceased friend to make his appearance. The hearse arrived and slowly pulled into the front of the church. The soldiers came to attention and stepped forward in unison to collect their fallen comrade. The Union flag-draped coffin was pulled out of the hearse and lifted onto the shoulders of the soldiers and taken to the church. The soldiers marched in unison under Sergeant X's timings, which he called out. Once in the church, the coffin was placed on a stand and the soldiers took their seats for the church service. A very sad time for all involved – as well as family and friends, every soldier in the church on or off duty had a lump in their throat and a tear in the corner of their eyes as the hymns were sung and modern songs played.

Once the service was over, the soldiers stood up and moved forward to lift the coffin onto their shoulders and take their young friend from the church to his final resting place. As they left the church, all of the family and friends stood up from the church pews and followed behind for the hundred metres to the newly dug grave. At the grave the six coffin-bearers had to shuffle up the sides of the grave and hold the coffin over the open grave. The funeral director would then come forward and place two wooden poles underneath across the hole so the soldiers could lower the coffin onto the poles. When the coffin was laid flat they would then thread the ropes through the coffin handles for lowering it into the grave, once the funeral director removed the wooden poles from over the hole.

When the coffin was over the hole and the six soldiers were straining with the weight of the coffin in their hands, Sergeant X gave a nod of the head to the funeral director – the signal to place the wooden poles under the coffin so the soldiers could put it down. The funeral director looked back at Sergeant X and his face went ashen – he had forgotten to bring the poles.

Sergeant X had to think quickly on his feet before the heavy coffin went crashing into the grave, as the soldiers couldn't hold it much longer because of the weight. He briefed the six coffin-bearers as quietly as possible so that the weeping congregation couldn't hear. On a count of three the soldiers on one side would need to step over the hole and the three soldiers on the other side would need to step back and then place the coffin on the ground and rethink from there. On a count of three the soldiers stepped across and placed the coffin on the ground, much to the sergeant's relief – he had visions of someone falling into the hole or dropping the coffin.

Sergeant X gave the soldiers a slight breather before carrying on with the remainder of the burial, which went without a hitch. At the end of the funeral the regimental sergeant major marched over and asked Sergeant X what happened to the wooden poles. The sergeant told him that the funeral director had been briefed and rehearsed, but he had forgotten to bring the poles to the funeral.

The regimental sergeant major could be seen at the corner of the graveyard waving his pace stick in the funeral director's face, giving him a telling off, and the funeral director could only listen in sheepish silence. The young soldier that was buried that day was well known for playing jokes on others and would have looked down smiling and giggling at the soldiers that very nearly dropped him into his grave.

The soldiers that carried the coffin of the young soldier still cringe to this day about what could have happened if they hadn't managed it across the hole. One of the songs played in the church that day was 'Tears In Heaven' by Eric Clapton, which is such a sad and haunting song, guaranteed to make grown men and soldiers cry at a funeral.

The platoon was halfway through a four-month tour of Southern Iraq and was ordered to patrol and monitor an area of desert approximately a hundred kilometres west of Basra, inside Iraq near the Saudi Arabian border. There had been reports and information that weapons and ammunition were being smuggled across the border into the southwest of Iraq from Saudi Arabia before distribution in to the Iraqi towns. The platoon's task was to ascertain likely routes and search all people that were in the area.

This particular part of the world is empty desert and the only inhabitants are the Bedouin tribes who transit across the area, regardless of national boundaries. They have done this for centuries and live off the land as they travel. Nowadays a lot of them have joined the twenty-first century and own four-by-four vehicles as well as camels and sheep. They still live in large black tents made out of very thick woollen material which are surprisingly cool in the extreme temperatures of the desert. From a distance their camp is a cluster of tents surrounded by various types of vehicles, while scattered nearby are camels and sheep grazing on anything they can scavenge. There is no fencing and lots of kids run around the place; it looks very untidy, and there could be as many as twenty or thirty of these tribes people in one location.

Sergeant X was allocated a sector of twenty square kilometres to patrol for two weeks at a time before being relieved by another platoon. His guys would then get back to barracks and sort out their administration and have a rest before going back out into the desert again. Due to the extreme heat it was soldiering at its toughest – fifty degree heat, no shade to escape under, Army rations, lack of water, vehicles continually breaking down, too hot to sleep and rest at night in the open desert. He had been out on patrol for about a week with his group of around twenty soldiers when he first spotted the Bedouin camp. Observing them through binoculars from a distance of about one kilometre away, he noted nothing out of the ordinary.

He decided to wait the few hours until the sun went down before he approached them to find out who they were and to search for any weapons or ammunition. Sergeant X briefed his platoon that he would place the vehicles with the mounted heavy machine guns to one flank and walk forward with the interpreter and another soldier so he could chat to the Bedouin. Everyone was briefed not to fire unless he ordered it over the radio.

Once it got dark and the sergeant was content that his soldiers were all in the correct position in case there was any trouble, he drove forward and stopped short, got out of the vehicle and started to walk towards the Bedouin camp.

When they were about two hundred metres away from the tented area they came under fire from several assault rifles being fired at them from the tents. The Bedouin were shooting wild inaccurate fire in their direction – the soldiers and the interpreter dived forward and lay flat on the sand. The interpreter shouted across at the Bedouin telling them who they were and what they wanted. The firing stopped and the interpreter and sergeant cautiously walked forward to meet and chat to the Bedouin.

It turned out the tribesmen thought the soldiers were raiders who had come to steal the sheep and children, which they would defend until death if necessary. The Bedouin were very apologetic and welcomed the soldiers into their camp. They explained that they had no weapons apart from their own personal weapons for protection.

In the morning the soldiers were treated as guests and invited to a special lunch by the head tribesman as a gesture of apology for shooting at them the previous night. The soldiers were invited into the tents, where they all sat cross-legged on the tent floor, which was covered in large, red-patterned carpets. The tribal elder had ordered the slaughter of a sheep and a small feast had been prepared for the soldiers. In the middle of the tent was a large round metal tray about four feet in diameter piled with rice, chopped-up mutton and mixed with spices about a foot high. There were no knives or forks, so everyone just had to lean forward and put their right hands into the pile of food and grab a handful. The tribesmen showed them how to roll the rice and greasy mutton into a ball before eating it, surprisingly very tasty.

The tribesmen never knew how lucky they were that Sergeant X had not given the order to fire to his cover groups – under the rules of engagement at the time, he was entitled to. He never ordered the soldiers to fire because he suspected they were just normal Bedouin living in the desert going about their own business, which turned out to be the case.

Sadly, five years later Sergeant X was killed in action by an IED in Helmand Province, Afghanistan, whilst on foot patrol. By then he had been promoted to warrant officer and was serving in the same company in the appointment of company sergeant major.

99   HALLELUIAH

The padre (Army religious minister) for the battalion decided that he would visit and hold a field service for each of the companies that were currently living out on the Canadian plain on exercise. The companies had already been living out under their ponchos for about four weeks before he came to visit this particular company. The reason they were camped out was the simple logistical issue of transporting the company two hours daily each way by truck over the bouncy tracks to get to the training areas. By living out on the prairie they were on the ranges, which saved a lot of time, negating early starts and late finishes by the time they got back to camp each night.

The camp location was very spartan but adequate for the company. Each platoon had its own living area where they all slept under their ponchos and mosquito nets. There was a small field kitchen tent manned by Army chefs to prepare the food, and wooden tables outside to sit at and have breakfast, lunch and dinner. There was a volleyball court scraped out of the scrubland and marked with mine tape – volleyball has to be the British Army's favourite sport. Off to one side was a fire pit surrounded by large fallen logs which had been dragged in to make a seating area; all the soldiers would gather here at night to sit and chat after a hard day's training or shooting on the ranges.

By the time the padre arrived, the company was an extremely close-knit group of men due to the fact they had all lived so closely together for the previous weeks and teamwork was at its best.

The padre was a very nice, genuine person who was well respected by the soldiers – he was a true believer and was intent on spreading the word of God to his flock. Some padres I have met in the past were maybe not quite as committed religiously as this gentleman, in my opinion.

The padre had agreed with the company commander that he would hold the service on a hill near the camp, overlooking the valley and the river below. It would take place on the coming Sunday and everyone in the company would attend the church service. The day before the service the padre worked hard, dragging trunks of wood around and lashing them together. By the end of the day he had made a cross about ten feet high and five feet across – it looked quite impressive as it stood on the hill towering over the valley.

The only flaw in the padre's plan was that he completed the task on a Saturday afternoon. On Saturday nights the company finished slightly early from training and had a communal BBQ, an inter-platoon volleyball competition, alcohol, bonfire and generally chilled out for the night – great fun and merriment was had by all.

The guys were sitting around the camp fire in the dark, singing songs and having a great time enjoying the normal banter. One of the soldiers shouted out, "Holy shit, look at that over there." When the soldiers turned around they could see that the cross that the padre had spent all day building and erecting was now in flames from top to bottom. Someone had obviously sneaked over in the night and covered it in petrol before setting it alight: a flaming cross blazed out of the darkness of the night, glowing over the valley below. The soldiers found this hilarious and they all rolled around laughing at the flaming spectacle on the nearby hill – the padre went mad and was even rumoured to have cursed and sworn (although not confirmed).

The field service the next morning still took place, albeit below a scorched and blackened wooden cross, but it was enjoyed by the soldiers and officers present. The padre, who held great affection and admiration for his soldiers, was only too happy to see his flock seated before him as he spread the word of God, even knowing one or more of the little angels in the audience had set fire to his cross.

Soldiers come from all religions and can have some very differing beliefs. However, you can be rest assured when the bombs and bullets start to fly the vast majority of soldiers look for God – only a very, very, very small minority of soldiers do not.

100   NAVAL RULES

For the twentieth anniversary of the Falklands War, the commanding officer decided to send all of the soldiers that were currently still serving in the battalion and had fought in the campaign, back to the Falkland Islands for a battlefield tour to mark the anniversary. The regimental sergeant major was asked to plan and organise the trip, which wasn't very onerous as there were only six members still serving in the battalion at the time. Of the six members, some had fought at Goose Green and Darwin, Mount Longdon and Wireless Ridge. So the battlefield tour was planned to include all three very separate battles.

All six of the soldiers were asked to prepare a talk on the attacks which they took part in and to brief the whole group, so everyone would get a better picture of the whole battle and not just the part they were involved in. The battlefield tours were absolutely outstanding due to the fact that all of the soldiers could remember almost every detail of whichever battle they were part of.

The first battlefield tour was Goose Green and Darwin. The group was fortunate to have Captain X, who had been a platoon sergeant during the battle. He briefed everybody and pointed out the locations and routes that the companies had moved across, and where they had formed up twenty years previously to attack the Argentinian trenches. The land they fought over was relatively flat and undulating; there were no trees or rocks to use as cover, which caused them difficulty whilst moving once the battle had started. Whenever they stood up and moved, it attracted a lot of incoming fire from the Argentinian positions.

He explained that the attacks all started in the hours of darkness and finding the Argentinians initially was quite difficult. They came upon some of them quite suddenly, which resulted in vicious, close-quarter fighting – bayonet, grenade, explosions, screaming, shouting, confusion, flashes and hand-to-hand fighting.

The battalion lacked artillery and mortar fire and only had the ammunition the soldiers carried with them. He explained that as the battle turned into an enduring daylight fight, the battalion was starting to run out of ammunition, water and rations, and the large number of friendly casualties was starting to make it look quite grim. However, they persevered and finally won the day at great cost to the battalion in dead and wounded officers and soldiers. When they accepted the surrender from the surviving Argentinean commander, they couldn't believe how many troops had been taken prisoner – there was more than three times the number of the battalion. The enemy was only supposed to be in company strength according to the troops from another unit that had completed the initial recce of enemy positions.

At Goose Green there is an Argentinian cemetery where the majority of their dead are buried; all of the soldiers and the regimental sergeant major went in and paid their respects. They may have been the enemy twenty years previously, but all of the soldiers found walking around the cemetery quite moving, particularly when they read the engraved white crosses and noticed the ages of the men that lay under the grass at their feet for eternity.

The next battlefield tour was Mount Longdon, which is part of a series of mountains that surround the capital Port Stanley – it became infamous for being the most costly battle in British lives during the liberation of the islands.

The mountain rises up from peat bog and tussock grass to a height of approximately five hundred feet; it is one hundred metres at its widest part and approximately one kilometre long. There are large boulder rocks scattered over its slopes, plus rock walls that reach up to about thirty metres in height. From a distance it looks as though it has a spine of rock similar to a dinosaur running up its back from west to east. It is totally different to the ground at Goose Green, where the first battle had been fought two weeks earlier.

Sergeant Y was a private soldier during this battle and gladly explained to and briefed all the soldiers on the part of the battle that he was involved in. He explained that the attack started out as a silent night attack before it went noisy – meaning there was no artillery or mortars fired onto the mountain that might alert the enemy of an impending attack. Once the attack went noisy, every weapon system available would be brought to bear on the mountain and used to devastating effect.

On the night of the attack, as they approached the shape of the mountain through the darkness, one of the corporals stood on an anti-personnel mine, losing his leg, and the attack became noisy very quickly. The soldiers ran forward through a minefield and into the rocks for cover; by now the Argentinians were alerted and were pouring fire down onto the British soldiers. The paratroopers fired back at every muzzle flash that they could see with rifle, machine gun and anti-tank rockets to silence the enemy. During the remainder of the night, the battle was mainly conducted by small groups of soldiers crawling forward, identifying the enemy positions, and then attacking the positions using grenades, rifle, machine-gun fire, and bayonets to silence the enemy.

The Argentinians were well dug in and fought back relentlessly using rifle, machine guns, grenades, recoilless rifles, artillery, and mortar fire. Due to the close proximity of the enemy, they could be stumbled upon by rounding the corner of a rock and the battle descended into vicious hand-to-hand fighting. The battle was very confusing throughout because some Argentinians had been bypassed in the dark and some hid in the rock crevices, only to appear fighting later in the night. As the battle moved along the mountain it became awash with the debris of battle – dead, wounded, the dying, parts of bodies, discarded clothing, smoke, weapons, screaming, shouting, simply mayhem.

When Sergeant Y finished his brief, he explained that he was only seventeen years old at the time of the battle and three of his best mates from his company had been killed during the night fighting – none of them over the age of eighteen years old.

Standing on top of the mountain beside the large silver cross that had been placed there after the battle, Sergeant Y took time to reflect and pay his respect to his fallen comrades. He placed a brass plaque dedicated to his three friends beside the cross. The audience of veteran soldiers all had a lump in their throats and a tear in the corner of their eyes. Sergeant Y was more open than the others and tears just ran down his face, as he thought of the battle and the memories of his lost friends that would stay forever young.

The last battlefield tour was Wireless Ridge, which runs away from Mount Longdon to the east and is lower in height by a hundred feet or so. The ridge is only a few contour rings on a map and is mainly tussock and peat bog; it lacks in cover from view or fire. It is approximately one hundred metres wide and one kilometre long, and from its top you can see right into the capital, Port Stanley, which is only about five or six kilometres away.

After the lessons learned at Goose Green and Mount Longdon, it was decided that the attack on Wireless Ridge would be a night, noisy attack from the outset – they would pound it with everything they had available before the troops attacked, which should hopefully reduce friendly casualty numbers.

Captain X had fought at this battle as well as Goose Green and briefed the audience that the battalion attack was supported by light tanks, artillery, mortars, anti-tank Milan missiles and heavy machine guns, which was co-ordinated to be unleashed upon the enemy for maximum effect. Once the battalion had marched behind Mount Longdon and was in position, the ridge was pounded by all available weapons, before the soldiers stood up to advance on the enemy that were still alive or dying on the position. The battalion suppressed the ridge whilst a company went right flanking and cleared along the ridge to its limit of exploitation. There was still heavy fighting as they fought through the positions, but not to the same level as Goose Green. When they had finished the attack and pushed the Argentinians off the ridge, the troops regrouped. Whilst they were in the middle of regrouping, the enemy counter-attacked in company strength, which was dispersed with artillery and mortar fire at great cost to the Argentinians.

At the end of the three battles the battalions and regiment had lost over forty soldiers killed in action and over one hundred injured – many severely wounded with life-changing injuries.

The battlefield tours had brought back so many events, emotions and memories of their fallen comrades for the veteran soldiers – the dead, the injured, the killing and for surviving the battles; they all felt in the mood for a good drink to toast the dead and celebrate surviving.

The captain of HMS *Leeds Castle,* which was the Royal Navy guard ship deployed to patrol the waters of the South Atlantic, was docked in Port Stanley for a few days taking on provisions at the time of the anniversary. He had heard that veterans from the regiment that fought in the war were in Port Stanley and passed a message inviting them on board his ship for a bite to eat and drinks – they, of course, accepted.

At 1800 hours that evening, the soldiers went along to the harbour where the ship was docked and were met at the gangway by a lieutenant who introduced himself as 'Paddy' and he was the ship's navigator. The officer looked every part the naval officer, with his white uniform and full beard. Before the soldiers were allowed on the ship, Paddy briefed them that on Her Majesty's ship tonight there were only two rules. The soldiers were not allowed to buy any beer and secondly they were not allowed to leave the ship sober. After the traumatic day the soldiers had endured, it was a challenge that was gladly accepted.

Paddy took them all below deck and into the wardroom, where all of the ship's officers and petty officers had gathered to meet the soldiers. The hosting from the sailors was second to none; as the night progressed it was clear that a long night was in the making. The sailors could drink and the soldiers were drinking like the best of them – beer, wine, port, and whisky were all out on display and drunk. There were inter-service drinking games organised and challenges made, all in fantastic spirit, and a great night was had by all. As the night progressed, drunken sailors drifted off to their beds and some of the soldiers crashed out in the soft chairs in the wardroom.

The regimental sergeant major decided it was time for them to leave the ship when he noticed Paddy lying in the corner under a table sound asleep; his beard was matted with what looked like sick. He wrote and left them a note thanking them for their outstanding hospitality, gathered up his soldiers and officers, before taking them back to barracks as the sun came up over the South Atlantic Ocean.

Out of the six soldiers on the battlefield tour, Captain X had been awarded the Distinguished Conduct Medal (DCM) for his gallantry and leadership as a platoon sergeant at Goose Green, Darwin and Wireless Ridge. Another of the soldiers in the group had been awarded a Mention in Dispatches (MID) for bravery during the battle for Mount Longdon and one other had been injured by shrapnel at Goose Green.

The commanding officer, the battalion second-in-command and the battle group logistics officer had deployed to Kandahar airfield, Afghanistan, for a pre-tour deployment recce – one lieutenant colonel and two majors. The recce was only for a week so that they could fully understand what their task was going to be and to gain any advice from their opposite numbers in the unit that they would be replacing in a few months' time.

This is normal standard practice throughout the British Army and a necessity before any operational tour. Each night the three of them would meet up in the coffee shop and discuss their day and highlight any good ideas that they had managed to spot or glean from the off-going unit. On the back of this recce they would finalise the training of their own battalion to meet the forth-coming challenges. With only four months until their deployment, they didn't have much time to waste.

The coffee shop was made from thin-planked wood, glass windows which had absolutely no ballistic protection, which was surprising as most nights it was full of servicemen if they were lucky enough to have some downtime for a brew. At this time in the Afghanistan campaign, Kandahar airfield was being shelled most nights with rockets fired from five to ten kilometres away. The rockets being fired were generally the Chinese 122mm rocket, which was placed on an elevated piece of earth and roughly aligned in the direction of the airfield, fuse lit and after a delay the rocket would launch on its path of death and destruction.

Considering the airport was the main entry for all nations' soldiers into the southern part of Afghanistan, it was quite unbelievable that this was still being allowed to happen. A direct hit on an aircraft full of servicemen would have had catastrophic implications on the nation that the servicemen belonged to – some of the smaller nations would likely have withdrawn all their remaining troops in this event.

As the three officers took their turn briefing each other on what they had been doing during the day and what would be best practice for their own troops, the wailing 'incoming rocket' alarm was sounded. The drill is simple – fall flat on the ground until the all clear and then get to hard cover. Hard cover was in the shape of concrete bunkers that looked like the upturned letter U. It has been proven that more casualties were injured from shrapnel whilst running to the shelters than if troops had just lain on the ground wherever they were. As a shell or rocket bursts, the shrapnel goes outwards and upwards, so unless the shell lands extremely close to you, your chances of survival are much better if you just lie flat as they explode all around you.

All three dropped to the floor in the coffee shop, looking at each other as they anticipated the rocket impacts. This is quite a surreal situation for people who have never experienced it, as there is absolutely nothing you can do apart from hope there is a God and if there is you weren't a bad person in his eyes.

The battle group logistics officer, who had been in the Army for about twenty-four years and had experienced being shelled a few times in the past, was not particularly fazed by the odds of getting hit because it was a very large airfield. As the rockets started to land and explode around the area, some of them were close enough to kick up the earth and stones and pepper the coffee shop roof. He lent across to the other two and said, "If we get a direct hit and I am killed, can you please drag my body out of this café. I don't want to be remembered as the paratrooper that was killed in the coffee shop in Kandahar." At this statement, the other two officers started to laugh their heads off, which caused the other troops lying beside them on the coffee shop floor praying to look over and wonder who these lunatics were.

The lieutenant colonel on the recce had already been awarded a Distinguished Service Order (DSO) for his leadership of the battalion on a previous tour of Afghanistan eighteen months earlier. The battalion second-in-command was awarded a Queen's Commendation for Valuable Service (QCVS) for his hard work during the six-month tour.

Defence cuts hit the army very hard. In reality, the Sergeants' Mess of 3 Para – the battalion was employed to provide film extras for a day to raise money for a soldier who had sadly lost both legs in a landmine explosion in Northern Ireland.

EPILOGUE

The stories have hopefully given the reader an honest snapshot into the lives of soldiers and officers and what they get up to when they serve their Queen and Country 'On and Off' duty. All of the people that join the British Army are given chances to travel the world and to deploy on operations to interesting places that the general public avoids like the plague, due to the danger that exists there. The British public has been fortunate enough to have the privilege of having a hundred percent volunteer Army for many years, unlike most countries.

This should never be underestimated – Britain has willing volunteers that are content to step into harm's way at the request of the politicians currently serving in the government. The soldiers might disagree with the government of the day and its policies, but are all still willing to step onto the aircraft that transports them to faraway lands and danger, where they could be maimed or killed. Oddly, very few of today's politicians who are responsible for deploying troops have ever served in the Royal Navy, the Royal Air Force or the British Army, and have no idea of the capabilities that can or cannot be achieved by military force.

The same politicians are very quick to point out that they have the admirals and generals to advise them on the use of troops and capabilities. Sadly, when it comes to the advice given by the same admirals and generals regarding cost-cutting and manning numbers, it would appear they prefer to listen to the treasury and save money, regardless of what their military advisers say.

The sad fact is, when troops get deployed they do get wounded and killed; there is no such thing as a deployment of troops into a conflict zone without shots being fired. There is no other employment in the country where employees get on an aircraft and make the conscious decision to step into harm's way.

The point that the politicians and general public need to remember is when Private X is down the local pub he has been places and seen a lot of things that the majority of the public will never see or should see. When soldiers return from conflict, the first thing that some civilian mates normally ask is "How many did you kill?" This is the last thing he needs to be asked; if he has been in the frontline and seen or caused some gruesome sights, he would rather have a beer and forget it. Normally they only talk about these things amongst their friends who were with them at the time and understand exactly what went on.

In the local papers up and down the country you will always read stories saying that Private X from the Parachute Regiment was in the pub and got into a fight, he was arrested and fined two hundred pounds by the local magistrate. Very rarely will you see 'Billy Smith from Todds the Butchers' listed as being in the same fight. When you analysis it, they were both young men who had got themselves into a fight, but one was identifiable to the Army and gets named and shamed. In reality they were both young men fighting – probably over a girl, which has gone on since Adam and Eve.

Soldiers should not be painted as saints or sinners, but looked upon as normal members of the public that are distinguishable only by the wearing of the uniform which they are proud to wear on behalf of the general public.

They are the youth of today that have decided to step forward for their own reasons and joined an organisation that gives plenty but can ultimately take back the gift of life.

It was a privilege to have served with so many good people that were always a credit to their regiment, battalion and country. We do remember the good times and not the bad, but when the chips were down and things got sticky, we all knew we were surrounded by a band of brothers that would fight until the very end if necessary.

Private soldiers are men of violence. Non-commissioned officers and commissioned officers are leaders of men of violence.

Major G Muirhead MBE Para

UTRINQUE PARATUS